The Swans

Peter Scott 1970

The Swans

Peter Scott
and the Wildfowl Trust

HOUGHTON MIFFLIN COMPANY BOSTON
1972

Contents

Acknowledgements — vii

List of Plates — ix

1 *Introduction*   Peter Scott — 1

2 *Classification*   Hugh Boyd — 17

3 *Distribution, numbers and migration*   M. A. Ogilvie — 29

4 *Food and feeding habits*   Myrfyn Owen and Janet Kear — 57

5 *Reproduction and family life*   Janet Kear — 79

6 *Mortality*   J. V. Beer and M. A. Ogilvie — 125

7 *Art and mythology*   Mary Evans and Andrew Dawnay — 143

8 *Exploitation*   Andrew Dawnay — 167

9 *Conservation*   G. V. T. Matthews — 181

Appendix 1   Body weights — 198

Appendix 2   Linear measurements — 199

Appendix 3   Life expectancy — 201

Appendix 4   The food of adult swans — 202

Appendix 5   Egg dimensions — 206

Appendix 6   Fresh egg weights — 208

Appendix 7   Clutch sizes — 210

Appendix 8   Incubation periods — 212

Appendix 9   Cygnet weights at one day old — 213

References, which also form an alphabetical bibliography to the text, are referred to by number throughout.

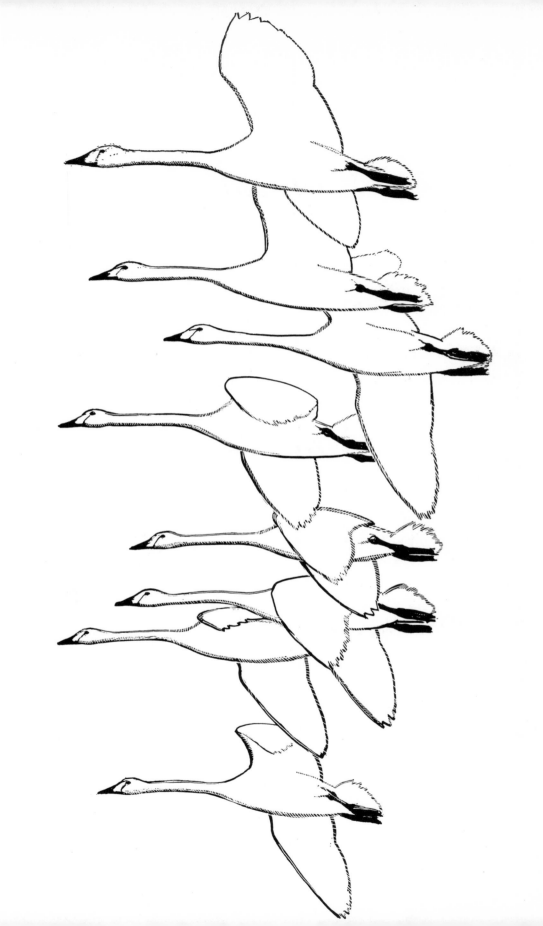

Acknowledgements

Our grateful thanks are due to the very many people who have helped in the preparation of this book; the Wildfowl Trust is heavily in their debt.

Mr. J. Lewis, Mr. C. Sellick and Dr. M. W. Weller advised on aspects of the biology of Coscoroba and Black-necked Swans in the wild, and Mr. J. A. Griswold on Coscorobas in captivity. Mr. R. Adams and Mr. E. S. Bucknell of the New Zealand Wildlife Service, and Dr. H. J. Lavery and Dr. E. R. Guiler of Queensland and Tasmania provided unpublished data on the breeding of the Black Swan. Information on the interaction of Black Swans and agriculture was given by Dr. H. J. Frith, C.S.I.R.O., Mr. R. J. Scarlett, Christchurch Museum, and Dr. C. A. Fleming answered many queries on the extinct New Zealand species. Dr. C. R. Schmidt and Mr. J. P. Williams gave information, respectively, on breeding Black Swans and Trumpeter Swans in captivity. Dr. C. D. T. Minton made available much useful material on Mute Swans, Mr. C. M. Reynolds allowed us to use his unpublished Mute Swan weights and Mr. C. H. Willey his information on the introduced Mute Swans of Rhode Island. Notes on the status of Polish Mute Swans and other colour variants were supplied by Mr. T. Lebret and Mr. C. J. O. Harrison; and Mr. A. Timmerman, Major R. F. Ruttledge, Mr. O. J. Merne, Dr. C. A. J. Schmidt and Dr. A. Hilprecht helped us with information on the distribution of European species. Mr. C. J. Lensink and Dr. W. J. L. Sladen sent unpublished data on the Whistling Swan, and Dr. W. Troyer and Dr. W. E. Banko on the Trumpeter.

Mrs. H. Morriss compiled Appendix 3, Dr. R. Avery assisted with the section on parasites and Miss V. M. Thom on the effects of agricultural chemicals. The R.S.P.C.A. and S.S.P.C.A. supplied information on accidents to and treatment of swans, and Dr. C. M. Perrins advised on the section on clutch size.

A great deal of help and encouragement was received from Professor A. T. Hatto in the preparation of the chapter on mythology. The Bristol University Arts Librarian, the Folklore Society and the Irish Folklore Commission gave ready advice and permission to use their facilities. The Clerk of the Dyers' Company, Dr. D. R. Balfour Park, answered our queries on swan-upping.

Giles, Robert Gillmor, Harry Hargreaves, Colleen Nelson, Carol Ogilvie, Thierry Robyns de Schneidauer, Dafila Scott, Keith Shackleton and Valerie Shirley have given appropriately beautiful and amusing illustrations, for which we are particularly grateful.

The following people allowed us freely to use their photographs: Winston Banko, the Bowes Museum, Richard Burn, the City Engineer of Newcastle upon Tyne, J. T. Darby, Kurt Gloor, *Gloucestershire Gazette*, Dursley, E. R. Guiler, Pamela Harrison, Kiyoshi Honda, E. E. Jackson, Russ Kinne, H. J. Lavery, A. Middleton, Jane N. Miller, Newman & Newman (Antiques) Ltd., Edwin C. Peckham, R. Piechocki, N. O. Preuss, the Rijksmuseum, Amsterdam, Philippa Scott, Christopher Stringer, the Tate Gallery, B. Thyselius, Will Troyer, U.S. Department of the Interior Fish and Wildlife Service, M. W. Weller, G. K. Yeates, Shigeo Yoshikawa and the Zoological Society of Philadelphia. We are also grateful to Mr. R. Soame Jenyns and Mrs. J. V. C. Turner for permission to photograph paintings in their possession.

Our thanks are also due to the following publishers and authors who have allowed us to quote from their works: The Loeb Classical Library, for a quotation from *Metamorphoses* by Ovid, translated by F. J. Miller; Bowes & Bowes, for a quotation from *The Prose Edda* translated by Jean Young; Thames and Hudson Ltd., and Random House Inc., for a quotation from *Fabulous Beasts* by B. P. Lum; Angus & Robertson Ltd., for a quotation from *Three Swans Went By* by Mary Gilmore; University of Missouri Press for a quotation from *Swans, Cygnets and Owl* by E. G. Martinez, translated by M. E. Johnson (copyright 1956 by the curators of the University of Missouri); University of Chicago Press, for a quotation from *Early Irish Literature* by M. Dillon; Wm. Collins Sons & Co. Ltd., for a quotation from *The Inner Hebrides and Their Legends* by O. F. Swire; George Allen & Unwin Ltd., for a quotation from *Iphigenia in Tauris* by Euripides, translated by Gilbert Murry; to W. M. Bannerman (formerly Priestley) and Victor Gollancz Ltd., for a quotation from *A Book of Birds*, and to Robert Graves for quotations from *The Greek Myths*.

Colleagues at Slimbridge who have advised and assisted include Chris Beale, Maureen Bower, Bram and Sybil Branford-White, Erik Carp, Diana Fowler, Michael Garside, Tim Gibson, Patrick Humphreys, Tommy Johnstone, Charles Martell, Malcolm Penny, Niels Preuss, Dafila Scott, John Secrett and Nick Wood. We have also relied to a great extent on the help of Eleanor Temple Carrington who typed the manuscript and most of the correspondence.

Lastly, our warmest thanks go to George Atkinson-Willes, who edited the final draft, and to Janet Kear who planned the book, browbeat the contributors and carried the project through to completion.

Plates

Frontispiece   COLOUR PLATE   Bewick's Swans.
From an oil-painting by Peter Scott

Photographs. Selected by Philippa Scott and E. E. Jackson

Between pages 6 and 7
1 Coscoroba family
   Coscoroba Swans on nest
2 Coscoroba Swans in flight
   Head of adult Coscoroba
   Head of juvenile Coscoroba
   Immature Coscoroba

Between pages 22 and 23
3 Black Swan family
4 Black Swan colony
   Black Swan nest
   Black Swan cygnets

Between pages 38 and 39
5 Black Swans in flight
   Black Swan flock
6 Mute Swan defending nest

Between pages 54 and 55
7 Mute Swan carrying cygnet
8 Mute Swan family
   Mute Swan up-ending
   Bewick's Swan up-ending

Between pages 62 and 63
9 Mute Swan on nest with eggs

   Mute Swan on nest with
   cygnets
10 Mute Swan courtship
    Mute Swan family
11 Mute Swan in aggressive
    display
    Mute Swan attacking
12 Mute Swans fighting

Between pages 70 and 71
13 Black-necked Swan carrying
    cygnet
    Black-necked Swan family
14 Black-necked Swan nest and
    eggs
    Black-necked Swan sitting on
    nest

Between pages 86 and 87
15 Black-necked Swan flock
    Black-necked Swan and
    juvenile
16 Black-necked Swan family in
    ice

Between pages 94 and 95
17 Whooper Swans in display

18 Whooper Swan pair
    Whooper Swan nests and eggs
19 Whooper Swans with cygnets
20 Juvenile Whooper Swans
    Stained Whooper Swan

Between pages 102 and 103
21 Whooper Swans feeding on
    land
    Whooper Swan courtship
22 Whooper Swans displaying
    Whooper Swan 'ground
    staring'

Between pages 118 and 119
23 Whooper Swans in flight
24 Head of Whooper Swan

Between pages 126 and 127
25 Trumpeter Swan on nest
26 Trumpeter Swan nest and
    eggs
    Trumpeter Swan cygnet
27 Trumpeter Swans in flight
    Trumpeter Swans defending
    nest
28 Immature Trumpeter Swans
    Trumpeter Swan preening

Between pages 134 and 135
29 Trumpeter Swans displaying
    Trumpeter Swan flock
30 Trumpeter Swan pair

Between pages 150 and 151
31 Heads of Whistling Swans
32 Whistling Swan nest and eggs
    Whistling Swan cygnets

Between pages 158 and 159
33 Whistling Swans in flight
34 Whistling Swan 'ground
    staring'
    Whistling Swan pair
35 Bewick's Swans at Slimbridge
36 Bewick's Swan with cygnets

Between pages 166 and 167
37 Bewick's Swans calling
38 Bewick's Swans displaying

Between pages 182 and 183
39 Head of Bewick's Swan
40 Adult and immature Bewick's
    Swan
    Head of immature Bewick's
    Swan

Between pages 190 and 191
41 Bewick's Swans preening
42 Bewick's Swans in flight
43 Oiled Bewick's Swans
    Oiled Mute Swans
44 Inn sign
    Swan Service dish and cover
    Mechanical silver swan

Between pages 198 and 199
45 *The Threatened Swan* by Jan
    Asselyn
    Swans in Flight by David
    Wynne
46 Chinese painting on silk

Between pages 214 and 215
47 *The Wild Swans* by Arthur J.
    Gaskin
48 *Swan Upping* by Stanley
    Spencer

I

Introduction

Peter Scott

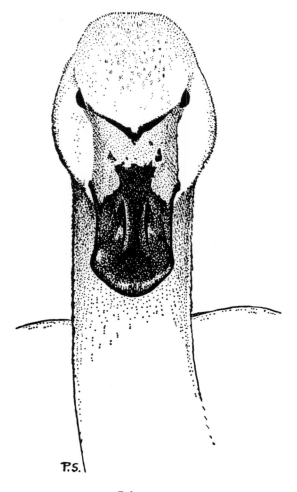

Sahara.

'What is your favourite bird?' My current answer to the question is Bewick's Swan. Ornithology calls, like any other science, for objectivity, whereas the selection of a favourite bird is wholly and delightfully subjective. With more than 8,000 species to choose from one may perhaps be allowed to answer the question differently at different times of one's life. My answers have always, I think, been within the family Anatidae – the ducks, geese and swans. For example, for a long period the Pink-footed Goose held my allegiance – the wild grey goose of the fenlands and the Wash where, as a hunter, I made my first acquaintance with wildfowl, the bird I subsequently studied all over Britain and for two summers on its remote breeding grounds in central Iceland, the species of which I helped to catch, ring and release 25,000 individuals.

Then there was my Red-breasted Goose period, back in the 1930s when I travelled to Hungary, to the Danube Delta and to the Caspian Sea to find these exquisite miniature harlequin-patterned geese. In the two winters of my search I found no more than a handful – fourteen in the largest flock – though in almost the same place in Romania we found, in December 1969, no less than 4,000 of them on a rolling field of sprouting wheat.

Soon after the war my favourite bird was the elegant Lesser White-fronted Goose, two of which we discovered among a flock of 2,000 European Whitefronts on the Severn estuary. Those two birds played a significant part in the selection of Slimbridge as the headquarters of the Wildfowl Trust, for they were the second and third official records of the species in Britain. Something like sixty Lesser Whitefronts have been recorded there during the twenty-five years since that first discovery, and it remains the only place in Britain where, in most winters, one can reasonably expect to find one of these delightful little geese.

Lesser White-fronted Goose.

3

It was not until 1964 that we persuaded the Bewick's Swans, which had been coming from their Siberian breeding grounds to the Severn estuary each winter in small numbers for ten years, to land on the pond in front of my studio window. Early in February of that year twenty-four of them, decoyed by tame birds, found the wheat we put out for them and came regularly until their departure in March, and during that period we discovered the striking variations in the yellow and black bill patterns which make every individual Bewick's Swan distinguishable from every other. In the next eight winters the numbers visiting 'Swan Lake' built up from twenty-four to 626, and Bewick's Swans became my favourite birds.

If brilliance of colour had been the only criterion I might have chosen a Pitta, a Tanager or a Kingfisher; colour combined with grace of form – a Bee-eater, a Sun-bird or a Humming-bird; beauty of movement – a Tern or a Tropic Bird; power – a Peregrine; mystery – a Swift; sound – a Curlew or a Blackcap; humour – a Parrot. But for a combination of fascinating and wholly admirable characteristics give me these small migratory swans from the Arctic, which travel vast distances each year, which pair for life and travel *en famille*, and which delight the ear as much as the eye when they swing in from the estuary to land on Swan Lake.

To most people swans are large white birds (except in Australia and New Zealand where they are large black birds and in South America where one kind is a large white bird with a black neck). To most people they look graceful and beautiful – some think there are too many, though for what is not usually disclosed, and others regard them, especially the wild migratory ones, as fascinating, mysterious and intensely romantic. Sometimes they have undoubtedly been seen as legitimate quarry, to be hunted for their large size, if nothing more. But at the same time, their whiteness has been linked with purity and characterised as the 'good spirit' in legend throughout the northern hemisphere. They carry, perhaps, the souls of our ancestors and this belief has protected them as it protected at times the Albatross.

My earliest recollection of swans is of feeding the Mute Swans on the Round Pound in Kensington Gardens – huge sedate birds around which sped innumerable ravenous Pochards just arrived from the far side of the North Sea. Later I paid a visit to Abbotsbury on the Fleet in Dorset, where some 900 years ago the monks established a colony of swans whose descendants still breed today at barely two necks distance from each other. All Mute Swans (scientifically *Cygnus olor*, both Latin words for swan) were probably brought into domestication in Britain long ago and were marked on the bill or foot to indicate their ownership. Any wild, unmarked swan then became the property of the Crown, and although Her Majesty the Queen is now to lose her rights to Sturgeon, happily she retains unmarked Mute Swans as Royal Fowl.

In 1952 I was commissioned to paint a set of large pictures of Mute Swans for the entrance hall of the Worshipful Company of Dyers in the City of London. The Dyers' Company is one of the two City livery companies (the other is the Vintners) which still retain a Royalty of Swans and have the right to mark them on the River Thames. Having painted the series, I was invited to join a swan-upping party on board a pleasure-steamer to watch the traditional ceremony in which the Thames swans are rounded up and apportioned between the two livery companies and the Crown. This colourful affair has no parallel elsewhere. Nevertheless, on the tomb shrouds of a Scythian chieftain, recently excavated in central Siberia, are beautiful *appliqué* representations of Mute Swans tethered by their feet. Were these people the first to round up swans 2,500 years ago?

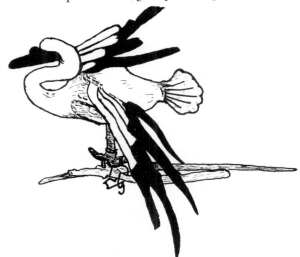

Tethered swan, from the Pazyryk tombs, Siberia. *John Secrett*.

The Australian Black Swan *Cygnus atratus* – *atratus* meaning 'clothed in black' – habitually nests in colonies, and is often found in enormous flocks. I remember at Lake Ellesmere in New Zealand, where the introduced Black Swan has been even more successful than in its native land, my wife and I saw more than 20,000 in a day, and that may have been only about a quarter of the population of this fifteen-mile-long lagoon.

The Black Swan, which for many centuries had been regarded as a natural impossibility, was 'discovered' on 2 January 1697 when the Dutch navigator Willem de Vlaming came across a small flock in an estuary, later named Swan River, in Western Australia. One can imagine the interest they aroused when they reached Europe. The Empress Josephine had several on the ponds at Malmaison, and they figured in the first list made of animals kept at the London Zoo. For several years we had an unmated female at the Wildfowl Trust; then in 1953 we heard that the swan pool at Chartwell was becoming overcrowded and that an unattached cob was making trouble. We wrote to Sir Winston Churchill asking if we might borrow the bird, and he replied that we could have him 'until such time as I may need him again'. He is a splendid creature and must have sired more than thirty cygnets before, with advancing age, he became infertile. His mate still lays a clutch each spring so for the last eight years we have substituted a clutch of Black-necked Swan eggs, and they have raised a foster-family instead.

In Patagonia I have been lucky enough to see wild Black-necked Swans *Cygnus melanocoryphus* (*melano* – black and *coryphus* – helmeted). My best sight of them was in the Fitzroy Channel where there were flocks of up to a hundred, and at times nearly every bird was up-ended, looking very droll. Years later I saw them there again in a rough sea, bobbing about among the huge waves. The first European to see this bird was the English naval commander Sir John Narborough, on 2 August 1670, while he was sailing towards the Straits of Magellan. Specimens reached Europe alive in 1846 and a pair bred at the London Zoo eleven years later. This was the first swan species to produce young at Slimbridge and two pairs still do so regularly, the early clutch of one of them going to the Black Swans and its replacement being hatched by the real parents.

Oscar – the juvenile
Coscoroba at Slimbridge.
Dafila Scott.

6

PLATE I Coscoroba Swans. ABOVE: with newly-hatched conspicuously patterned young at Philadelphia Zoo. *Zoological Society of Philadelphia*. BELOW: aggressive wing raising of the adults. The feather-down around the eggs is very noticeable. *Zoological Society of Philadelphia*.

PLATE 2 Coscoroba Swans. ABOVE: in flight in Argentina, showing black wing tips. *M. W. Weller*. LEFT: unique among swans is the feathering between eye and bill in the adult. Dark marks on plumage are due to bird feeding in mud. *Russ Kinne*. RIGHT: the dark crown, seen in Plate 1, is still obvious in this juvenile. *Philippa Scott*. BELOW: this older cygnet shows the greyish feathering of the first plumage. *Philippa Scott*.

The other South American swan, the Coscoroba (which is perhaps only a swan by courtesy) seemed to be less common in Patagonia and less gregarious. A scattered thirty-two was the most we ever found there, though I recently saw rather more in the pampas quite near Buenos Aires. The Coscoroba was scientifically described in 1782, and first reached Europe in 1870. In 1952, one of the pairs at Slimbridge built a huge nest, and in due course produced a cygnet, inevitably named Oscar – the first to be reared in this country for over half a century. In the breeding season the male Coscoroba is quite aggressive and rushes up to stand against the fence with a cry of Cos-cor-oo (from which no doubt its name must be derived).

The migratory Whooper Swans, which winter in many parts of Britain, have long delighted me with their grace and music. I knew them well from my early excursions along the Norfolk coast, and have painted them many times against waves and snow, and grey skies and sunsets. I have also seen them far out on the Transcaspian steppes of northern Persia, and later, during our study of the Pink-footed Geese in central Iceland, encountered them again, this time on one of their remote breeding grounds. We arrived there just as the eggs were starting to hatch, and were amazed by the tameness of the pale grey cygnets. On several occasions we were followed by newly hatched babies who evidently mistook us for their parents, and we had to retreat hastily to avoid leading them away from the nest. Some older cygnets, which we caught for marking, at first feigned death and then rushed away to their mother, whose relief at their return was delightfully reflected in the changed note of her almost continuous calls. One cob apparently tried to lead us from his family by repeatedly flying from us and settling a few hundred yards ahead.

Whooper with blue eyes (the iris is
normally brown) found breeding in Iceland.

The Whooper Swan *Cygnus cygnus cygnus* is the 'type' species of all the swans; that is, it is the one described first by the great Swedish taxonomist Linnaeus in the middle of the eighteenth century. Surprisingly, he did not distinguish between it and the Mute Swan, apparently thinking that they were the same species of which some were wild, *ferus*, and others tame, *mansuetus*.

The Whooper's North American relative (I am inclined to think not a *very* close relative) is the still rather rare Trumpeter Swan *Cygnus cygnus buccinator* (*buccinator* meaning literally a trumpeter). This magnificent bird, the largest of the waterfowl, was first distinguished from the Whistling Swan in 1831. At that time, and for many years before and afterwards, it was ruthlessly hunted for its meat and skin and appeared to have been brought to the verge of extinction. Thanks to vigorous protection in the United States, it has since made a remarkable recovery, and some new breeding groups have recently been discovered, which may mean that it was never in quite so much danger as had been supposed. In view of this, the Trumpeter Swan has now been removed from the list of endangered species which makes up the Red Data book of I.U.C.N.'s Survival Service Commission.

Trumpeter Swan.

One day when Her Majesty the Queen, then Princess Elizabeth, visited the Wildfowl Trust she told us that she was shortly to set out on a Royal Tour of Canada. Were there, she asked, any birds that she could bring back for us? I murmured that for some time we had been trying unsuccessfully to acquire some Trumpeter Swans. A couple of months later a cable came from Canada saying that three pairs of Trumpeter Swans had been presented to Her Royal Highness and asking whether the Trust would look after them for her. In due course five swans arrived (PLATE 30) and Her Majesty came down to see them only a few weeks after her accession to the throne. Wild swans do not usually breed for some years after being brought into captivity, so we settled down for a long wait. The first eggs were laid in 1959, but it was not until 1964 that any hatched. Since then, we have reared some cygnets nearly every year.

In the summer of 1969 I flew in an amphibious aircraft over southern Alaska, to see my first wild Trumpeters. We visited one of their forest-girt breeding lakes, skimming in over the trees and doing a 'ducks and drakes' landing. The swans with their two well-grown cygnets, which we had spotted from the air, made off into the cover of tall grass, but presently the cob emerged swimming out to lead us away from the brood. After looking at the vast pile of reeds which had been their nest we took off again, just topping the fringing spruces and looked down on the mother crouching with her cygnets as we turned to head for nearby Anchorage.

The smaller and much commoner North American species is the Whistling Swan, known to science since 1815 as *Cygnus columbianus* after the River Columbia where it was found. The first birds to reach Europe were imported in 1903, but it has not yet been bred there in captivity and is seldom seen in zoos and collections. At Slimbridge a pair nested in 1955 but the female died 'egg-bound' on the nest before laying. I first saw them breeding in the wild on the tundra pools of the Canadian Arctic near the Perry River in 1949, when we were studying the nesting of the lovely little Ross's Geese. The swans were sometimes remarkably curious about us, and one day, I remember, in bright sunshine an adult and two yearlings swam to within sixty yards to take a good look at us. It was a summer of unusually bad weather and we were often confined to camp by snow-storms, but the trip was entirely successful. One of the most memorable sights was a tundra pool soon after the break-up of the ice. It was a small pool covered with birds – seventy King Eiders and almost as many Long-tailed Ducks, a few Pintails, seven Whistling Swans and dozens of tiny Red Phalaropes swimming about in among them all. At the back were three Little Brown Cranes and a pair of White-fronted Geese. It was an unforgettable scene.

More recently, I have flown over the Kuskokwim Delta in Alaska and seen hundreds of nesting Whistlers below, and once we landed from a helicopter beside a pair which seemed to have a nest but turned out just to be sitting down, perhaps occupying a territory for the following year.

The slightly smaller Bewick's Swan *Cygnus columbianus bewickii* fills the same place in Europe and Asia as the Whistling Swan in North America. It was named by Yarrell in 1830 in honour of Thomas Bewick of Newcastle, the eighteenth-century ornithologist and engraver, whose telescope, dated 1794, is now used for watching Bewick's Swans at Slimbridge. As I said earlier, the Bewick's Swan is now my favourite bird, and the saga of their build-up on Swan Lake is, to me, one of the most exciting events in the history of the Wildfowl Trust. Before the establishment of the Trust in 1946, Bewick's Swans were almost unknown on our part of the Severn estuary, though a few were often found on the Somerset 'moors' fifty miles away. It was quite an event, therefore, when a single male dropped in to join the Whistling Swans which we kept in our collection of captive waterfowl. The date, I remember, was 3 November 1948. We decided to catch him, because at that time we needed his kind to add to the collection; a mate was procured from Holland, and in 1956 the pair bred – the first ever to do so in captivity (PLATE 36). Over the next few years an increasing number of wild Bewick's Swans began to appear in the enclosures, attracted by the birds already there. By the winter of 1963–64 about twenty were coming in each day in pairs and family parties, mostly to pools where they were constantly disturbed by visitors and had to fly out to the estuary several times a day. Then on 9 February 1964 I had the idea of moving all the tame swans on to the pool in front of my studio window, in the hope that the wild birds would join them so that we could have the opportunity of watching them at close quarters. On the very next day the first one appeared, and within a week all twenty-four swans then in the neighbourhood were flighting in daily from the estuary half a mile away. We gave them peace and food – no disturbance except for the warden twice a day pushing a wheelbarrow full of wheat. Almost immediately we realised that the swans could be recognised individually by the variations of the yellow and black patterns in their bills. These were like finger-prints but much more obvious and enabled us to give a name to every bird (which we thought easier to remember than numbers).

Bewick's Swan.

In mid-March the swans left for their breeding grounds 2,600 miles away on the tundra shores of the Kara Sea and the Yamal Peninsula. Next November they returned to Swan Lake, bringing their young and some of their 'friends'. In 1964–65 there were fifty-five at peak, and sixty-eight different swans were recorded during the winter. In January 1966 when I telephoned to my wife from the Antarctic she reported that for the first time 100 Bewick's Swans had been counted on Swan Lake, and that year the total for the season was 147. And so the build-up continued. By the winter of 1970–71 – the eighth year of the study – the maximum day total was 411 with 626 recorded in the season, and by then names had been given to

1,315 birds (PLATES 35 to 42). Each bird has a dossier containing a drawing of its bill pattern, its family connections, its yearly arrival and departure dates and, for most of them, a series of portrait photographs taken by my wife from the studio window with a 600-mm. lens (PLATE 39). Seven people have so far been involved in the study and have had to learn the names and face patterns of many swans – three members of the Scott family and at various times four members of the Wildfowl Trust's scientific staff. The task, however, has become increasingly difficult and in the winters after 1968–69 only Miss Mary Evans and my daughter Dafila could recognise every swan.

One of the most beautiful aspects of Swan Lake is from dusk until midnight, when the pond is floodlit. The lamps had been installed long before the first swans came. We little knew then that we were to be adopted by a great mass of birds which, being white, shine with marvellous brilliance under the light. This artificial illumination does not seem to affect their behaviour, except that they are able to continue feeding after dark.

On first arrival in late October the birds spend most of their time, day and night, on Swan Lake, resting and feeding to recover the weight lost on migration. But after two weeks they begin going out to the river, and later most of them leave under the floodlights to spend the night on the sandbanks or drifting with the tide. When they come in again at sunrise they often circle again and again before landing. The pool has been specially extended to give them an adequate approach in all winds but flying is still difficult so close to the buildings. In frosty weather the water is kept from freezing over by submerged propellers, and in the early morning the combination of food and open water produces an impressive concentration of wildfowl in an area of not much more than an acre. During this morning assembly, when the Bewick's Swans are mixed with up to sixty Mute Swans, a few Whoopers, 100 feral Canada Geese and several hundred wild ducks – mostly Shovelers and Pintail, a 'roll-call' is made of the Bewick's and the presence of each swan ticked on a chart. Any newly arrived swans are drawn and named. The choice of self-explanatory names is difficult, especially as behaviour is almost the only clue to sex unless the bird is in the hand. The names of most single swans are descriptive like Lemon, Splodge, Y-front, Primrose. Puns are frequent and mates are often given names which go logically together, for instance Kon and Tiki, Swan and Vesta, Antony and Cleopatra, Stars and Stripes, Pote and Tate, Hyle and Fling, and Harvey and Maria.

Pink and Rebecca, one of the early faithful pairs.

The study has already taught us quite a lot about social structure, aggression, dominance, winter territorialism, stress, hereditary flying skill and family devotion. In eight years we have not had a single case of divorce, and the families are extraordinarily tightly knit. Some swans when bereaved take up to three seasons to find a new mate, though some re-pair much sooner. The cygnets are only three months old when they are led by their parents on the first of their flights from Siberia. We have discovered that some cygnets join up with their parents in the second and even the third winter of their lives. On present evidence we think that Bewick's Swans normally breed first when they are four years old and some at least not until five. We do not yet know how long their breeding life may be, or indeed their expectation of life in the wild state, but suspect it may sometimes be as high as twenty years. In captivity swans can live to thirty years and it is this potential longevity which makes a long-term study of individuals so rewarding. One unexpected finding of our study has been that several swans have missed a winter with us and a few have missed two. We do not know why, or where they went instead. But most of all we want to find out more about the migrations of these tundra swans, and to this end we are catching as many as possible for ringing. At first they used to catch themselves by flying into the trees in the darkness behind the floodlights and falling unharmed into the garden or into some of the smaller pens from which they could not escape. Now the trees (as well as the pool) are floodlit so that the birds can see and avoid them. Instead we have built a screened ditch like a duck decoy pipe into which the birds are attracted by food and then driven along it to a holding pen at the far end. By the spring of 1971 we had ringed 304 Bewick's Swans in these various ways. Recoveries have been recorded from the Soviet Union, East Germany, Denmark, Northern Ireland and Eire.

In addition to the standard metal rings we now use our own design of white or coloured plastic rings engraved with large black numbers that can be read through binoculars (PLATES 9 and 38). Recognition of known individuals away from Slimbridge by other observers not involved in the recognition of bill patterns is also being assisted by the use of dyes. All the 115 swans caught in the winter of 1970–71 had their tails, scapulars and wingtips dyed yellow. This lasts, of course, only until they moult in the summer. By 1971 Slimbridge swans had been recognised in several places away from Swan Lake. The first of these to be discovered was Ashleworth Ham – an area of floodwaters about fifteen miles further up the Severn. Here in the 1970–71 winter some twenty-five of 'our' swans were to be seen.

On the Wildfowl Trust's Welney Reserve in Norfolk, where up to 1,200 Bewick's Swans appear in some winters, one bird was seen which had been ringed at Slimbridge in the previous year, though it was too far-away for the individual ring number to be read. In March 1970 after the swans had left Slimbridge on migration my daughter Dafila followed them to the Netherlands to see how many she could recognise there. At various points along the flooded River Ijssel she found six, including a favourite pair Peasant and Gypsy (PLATE 40), which subsequently returned to Slimbridge the next winter. Three of the six were ringed and the black number on the tall white ring of one named Raquello could be read by the Dutch ornithologists present who until then had been not unreasonably sceptical of her recognitions. In March 1971 the River Ijssel was not flooded and so Dafila, paying a return visit, found no swans there, and only a few in fields further south. In Denmark she saw three dyed swans (two in Jutland and one in Zealand), but only two of them were close enough for recognition by the bill pattern.

Before long we hope to extend the study of the Bewick's at our reserve on the Welney Washes, by feeding them close to the new observatory building; we also have plans to follow the spring migration route through the Netherlands again, to Germany, and Sweden. Ultimately, perhaps, we might even reach the shores of the Kara Sea and the Yamal Peninsula. To find and study our Slimbridge friends at their nests on the tundras of the Siberian Arctic would surely be the greatest thrill of all, perfectly completing the work made possible by the technique of individual recognition.

Unbeknown to us another 'Swan Lake' has been developing in Japan. At Suibara, near Niigata, Whooper and Eastern Bewick's Swans have been building up rapidly during the last fifteen years, in response to winter feeding and protection. From fifteen birds in 1955 the concentration had reached 687 by 1967 and over 1,000 by 1970. The initiative for all this came from a farmer, Jusaburo Yoshikawa, and his son Shigeo who continues the work of feeding the swans. The Hyoko (Swan Lake) at Suibara is at the edge of an industrial area and appears to be some 400 yards in diameter with rice paddies along one side. The lake became a National Monument and at times as many as 10,000 people come to see the swans.

Intimate knowledge of one kind of swan illuminates the study of the other seven, and indeed of other kinds of birds. But this monograph is concerned with swans. In the following chapters you will find all the information we and others have discovered about swans already. We know quite a lot about some of them: where and how they live, how they bring up their families, and the factors that threaten their survival. About others, we know comparatively little. Living in the more remote parts of the globe, they are almost beyond the reach of biologists and observers. But there are so many questions still to be answered. We hope that this book will stimulate your interest and perhaps you will come to share our enthusiasm for these beautiful birds.

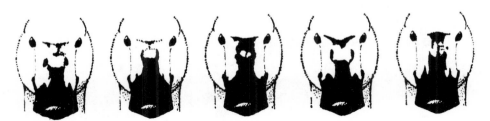

Pink and Rebecca, Owl and Pussycat, and Moody.

Whistling Swan.

2

Classification

Hugh Boyd

It is easy to recognise a swan. Swans are large, long-necked waterfowl with short legs and large feet, readily distinguished by the layman from all other birds. Unfortunately, if you ask any two or more taxonomists how many kinds of swan there are, the answers they give are unlikely to be the same. The classification of animals is a game, based on facts but dependent for its outcome upon the weight of opinion and so scarcely a scientific activity at all. Taxonomists are temperamentally inclined to be either 'lumpers' or 'splitters'. Lumpers are more interested in the resemblances than in the differences between closely related animals, and so are more helpful to the non-specialist. Among the lumpers who have addressed themselves to the study of the family Anatidae (the ducks, geese and swans), the most magisterial are undoubtedly Jean Delacour and Ernst Mayr, who published a major reclassification of the family in 1945 (65). Their work simplified the understanding of the relationships within the group a great deal. Additional facts discovered in the last twenty-five years have left their scheme relatively intact; it will therefore be followed here.

The fundamental taxonomic unit is generally held to be the species; species being grouped together into a larger unit, the genus, or further divided into subspecies or races. This kind of classification is expressed in the Linnaean system of binomial nomenclature, in which a species has two names, the name of the genus preceding that of the species. If several sub-species are recognised a third name is added. The species has been defined in a variety of ways, none being fully efficient. The essential notion seems to be that of a group of animals resembling each other in many ways and reproductively isolated from otherwise similar animals.

Coscoroba. *Dafila Scott.*

The lack of rigour in applying this idea is such that some present-day taxonomists recognise eight species of swans in the world while others see no more than four: they may use five genera, or only one. In my view it is most convenient to recognise six species in two genera. One species, *Coscoroba coscoroba*, from southern South America, is so unlike the rest that it may not be a swan at all but, as it is large and long-necked, and white, it seems a pity to segregate it too far.

Three other species are readily distinguishable: the Eurasian Mute Swan *Cygnus olor*, the Australian Black Swan *Cygnus atratus* and the South American Black-necked Swan *Cygnus melanocoryphus*. They live far apart, and they look very different when full-grown. In the evolutionary sense, however, they seem to be quite closely related, especially the first two.

Black-necked Swan.

The northern swans, breeding in or near the Arctic regions of Eurasia and North America, differ markedly from the southern species but resemble each other sufficiently to create difficulties for field observers as well as museum men. They form two groups of two: in North America the very large Trumpeter and the smaller Whistling Swan; in Eurasia the large Whooper and the small Bewick's Swan. The bill of the Trumpeter appears all black at a distance; that of the Whistling Swan usually has a small yellow patch close to the eye, while the Whooper and Bewick's Swans have much larger yellow patches. These swans have often been considered as four distinct species, but Delacour prefers to treat the Trumpeter and Whooper as two subspecies (*buccinator* and *cygnus*) of *Cygnus cygnus* and the Whistling and Bewick's Swans as subspecies (*columbianus* and *bewickii*) of *Cygnus columbianus*. All four forms are at present isolated reproductively. The breeding range of the Trumpeter, which has been much reduced in the last century, is now well south of that of the Whistling Swan, except in one small corner of Alaska (187), and even on migration the one can seldom encounter the other. The ranges of the Whooper and Bewick's Swans overlap, both in the breeding season and outside it, but no hybridisation takes place. This being so, the argument for Delacour's division is to emphasise that the differences between the large and the small form in each continent are greater than those between either the two large forms or the two small ones.

Whooper Swan cygnet.

The adults of the eight species and subspecies may be identified, at the most superficial level, by means of the following key. The most reliable, though not the most readily observed, characteristics for distinguishing between the northern swans are in italics.

1. Plumage pure white   see 2
   Plumage white and black   see 5
2. Bill reddish orange and black, with black knob   MUTE SWAN
   Bill black   see 3
   Bill black and yellow   see 4
3. Bill large and deep; little or no forehead; *length from eye to nostril equals length from nostril to bill tip*; very large bird, with proportionately long neck   TRUMPETER SWAN
   Bill slender; slight forehead; *length from eye to nostril longer than from nostril to bill tip*; small swan, with relatively short neck   WHISTLING SWAN
4. Small yellow spot close to eye   WHISTLING SWAN
   Yellow patch on bill does not reach nostrils, and generally has round or square distal end; small swan with relatively short neck   BEWICK'S SWAN

Yellow patch on bill extends to a point, and ends below or just beyond the nostril; large bird with proportionately long neck .... WHOOPER SWAN

5. Body plumage black .... BLACK SWAN
   Body plumage white .... see 6
6. Head and neck black .... BLACK-NECKED SWAN
   Head and neck white, wing tips black .... COSCOROBA SWAN

Such a key fails to make use of much of the available information on adult swans, including their internal anatomy, dimensions and behaviour; it also ignores the differences between the adult plumages and those of young birds. Most of the information on the appearance of the species at various ages is conveyed more effectively by the photographs throughout the book than by lengthy descriptions of the plumages. The latter are not, therefore, attempted here, but can be found in Delacour (64), and in the standard regional handbooks. For the species found in Britain, the detailed accounts by Mrs. A. C. Meinertzhagen, originally published in the *Practical Handbook of British Birds*, are still unrivalled in the English language (345).

Table 1. Body weights of adult swans

	MALE MEAN WT.			FEMALE MEAN WT.		
	kg.	lb.	oz.	kg.	lb.	oz.
Coscoroba Swan	4·6	10	2	3·8	8	6
Black-necked Swan	5·4	11	14	4·0	8	13
Black Swan	6·2	13	11	5·1	11	4
Bewick's Swan	6·4	14	2	5·7	12	9
Whistling Swan	7·1	15	10	6·2	13	11
Whooper Swan	10·8	23	13	8·1	17	14
Trumpeter Swan	11·9	26	4	9·4	20	12
Mute Swan	12·2	26	14	8·9	19	10

The average weights of male and female adults are shown in Table 1. The full data relating to these and some other frequently used measurements are summarised in Appendices 1, 2 and 9. These go a little further than verbal descriptions in establishing the differences between one swan and another, though a much larger battery of measurements would be needed to do so thoroughly. And how many watchers of swans can catch and handle them alive? Dead swans are too big to be welcome in museum collections and get stuffed in the most curious ways. It is extremely difficult to determine the length of a swan's neck; yet the length of the neck, both in absolute measurement and in relation to that of the body, is the most effective means of distinguishing a Bewick's Swan from a Whooper, or a Whistling Swan from a Trumpeter. In each case the larger bird has the relatively longer neck.

Newly hatched cygnets are a little harder to identify than adult swans. In all species the down on the undersurface is white, while the hues of the upper parts and the bill and feet differ from one to another:

Black-necked Swan cygnet (left) and Black Swan cygnet (right).

SPECIES	DOWN OF DORSAL SURFACE	BILL	FEET
Coscoroba Swan	Greyish white, strongly marked with white and blackish grey on front of head; back and wings clearly patterned grey	Grey, pink patches at tip and near gape	Pale pink tinged grey
Black Swan	Light brownish grey, rather darker on neck	Nearly black with light grey tip	Dark grey tinged brown
Mute Swan	Nearly uniform light grey; or white in leucistic phase (see page 105)	Dark bluish grey	Bluish grey (or pale grey/pink)
Black-necked Swan	White, faintly tinged pale grey	Bluish grey	Bluish grey

PLATE 3 Black Swan family. *Jane J. Miller*.

PLATE 4 Black Swan. ABOVE: nest within a colony at the edge of Lake Ellesmere, New Zealand. *J. T. Darby, Otago Museum, N.Z.* LEFT: nest in Tasmania, neatly constructed and with little feather-down. *E. R. Guiler.* RIGHT: newly-hatched cygnets in Queensland. *H. J. Lavery.*

Whooper Swan/ Trumpeter Swan	Pale greyish white, rather darker on lower nape, shoulder and rump. Trumpeter also has a pale phase (page 108)	Flesh pink, grey at tip and along sides	Pale orange to flesh coloured
Bewick's Swan/ Whistling Swan	Pale greyish white, with vague darker patterning	As Whooper; but bill already relatively smaller and with down extending less far along it	Pale orange

Bewick's Swan cygnet. *Dafila Scott.*

Trumpeter Swan cygnet. *Peter Scott.*

The first feathered plumages of all species of swan differ from those of mature birds by the inclusion of more or less brown or grey colouring. Some of these brown or greyish feathers may be retained into the second and occasionally the third year. Because of the brown colouring, young Black Swans look lighter than adults but in the white swans the young birds are obviously darker than adults. The yearling Black-necked Swan has black wing tips. After fledging, the colours of the soft parts resemble those of the cygnets but these change more or less speedily into dull versions of the adults during the first two years of life. The greyish plumage of the young northern swans is not to be confused with the russet staining of the head and neck which occurs in many adults and immatures. This is commonest in birds which are feeding in shallow lakes and marshes, and is caused by ferrous organic compounds in the water or mud. The Trumpeter Swans in North America become stained almost as soon as the moult is complete, and few, if any, are ever entirely free from some discoloration (14). Many of the migratory swans wintering in Britain are also discoloured (PLATE 20), particularly the Whoopers in the north of England and in parts of Scotland (3).

Whooper Swan with iron-stained head and neck.

The appearance of swans does little to explain why their closest relations are thought to be the geese. For that it is necessary to look at the internal anatomy, particularly the skeleton. But anatomy cannot be described in any detail without the use of a specialised and alarmingly polysyllabic vocabulary that would be out of place here. The general point to be made is that, when resemblance is measured by the extent to which two species or groups of species possess, or lack, analogous anatomical features, the swans and the geese are found to be extremely similar. With respect to internal structures, the differences between them are very largely in their relative proportions, rather than in presence or absence.

The recent growth of interest in the behaviour of animals has led to the realisation that studying what birds do and how they do it is as helpful in understanding their affinities and their ancestry as looking at their anatomy. Just as some features of their construction show little variation between one genus and another, while others differ greatly in proportions, so it has been found that the range of behaviour patterns involved in, say, the care of plumage is more 'conservative' than the variety of displays associated with the formation and maintenance of pair bonds. It is thus possible to classify the species of waterfowl into genera, tribes and larger groups on the basis of how they do things, and to emerge with a picture which is not only as detailed as that assembled by the comparative anatomists but which looks, encouragingly, very much the same.

A particularly important resemblance between swans and geese is that both have a well-developed and prolonged family life. Pairs usually stay together as long as both birds remain alive. The male shares with the female in the care of the brood and the family remains together for nearly a year: some immature birds continue to associate with their parents even after the latter are caring for their next brood. This persistence of family groupings has profound effects on the social structure of 'herds' of swans and 'flocks' of geese. Perhaps more importantly, it enables parents to show their offspring what routes to follow and what places to live in on migration, in winter and on return to the breeding sites. Unlike the geese and swans, the ducks (with a few possible exceptions) have not exploited this opportunity for supplementing innate recognition of environmental characteristics by traditional example. In the geese it has resulted in a relatively high degree of genetic segregation between different groups within a species. The Canada Goose, for example, has split into many races, that look different and behave distinctively. The swans, however, have not subspeciated any more than, for instance, the diving ducks. The Whooper Swans of Iceland are rather smaller than those of the Eurasian mainland: the Bewick's Swans of eastern Siberia have larger bills than those further west, and for that reason are sometimes separated as Jankowski's Swan. No one has yet tried to carve up the southern swans into races, though it has been claimed that the extinct New Zealand Swan was a subspecies of the Black Swan.

Swans are conspicuous animals, emphasising their size by the boldness of their plumage. Their striking appearance is presumably used for intra-specific signalling at long distances, as well as at close quarters. The utterances of most swans also include bugling calls of great carrying power. Looking at, and listening to, northern swans dispersed over the tundra one can see why.

Geese and swans are alike, and differ from other waterfowl, in the simple structure of their vocal apparatus. Waterfowl do not show the complex musculature of the syrinx possessed by song birds. They achieve their characteristic qualities of voice by variations in the size and shape of the windpipe (trachea) and of the syrinx. Swans and geese have symmetrical tracheae, without the bulbous bullae of ducks, and with no appreciable difference between the sexes. In the Coscoroba Swan, as in the geese, the males have higher-pitched voices than the females. In the other swans the sexes have voices of similar pitch, or those of the males are lower. The earliest anatomical investigators of the northern swans found that they have extraordinarily long and convoluted tracheae. Presumably these account for the powerful calls, in the manner of a trombone. It has recently been found that the Trumpeter Swan lacks the internal tympaniform membranes, the vibrations of which have generally been held to produce sound.

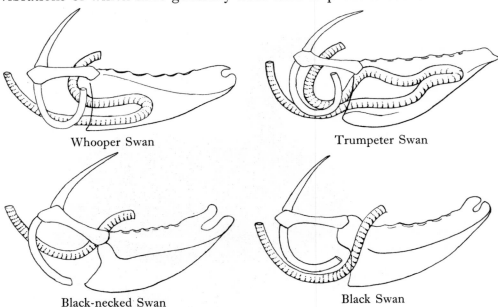

Whooper Swan   Trumpeter Swan

Black-necked Swan   Black Swan

Windpipe and breastbone in adults of four swan species.

The southern swans have tracheae of uniform diameter which lack convolutions. The Black Swan has a high-pitched musical bugle and an extensive vocabulary. Black-necked Swans whistle, rather than sing. Mute Swans are not mute but are relatively quiet, using hisses and snorts, and occasionally a quiet whistle. These three species all produce a loud singing note with their wings when in flight. Like the cries of the northern swans, these sounds may help to keep the birds in touch with one another.

The lack of sexual differences in the voices of swans parallels the lack of sexual dimorphism in their plumage. Males tend to be larger and to have more intensively coloured bills, but these are differences of degree, not kind.

The significance of the yellow patches on the bills of Whooper and Bewick's Swans (PLATES 24 and 39) is not altogether clear. The intensive observations on Bewick's Swans at Slimbridge have revealed that the patterning of black and yellow on the bills differs recognisably from one bird to another and remains nearly constant from year to year in most individuals. It seems unlikely, however, that this characteristic is of crucial importance for identification of one swan by another, since the Trumpeter and Whistling Swans can make little use of it. There are, of course, many other clues available, such as the proportions of the bill and head, which are hard to define by mensuration but can often be appreciated, even by an unskilled observer. No one has yet watched Whistling Swans (PLATE 31) closely enough to know whether their apparently greater similarity to each other makes their lives more difficult or less interesting.

3

Distribution, numbers and migration

M. A. Ogilvie

The swans, as a group, have an almost world-wide distribution, being indigenous to every continent except Africa and Antarctica. Of the eight species and subspecies, three are natives of the southern hemisphere, the South American Black-necked Swan and Coscoroba Swan, and the Australasian Black Swan. North America has the Trumpeter Swan and the Whistling Swan, and Eurasia, the Mute Swan, the Whooper Swan and the Bewick's Swan. The Mute Swan also occurs as an introduced species in Australasia, North America and South Africa. Most of the populations, especially in the northern hemisphere, are migratory, but except for vagrants there is no movement between continents, and none between the two hemispheres.

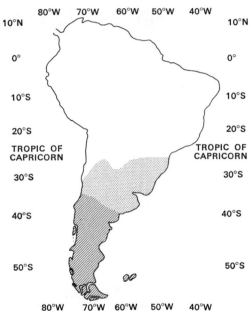

Distribution of Coscoroba Swan. Hatched, breeding range; stippled, additional wintering range.

Coscoroba Swan

The Coscoroba Swan is an inhabitant of southern South America. Its breeding range, shown in the Figure, extends from Tierra del Fuego and the Falkland Islands north through Chile and Argentina to Uruguay and southern Brazil (64, 247). It is fairly common south of 45° S, the greatest concentrations being in southern Chile and Argentina. In winter it is found a little further north in Brazil and into Paraguay, though probably not north of 25° S. The southern breeding birds are migratory, but the extent of their movements is unknown. It is possible that they travel long distances to the wintering areas north of the breeding range, this type of 'leap-frog' migration being not uncommon among waterfowl and waders. On the other hand, the northern birds could equally well be wanderers from the nearest breeding locality.

No attempt has yet been made to estimate the total population. Although there are no reports of very large flocks or colonies, the birds are widely distributed, and it seems not unlikely that they number some tens of thousands.

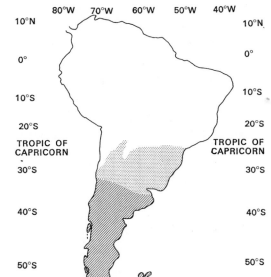

Distribution of Black-necked Swan. Hatched, breeding range; stippled, additional wintering range.

Black-necked Swan

The distribution of the Black-necked Swan is similar to that of the Coscoroba (see Figure). It breeds in southern South America, in Tierra del Fuego, the Falkland Islands, Argentina, Chile, Uruguay and the southernmost parts of Brazil (64, 247). The greatest numbers are towards the south. In winter the species has been found as far north as the Tropic of Capricorn, in Paraguay and the three southern provinces of Brazil. Birds breeding or summering in the south of the continent move north in winter, but their

31

destination is unknown. The origin of the birds which winter to the north of the breeding range is also obscure.

The Black-necked Swan is said to winter in larger flocks than the Coscoroba (291), but there is no indication as to whether it is more or less numerous.

Black Swan

The Black Swan is a native of Australia, and is also widespread in New Zealand, following its introduction there about a hundred years ago. In Australia, the breeding distribution is predominantly southern, the greater part of the population being concentrated in the extreme south-west of Western Australia, in the southernmost parts of New South Wales and South Australia, and in Victoria and Tasmania (see Figure). Small numbers also breed regularly throughout the west of Western Australia, and in central Queensland and northern New South Wales. Vagrants have been recorded in nearly all the remaining parts of the continent, wherever suitable habitat occurs (88).

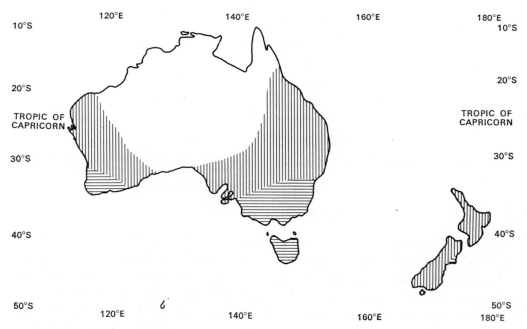

Distribution of Black Swan. Horizontal shading indicates normal range, vertical shading shows especially favoured areas.

Although no detailed estimate has yet been made of the total population within Australia, the species is certainly numbered in hundreds of thousands. In 1957 some 50,000 birds were seen on the Coorong, a brackish coastal lagoon in South Australia, and at the same time a further 50,000 were recorded on Lake Albert. Several other inland waters, such as Fletcher's Lake, and the Yanga and Cowal Lakes, are capable of supporting 15,000 swans, and many more attract up to 5,000 on occasion (88). In addition there are several districts, particularly in Western Australia, in which the species is described as abundant.

At one time the flocks were thought to be largely sedentary, but recent counts and visible marking schemes have revealed a good deal of movement (88). Many of the non-breeding birds perform moult migrations, and in addition there is a certain amount of nomadic wandering. This is prompted mainly by the weather and the availability of suitable habitat. The rainfall over much of Australia is erratic in both timing and quantity, and many areas become flooded only after periods of rain. These temporary wetlands are quickly exploited by Black Swans and other waterfowl, not only as feeding places, but also as breeding sites. Because of the irregularity of the rains, the timing of the breeding season and the pattern of movement varies considerably from year to year (page 119). The full extent of the movements is not yet known, but journeys of several hundred miles have often been recorded. During dry spells the birds concentrate on the coast, on sheltered lagoons and bays.

The Black Swan was introduced from Australia into New Zealand just over a hundred years ago (88, 228). The first four birds were released at Christchurch, South Island, in 1864, and were followed in 1865 by a further thirteen pairs. These initial introductions were made in the hope that the birds might help to control the water-weed in the rivers, but later on they were brought in mainly as ornamental birds or to provide sport. During the next five years about seventy swans were released in Otago, and a smaller number in the North Island. Shortly afterwards birds began to appear in areas several hundred miles away from the release points, and large flocks were being reported from some localities. By 1895, a colony of several thousand birds was established at the mouth of the Opawa River, near Marlborough. Some authors have suggested that the expansion of the species in New Zealand must have been aided by natural immigration from Australia, but this supposes a remarkable coincidence, as none had previously been known to wander that far. It seems, therefore, that the rapid increase was due solely to the ideal conditions prevailing at the time. The main factors were no doubt the abundance of suitable habitat, and the virtual absence of both predators and competitors.

At the present time, Black Swans are widespread on all suitable waters, both fresh and brackish. The largest concentrations are at Lake Whangape and Lake Ellesmere (228). At the latter resort the population is estimated at 60,000, and is kept at that level by strict control. In recent seasons not more than 20,000 eggs have been allowed to hatch each year; the remainder are gathered up and sold. Other major centres include the Otago Lakes in the South Island, and the Waikato Lakes in the North. No estimate has yet been made of the total population in New Zealand, but the evidence points to at least 200,000 birds.

Black Swans have been brought to Europe over a long period of years but have never become established in the wild. Most of the specimens are kept in zoos or private collections and, although odd pairs have presumably escaped from time to time, no one has attempted to release large numbers. Even escapes are rare, the reason being that the birds are expensive to acquire, and are usually well guarded.

Mute Swan

The Mute Swan is common and widespread in many parts of Europe and Asia, notably in the British Isles, the Netherlands, Denmark, southern Sweden, Germany and Poland (see Figure). It also occurs, less abundantly, in Belgium, northern France, Switzerland, Austria and Turkey. In many of the northern areas the present status and distribution has been greatly influenced by introductions and by the long history of domestication – so much so that it is often impossible to determine which populations are truly wild. In Iberia and Italy the species is rare as a breeding bird, and the same is true of Norway, Finland and the northern parts of the U.S.S.R. In the southern U.S.S.R. there are several breeding areas scattered at intervals from the Black Sea eastwards to 81° E and northwards to about 56° N.

Then, after a considerable gap, there are further breeding populations to the east of Lake Baikal and in the Ussuri Basin, and Mongolia. The species also breeds in Iran and Afghanistan (331, 64, 345).

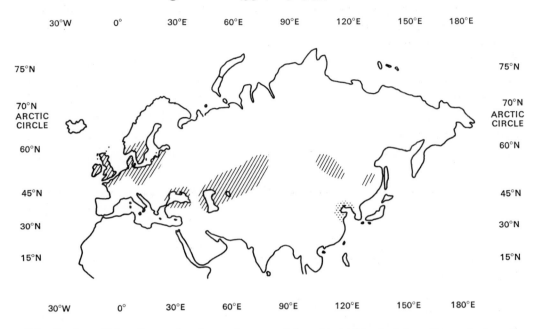

Distribution of Mute Swan, showing main areas of abundance. Hatched, breeding and wintering range; stippled, winter only.

The status and distribution of the Mute Swan has been studied in detail in several countries, mainly in north-west Europe where the species has increased greatly in numbers and range during the last forty years. In the United Kingdom it is found on all suitable habitats throughout the lowland districts, the largest numbers being in the south-east. The immature and non-breeding birds forgather on the larger lakes and reservoirs, and on some estuaries; they also show a preference for the rivers in the centre of large towns. The largest flock in the country is on the Stour estuary in East Anglia, where up to 1,000 swans congregate for the summer moult, and 500–700 remain throughout the year. The birds feed extensively on the waste grain which is tipped into the river from the nearby maltings. Another flock, almost as large, is located on the Fleet, behind Chesil Beach in Dorset, a site which includes the well-known breeding colony at Abbotsbury. Although the colony itself contains only 30–50 pairs, the Fleet as a whole has a winter population of up to 850 swans. Some of these are the immature and non-breeding birds associated with the colony, the others come from further inland and more especially from Radipole Lake, near Weymouth, where a further 30–50 pairs breed regularly. The birds feed largely on *Zostera*, which is abundant over much of the Fleet. Elsewhere there are many flocks of 100–200, mostly on rivers in towns, as for example, on the Thames in London, the Avon at Stratford and the Trent at Burton.

The total number of Mute Swans in Britain has been estimated with considerable accuracy. On two occasions during the past fifteen years a full-scale census has been made of the birds occurring in all the more important districts. Regular monthly counts have also been made each winter on a sample of several hundred sites throughout the country. The first census took place in the spring and summer of 1955 and 1956, and covered virtually the whole of England, Scotland and Wales. On the basis of the two years combined, the breeding population was estimated at 3,500–4,000 pairs; in addition there were rather more than 11,000 non-breeding birds. The total population lay between 17,850 and 19,250 (43, 271).

At the time of the census many observers spoke of recent increases, and shortly afterwards both farmers and fishermen began to complain of damage to their interests. A second census was therefore arranged during the summer of 1961, to discover whether the population was in fact increasing at the rate suggested. The study in this case was restricted to a sample of twenty-six important counties in England and Scotland, and was conducted largely by means of aerial survey. The total number of Mute Swans counted came to more than 12,000, a figure which corresponded almost exactly with the total obtained from the same areas in 1955 and 1956. Despite this apparent stability in the population, it was found from the regular winter counts that substantial changes had taken place between the two censuses. During the first four years up to 1959 the numbers had increased steadily, but thereafter showed a rapid decline, and by 1961 they had fallen almost to their previous level (77). There was a further decrease, of 25%, between 1961 and 1965 (242). Since then the population has become more or less stable (see Figure). The second part of the decrease coincided with the hard winters of 1961–62 and 1962–63, both of which caused heavy mortality. It is clear, however, that other factors are now preventing the numbers from increasing again (page 129).

As a part of the same study more than 14,000 Mute Swans were caught and ringed in Britain during the six years between 1961 and 1966. Several

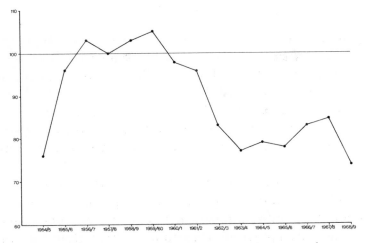

National indices of Mute Swans in Britain, based on 1959–60 = 100.

thousand of these were subsequently recaptured or found dead from various causes. The mass of information obtained in this way was used to discover the extent of the birds' movements, and to assess the mortality rates among different age-groups (page 128). The movements were nearly all restricted to distances of less than thirty miles, and usually followed the line of a watercourse (242). There was also evidence of a possible moult migration by small numbers of birds from the Thames Valley and West Midlands, and from Northumberland and Durham. The former appear to move to a site near Barrow-in-Furness, and the latter to Loch Leven, Kinross-shire. There is virtually no migration of Mute Swans to and from the Continent, except perhaps in very hard weather. During the severe winter of 1962–63 a few birds ringed in Sweden, Denmark and the Netherlands were caught or found dead in south-east England, and similarly a few of the birds ringed in south-east England in early 1963 were later reported from those three countries and also from Germany (125).

Migrating Mute Swans. *Robert Gillmor*.

37

The Irish population is again large and widespread. Breeding has been recorded in nearly all counties, and on some of the islands off the west coast. There are not many town flocks, but several large gatherings occur, especially on tidal waters. In Co. Wexford flocks of up to 500 are found regularly, and in 1946 one flock reached a peak of no less than 1,500 (282). The total population is probably in the order of 5,000–6,000. As in England, the birds are largely sedentary; there is certainly no evidence of migration across the Irish Sea.

In the Netherlands the Mute Swan has increased steadily over the past fifty years. The breeding population is at present estimated at about 2,500 pairs, and the winter numbers at 15,000–20,000. The birds show little sign of movement, except within the country, although in cold winters there may be some immigration from further east. About half the breeding pairs are concentrated in Zuid-Holland; the rest are distributed fairly evenly in all districts, except the drier south-east. Zuid-Holland also contains the largest wintering flocks, the numbers at times amounting to as much as three-quarters of the national total. Another important centre is on the Ijsselmeer.

By comparison the numbers in France are insignificant. Some 50–100 pairs are found breeding in the north of the country, and a further 50–100 individuals winter along the Mediterranean coast. The Belgian population is also small.

Further to the east another large population is distributed over Denmark, Sweden, Finland, the Baltic Republics, Poland and the northern parts of East and West Germany. At the onset of winter the birds move from the inland districts to the Baltic coast, and as the weather hardens continue westwards to the milder areas around the Danish islands. In January 1969 a synchronised count in most, if not all, the main resorts produced a total of just under 90,000, of which 66,000 were in Denmark, 14,800 in East Germany, 4,450 in West Germany and 4,200 in Sweden. Poland held 1,235 and Finland 116; the Baltic Republics had none. This distribution is probably typical of a rather cold January, but in other months and other years would certainly be different.

Counts of breeding swans have recently been made in all these countries, with the exception of Sweden and Germany. In each case the numbers have increased greatly over the past few decades. Prior to 1939 the Polish breeding population is believed to have totalled about 400 pairs. By 1956 it had increased to 1,000 pairs, and in 1958 stood at 3,600. There was also a big

PLATE 5 Black-Swans. ABOVE: in flight at Lake Ellesmere, showing their white wing tips. *Country Life*. BELOW: in Queensland. *H. J. Lavery*.

PLATE 6 Female Mute Swan defending her nest. Her open wings, ruffled neck and gaping bill are signs of imminent attack. She has some white ('Polish') cygnets. *Zoological Society of Philadelphia.*

increase in non-breeding birds from 1,500 in 1956 to more than 3,000 in 1958 (304). No recent information is available, but the increase has probably continued.

In Estonia, Latvia and Lithuania the Mute Swan was virtually exterminated during the late nineteenth century, but is now firmly re-established. The first breeding record from Estonia was in 1959; by 1963 there were 10 pairs nesting (161). In Latvia a few pairs bred on Lake Engure from 1935 onwards. These had increased to 12 by 1957, and scattered pairs were becoming established elsewhere. In 1964 there were 40–60 pairs in the country, and up to 70 non-breeding birds (334). In Lithuania, a few pairs nested sporadically during the 1930s, but it was not until the early 1950s that the numbers began to increase. By 1955 there were 35–40 pairs, and in 1960 about 100 (233). Here again the trend has probably continued.

Mute Swan with cygnets. *Robert Gillmor.*

The increases in Denmark have been even more striking. During the nineteenth century the species suffered a serious decline, and by 1925 was reduced to only three or four pairs. Next year it was afforded full protection, and the numbers began to increase. By 1935 there were 30–40 breeding pairs, by 1950 nearly 400 pairs and in 1954 about 750 (251). The latest figures are for 1966, when the number of pairs was estimated at 2;500 (31). The annual rate of increase over the thirty years between 1935 and 1966 was remarkably constant at around 17%. This presumably represents the normal growth-rate of a population under optimum conditions, with abundant food and virtually no interference. It could not have been maintained, however, had not the birds abandoned their normal territorial behaviour, and evolved the habit of colonial breeding. At the present time, there are many colonies with up to 100 pairs in each, mainly along the tideless Baltic coast. This allows large numbers of birds to breed in areas where food is particularly plentiful, but where the number of nest sites would be limited by territorial spacing (page 90). Before long the population will presumably begin to stabilise, perhaps through shortage of food; if the present rate of increase were maintained until 1976 the number of pairs would exceed 20,000.

In central and southern Europe the Mute Swan is somewhat restricted by lack of suitable habitat, but is common enough in some districts. Counts from Switzerland indicate a breeding population of about 250 pairs, and a winter total of around 3,500 (18). The latter apparently includes a proportion of migrants from further north, and in hard winters there is often a substantial increase; in the early part of 1963 nearly 4,000 birds were recorded on the Bodensee alone. Austria has only a small breeding population, and less than 1,000 are present in winter. The same is generally true of Hungary and the other countries in the region. In Greece 96 birds were introduced on to Lake Agras in 1965, and by 1969 had increased to 200. It is hoped that these will now spread to other sites.

Further to the east there are several small populations scattered across the southern regions of the U.S.S.R. The birds here are migratory, and in winter move from their inland breeding areas to the shallow bays and deltas of the Black and Caspian Seas. Recent counts from these two regions, and from the neighbouring resorts in Romania, Bulgaria and Turkey, suggest a total of 5,000–6,000 birds. There are also records of a few birds wintering in the regions beyond the Caspian, for instance on the Aral Sea, on the rivers above Tashkent and in the eastern parts of Kirgizstan. In each case the flocks totalled less than a hundred birds, the only exception being on Issyk-koul near Alma-ata, where up to 400 were recorded in both 1967 and 1968. This it seems is near the limit of this particular group. The far eastern population, between Lake Baikal and the sea, has not yet been censused. The birds from this area are presumably those which appear in winter along the Pacific coast, from Korea southwards to the Yangtze Kiang, and which on occasion wander to Japan. No details are known of the summer distribution within the U.S.S.R., even in the western regions around the Black Sea. It seems, however, that the majority of the juvenile and immature birds are left behind on the wintering grounds and remain there till the adults return the following autumn (66).

The Mute Swan also occurs, as an introduced species, in Australia, New Zealand, parts of North America and South Africa. The first birds reached Australia in the mid-nineteenth century and were released on to lakes in city parks. In addition a few pairs were released on more natural habitats, particularly in Tasmania and in the south-western district of Western Australia. These birds became established, but the species has not increased or spread to any marked extent. The main limitation appears to have been competition from the indigenous Black Swan. The situation in New Zealand is the same. The first introductions were made in the 1860s, but the species is still largely restricted to ornamental waters. There are, however, a few areas in both islands in which it has managed to establish itself in the wild (88). In the United States the Mute Swan is well established along the eastern seaboard, from Massachusetts south to New Jersey; there is also a sizeable flock in north-west Michigan. In a few areas the species appears to compete with the Canada Goose, but in general it has not succeeded sufficiently to become a nuisance. There is a small population of about 120 Mute Swans in Cape Province, South Africa, mainly on two estuaries. They are descended from a few birds introduced from Europe some fifty years ago (300).

Whistling Swan

The Whistling Swan breeds in Alaska and in Canada, mainly to the north of the Arctic Circle (see Figure). In the west its range extends to St. Lawrence Island in the Bering Sea and as far south as Bristol Bay, and in the east to Southampton Island and the northern parts of Hudson Bay. It may also breed on Baffin Land. The wintering grounds lie almost exclusively in the coastal areas on both sides of the continent. On the Atlantic seaboard the main resorts are between Chesapeake Bay and Currituck Sound, in the neighbouring states of Maryland and North Carolina; on the Pacific coast they are scattered more widely from southern Alaska down to California. Stragglers have also been reported from the far east of Siberia (66).

The division on the breeding grounds between the birds which winter on the east coast, and those wintering in the west has not yet been defined, but it probably lies quite far west. It is known, for example, that the swans which breed on the Mackenzie River in the North West Territories, migrate to the Atlantic coast. There are also reports from northern Alaska of birds moving eastwards in autumn before turning south along the eastern side of the Rocky Mountains. Birds marked on the east coast in winter have been seen in Alaska during the breeding season (302). During the course of their migration large numbers of swans concentrate on the Great Lakes; the

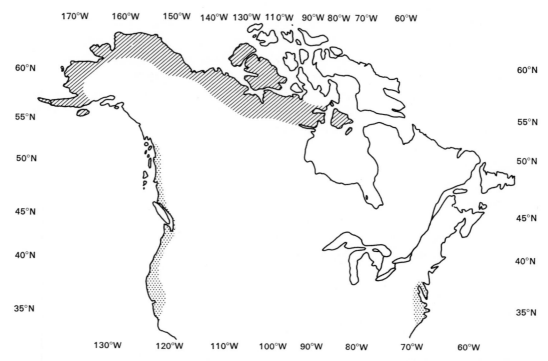

Distribution of Whistling Swan. Hatched, breeding range; stippled, wintering range.

majority of these move south-eastwards towards the Atlantic coast, though a small proportion may head south-west.

Censuses of the entire population of the Whistling Swan have been made annually for many years. During the period from 1964 to 1969 the numbers fluctuated widely from 81,000 in 1967 to 137,000 in 1968. The average for the six years was 103,000. The numbers on the east coast varied from 45,000 to 72,000, and on average represented 56% of the total; those on the west coast varied from 31,000 to 75,000 (211). The population may well have increased slightly in recent years. The average count for the period 1952 to 1956 was 86,000 (313). This annual variation in numbers is a common feature among wildfowl which breed in the Arctic, and is attributable to differences in the breeding success from year to year (page 98).

Bewick's Swan

The Bewick's Swan, like its North American counterpart the Whistling Swan, is an Arctic species with a wide range of breeding and wintering grounds (see Figure). Its numbers, however, are relatively small. The breeding range extends from the Pechenga River, near the Fenno–Russian border, eastwards along the north Siberian coast to about 160° E. The main centres in the west are on the Yamal Peninsula and in the districts around the Kara Sea, including Vaygach Island and the southern half of Novaya Zemlya. It also breeds on Kolguev Island. Further to the east it occurs on the lower reaches of the Lena, Yana and Indigirka, and also on the Kolyma River which is said to be about the limit of its range. There is, however, an unsubstantiated report of nesting on the Anadyr River in the district adjoining the Bering Sea. For the most part the breeding grounds lie to the north of the Arctic Circle, but in some parts, for example in the Yenesei Basin, nests have been found as far south as 61° N. Some taxonomists have claimed that the Bewick's Swans to the east of the Lena belong to a separate larger-billed race (64), but this has doubtful validity (326).

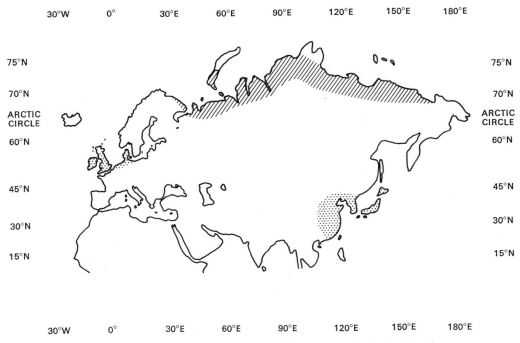

Distribution of Bewick's Swan. Hatched, breeding range; stippled, wintering range.

Bewick's Swans are wholly migratory, none wintering within a thousand miles of the breeding grounds. In Europe, the autumn migration follows the Gulf of Finland and the south coast of the Baltic Sea. The wintering grounds lie primarily in the Netherlands, but substantial numbers also occur in Germany, Denmark, England and Ireland. A few occur regularly in Wales and Scotland, and more occasionally in France, usually as a result of hard weather. Vagrants have been recorded from the Mediterranean, including Algeria (331). Many authorities have stated that the species winters on the Caspian and Aral Seas, and on some of the lakes to the east (64, 331, 345). There is no evidence, however, of large, or even regular, occurrences; in fact, the recent winter censuses have failed to record a single bird (9, 151). Occasional birds have been seen in north-west India, Kutch and Sind.

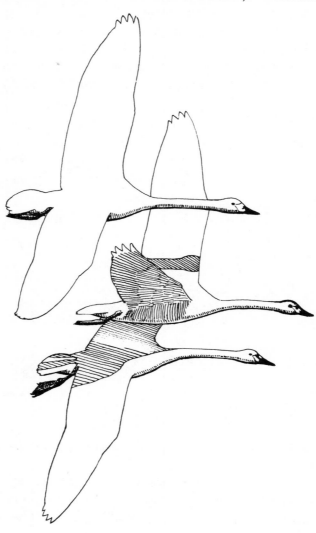

The Bewick's Swans from the eastern parts of the breeding range migrate to wintering areas in China, Japan and Korea. In China they have been recorded as far south as Kwangtung province, and inland up the main river valleys. Lake Bu-Yan on the Yangtze River is quoted as an important resort, but, in common with the rest of China, there is no recent information on the numbers present. On migration they are seen in Kamchatcka, the Kurile Islands and Sakhalin, and vagrants have reached Formosa (331).

Considerable changes in the winter distribution have taken place in north-west Europe, especially within the British Isles. The species was first distinguished from the Whooper Swan in 1830, and for the rest of the nineteenth century was said to be common in Scotland, particularly in Tiree and South Uist. Large numbers were reported migrating through the Shetlands in autumn and spring, and many moved on into Ireland (19). By the 1930s the pattern was completely different. The birds were no longer passing through Scotland on their way to Ireland, but were flying over England instead. As a result, the Scottish resorts fell into disuse, while in England, where the species had never wintered regularly, there were many more reports of birds being sighted. This trend continued until the winter of 1938–39, when a period of severe frost in north-west Europe resulted in a large influx of birds into southern England. Further influxes took place in the hard winters of 1953–54 and 1955–56, and at the same time small numbers of birds were beginning to appear regularly, irrespective of the continental weather. In this way a wintering tradition was built up, the main centre being on the Ouse Washes on the Cambridge–Norfolk border (240, 241). At the present time there are five or six localities in Britain which hold appreciable numbers of birds throughout the season, and many more are used by smaller flocks for varying lengths of time. The total number of birds wintering in the country is now over 1,500, about five times as many as in the early 1950s. In Ireland on the other hand the numbers have fallen from 1,500–2,000 to less than 1,000, due largely to the loss of habitat through drainage and disturbance (243). Still larger numbers may winter in Britain in the future as an alternative both to Ireland, and to the Netherlands where the habitat is being reduced by reclamation projects.

In north-west Europe as a whole the winter population is estimated at 6,000–7,000, of which about 3,000 are normally located in the Netherlands, 2,000 in the British Isles, 700 in Denmark and 300 in West Germany. No marked trend has been observed, at any rate during the past ten years, though the total number may fluctuate considerably from year to year depending on the success of the breeding season. After a good summer the proportion of young birds in the winter flocks has been as high as 44%, and in a bad year as low as 8% (243). The size of the eastern population is unknown, but it seems unlikely that the numbers are substantially greater than those in the west. The only positive information comes from Japan, where a total of 540 was recorded during a recent winter survey of the main resorts.

Trumpeter Swan

The Trumpeter Swan at one time bred over a wide area of North America, from Alaska and Arctic Canada south to Iowa and Missouri and eastwards as far as Indiana. The wintering grounds were also extensive, lying mainly along the Atlantic seaboard, along the valleys of the Ohio and Mississippi and around the shores of the Gulf of Mexico. In the nineteenth century, however, their numbers and range were drastically reduced by excessive shooting. This trend has since been reversed, but even now, after many years of protection, the species is still confined to a series of small and often isolated localities in Alaska, British Columbia, Alberta, Wyoming and Montana (see Figure).

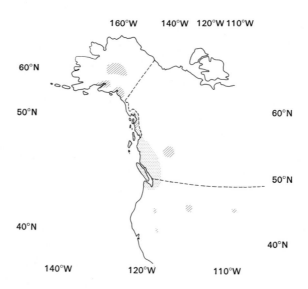

Distribution of Trumpeter Swan. Hatched, breeding range; stippled, wintering range.

Most of the Trumpeter Swans surviving today are descended from non-migratory stocks, which remained throughout the year in areas remote from the heaviest of the shooting. This tradition continues, and except for the Alaskan birds which move to the coast and down into British Columbia, the population is virtually sedentary. This applies particularly in Montana and Wyoming, where the presence of hot springs enables the birds to remain in the one small enclave, even through the hardest winters (14).

The present population of the Trumpeter Swan is estimated at not more than 5,000 individuals. Even at this low level it is much more numerous now than thirty years ago. In 1932 the important centre in Montana and Wyoming held a total of only sixty-nine birds. Three years later a reserve was established, and the flock began to increase, reaching a peak of about 600 in 1955. Since then the population has remained stable, suggesting that the area is incapable of supporting more. In view of this, a number of birds were transported to sites in Oregon, Nevada and South Dakota, where new breeding populations are now successfully established. The numbers in Alaska have also increased steadily, from less than 1,000 in 1958 to an estimated 4,000 at the present time. Elsewhere the numbers are small (14, 297).

Whooper Swan

The Whooper Swan replaces the Trumpeter throughout Europe and Asia. The main breeding range extends from Iceland and northern Scandinavia across the U.S.S.R. to the Urals and on through Siberia to the Pacific coast (see Figure). Unlike the Bewick's Swan, it is not normally found on the northern tundra, the majority of the nest sites being on the rivers and lakes of the taiga and scrub zone. Further to the south a few pairs may breed sporadically on the northern shore of the Caspian Sea, in one or two districts of Kirgizstan, Altai and Outer Mongolia, and northern Manchuria eastwards to Sakhalin. It also breeds very occasionally in southern Greenland, and even more rarely in Scotland (331).

The Icelandic population totals between 5,000 and 6,000 individuals. Of these about 2,000 winter in Ireland, up to 2,000 in Scotland, and not more than 500 in the northern and western districts of England and Wales (39). The remaining 1,000–1,500 winter in Iceland, for the most part on the brackish lagoons along the south-east coast and on certain inland waters which are fed by hot springs. Although most of the migrants leave Iceland

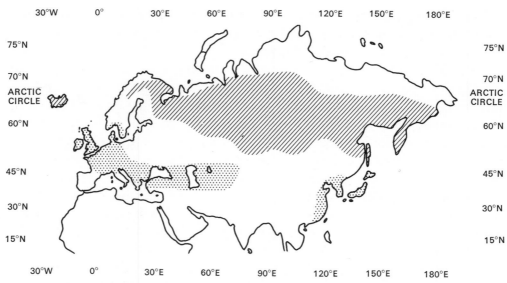

Distribution of Whooper Swan. Hatched, breeding range; stippled, wintering range.

in October, it may well be that further movements take place during the course of the winter, depending on the weather. There is also a considerable interchange of birds between Scotland and Ireland which leads to substantial variation in the winter distribution. In addition to the Icelandic birds, a few Scandinavian migrants are believed to reach Britain each winter.

Central Iceland.

Recent counts in north-west Europe indicate a total winter population of about 14,000. In January 1968 there were 10,000 in Denmark, 1,500 in Sweden and 1,200 in Germany; small numbers were also present in Poland, the Baltic Republics, Norway and the Netherlands. These presumably represent the bulk of the population which breeds in Scandinavia and

48

western Russia. The birds from further east winter mainly on the Black Sea and the Caspian. Counts from these areas suggest a total of at least 25,000, of which more than half are normally located in the south-west corner of the Black Sea, between the isthmus of the Crimea and the delta of the Danube. There are also records of up to 400 birds in Greece, and of up to 1,000 in the area between the Aral Sea and the western border of China. The main resort in this case is on Issyk-kul where 500–700 were reported in two successive seasons.

The populations breeding in eastern Siberia winter predominantly in Japan and Korea, and in China south to about Shanghai. No information is available on numbers, except from Japan where upwards of 11,000 were recorded in a recent census.

Aspects of Swan Migration

Tradition plays an important role in the life of swans. Each spring the breeding pairs return to the same nest sites, and each autumn follow the same migration routes to the same familiar wintering grounds. By doing so they benefit from the accumulated experience of their own and previous generations. As young birds they remain with their parents during most of their first year of life, and learn from them the elements of survival; as parents they, in turn, pass on to their cygnets the details of the well-tried migration routes, and the equally well-tried breeding and wintering grounds. During the course of each winter the families may move from place to place, depending on the weather, the availability of food and the amount of disturbance, but usually keep to sites which they know to be suitable. Some birds, however, may wander more widely and sometimes discover new wintering places, to the benefit of the population at large.

In some species the young birds remain with their parents until the spring migration to the breeding grounds is almost complete; in others they stay behind on the wintering grounds or move only part of the way before congregating at some suitable place. Observations on the Bewick's Swans at Slimbridge have shown, not unexpectedly, that the birds in their second autumn return to the winter quarters independently, but if the parents appear the family reunites. This happens even when the parents are accompanied by a new brood. The group then spends the winter together, and in due course departs for the spring migration, still as a family party. As in their first year, the second-year birds probably follow their parents all the way to the breeding grounds, thus reinforcing their memory of the route, and increasing the likelihood that they in turn will breed in the same general area.

Some swans, although capable of breeding, are inhibited from doing so by various factors, such as adverse weather, the loss of a mate or changes in the breeding habitat. Many others start to breed, but lose either eggs or young to predators or natural hazards. These non-breeding and unsuccessful pairs usually gather into flocks in company with the birds which are still too young to breed, and make their way to traditional moulting grounds. This movement, known as moult migration, sometimes entails journeys of several hundred miles, and is prompted presumably by the need for ample food and minimal disturbance during the flightless period (page 118). It is also to the advantage of the nesting pairs and young that the birds without family ties should not remain on the breeding grounds throughout the summer. Their departure relieves the pressure on the local food supplies, and increases the chance of survival for the parents and cygnets, which together form the most important segment of the population (283).

Migrating swans fly high and fast. The speeds at which they travel have been measured with some accuracy by timing them over known distances, and by pacing them in cars and aircraft. In still air, all species attain an average of between 35 and 50 m.p.h., the rates being somewhat higher on migration than on local flights. The speed in relation to the ground depends on the force and direction of the wind: with a following wind a bird might well cover sixty or seventy miles in an hour, and with a strong headwind, not more than twenty or thirty. The height at which they fly is more difficult to determine. Most swans migrate at night, leaving the daylight hours for feeding, and the details of their flights are seldom observed. In good conditions they probably climb to an altitude of between 2,000 and 5,000 feet, and exceptionally to as much as 10,000 feet, the turbulence there being much less than at lower levels. If the weather is bad, with low cloud or strong headwinds, they usually fly quite close to the ground. Although the turbulence there is greater, the wind force is less, and the visibility better.

Migration is more frequent in clear weather than in cloud, probably because the birds rely on the sun, moon and stars as their main aids to navigation. This applies in particular to sea crossings, and in regions which lack any obvious landmarks, such as rivers, coastlines and mountain ranges. It is often said that the birds wait until the full moon before moving, but there is no evidence that this is so; provided that the nights are clear, migration can take place at any time. The moon, in fact, is a less satisfactory aid to navigation than the stars, and it may well be that its only value is to light the way.

Most of the migrations undertaken by swans are over land, and the birds are able to stop at intervals for rest and food. Some journeys, notably those undertaken by the Whistling Swans in North America, and by the Bewick's Swans in Eurasia, involve distances of up to 2,000 miles, and take several weeks to complete. During this time, the birds make use of a series of traditional stopping-places along the way. In North America the progress of the Whistling Swans has been studied by attaching miniature radio transmitters to individual birds, which can then be followed in light aircraft. This has shown that even over land the flocks are likely to cover several hundred miles at a single flight.

The longest non-stop flights are probably those undertaken by the Whooper Swans which migrate between Iceland and the British Isles. The journey in this case entails a sea crossing of at least 500 miles, and some birds may well add an extra hundred miles at either end. In calm conditions the crossing itself ought not to take more than ten hours, but much depends on the strength and direction of the wind. If the weather at the starting-point is bad, the birds delay until it improves or until shortage of food forces them to leave. Even if they leave in good weather, they are not unlikely to run into storms on the way; the north Atlantic is seldom calm for long and it seems improbable that the migrants can predict the rapidly changing weather situations which lie ahead of them. Not enough swans have yet been ringed to show how often they run into difficulties, but the geese which make the same journey have sometimes been found far off course. On several occasions, after a westerly gale, observers on the east coast of Scotland have seen flocks of Pink-footed Geese struggling in from the North Sea to make their first landfall. A few birds have even been swept as far east as the coasts of Norway and Denmark.

Spring observations from the northern tip of the Outer Hebrides have shown that both geese and swans often leave for Iceland in anticyclonic conditions, when calm air and clear skies will aid their passage. At such times, however, there is often a depression centred over Iceland, and the birds are therefore likely to encounter cloud and rain on approaching their destination. It is not yet known whether this results in losses. Swans are more powerful fliers than many of the migrants making the same journey but, even so, some of them probably perish through exhaustion.

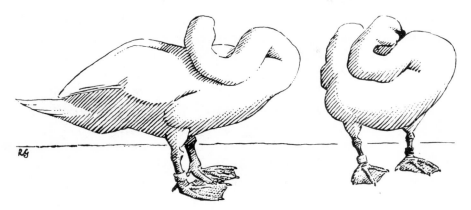

Ringed Mute Swan pair. *Robert Gillmor.*

Counting and Ringing Techniques

Most of the detailed information on distribution, numbers and migration has been gained through the two study techniques of counting and ringing. The first adds the all important facts of status to the bare outlines of distribution and enables populations to be measured and monitored; the second is the main source of information on migration, and on the age-structures and mortality rates within the various populations (page 128).

The system of counting varies considerably depending on the type of information required. The main aims are to detect and measure changes in the level of population, and to estimate the total numbers of the species in various parts of their range. Both these aspects are essential aids to conservation; the first shows the extent and urgency of the problem, the other indicates the areas in which measures can most usefully be applied.

Censuses of a species over the whole of its range are generally impracticable, because of the effort involved; they have, however, been undertaken with notable success in cases where the population is restricted to a few well-defined areas at certain stages in the year. The Whistling Swan provides an obvious example. Successful censuses have also been made of the small discrete populations which occur in some regions. These include the Icelandic population of the Whooper Swan (page 47), and the resident population of the Mute Swan in England, Scotland and Wales. Similar censuses of the birds occurring in a particular country or region are sometimes quite easy to arrange. In Britain, for example, the wintering Bewick's

Swans are concentrated on to less than twenty sites, and a simultaneous count on these few places will provide an accurate national total. In this case the organisation is so simple that the census can easily be repeated each winter; with most other species, however, the interval between censuses may be as long as ten or even twenty years.

The detection of trends requires a different approach. The counts in this case can be restricted to a relatively small sample of important sites, and should, where possible, be repeated on several set dates each winter. If the same sites are covered on each occasion, a direct comparison can be made of the numbers present in different months and in different years. These comparisons will give a reliable indication of any trends which may be taking place in the population as a whole, provided always that the sample of sites is reasonably representative. The results of the British Mute Swan counts, shown on page 37, are a good example of the high quality information which can be gained without undue expenditure of effort.

The counting of swans presents fewer problems than the counting of most other wildfowl, except in the few localities which hold more than one species. Unlike geese and ducks, they seldom have to be counted in flight, or in large concentrations. They are also an ideal subject for aerial censuses, being readily visible, whether on the nest or in winter flocks. This technique has been used extensively in Britain, Denmark, America and Australia, and is particularly useful in areas where observers are scarce, or where the terrain makes ground counts impracticable.

The marking of birds by means of numbered leg rings was first attempted more than seventy years ago; it is only in the past ten to fifteen years, however, that swans have been ringed in large numbers. The standard ring is made of a light alloy, and is stamped with a serial number, and with an address to which the finder is asked to send details of the place and date of recovery. Such recoveries depend on the bird being found dead, or being caught for a second time, and because of this the majority of the rings placed on birds are never seen again. The highest recovery rates come from the species which are hunted extensively, like most of the ducks and geese. Although swans are not normally a quarry species, the recovery rate is

PLATE 7 Female Mute Swan carrying a cygnet. *Jane J. Miller*

PLATE 8 ABOVE: family of Mute Swans in Sweden with one 'Polish' (third from left) and several grey-brown cygnets in their first plumage. *B. Thyselius.* LEFT: Mute Swan upending to feed underwater. *Philippa Scott.* RIGHT: Bewick's Swan upending. The longer wings of this migratory species are noticeable. *Philippa Scott.*

relatively high; obviously a dead swan is much more likely to be noticed than a smaller and less conspicuous bird.

The standard ring has the limitation that the number on it is illegible at ranges of more than a few yards. The bird cannot, therefore, be identified under normal field conditions. This difficulty can be partly overcome by the addition of coloured rings or neck-bands. In a small population a different colour or combination of colours can be allotted to each individual, but where larger numbers are involved, the colour system can be used only for generalities, such as the place of capture, the year of hatching, or the status of the bird within the population. A recent development has been the use of large plastic rings, with numbers which are visible through binoculars at distances of well over a hundred metres. Rings of this type have been used with considerable success on Mute Swans (PLATE 9) and Bewick's Swans in Britain (PLATE 38), and on Whistling Swans in North America.

An easy time to catch swans is in July and August when the cygnets are too young to fly, and the adults are flightless during the annual moult. The birds can then be rounded up and herded into temporary pens erected near the water's edge. If this proves impracticable, they have to be caught individually, by pursuing them in a boat. Mute Swans, particularly in the neighbourhood of towns, are often tame enough to be caught without pursuit, either by hand or with the aid of a crook attached to a long pole. Baited traps have also been used with success on the wintering grounds of some species. All these methods require considerable experience; swans are powerful birds, and can hurt both themselves and their captor, unless handled properly. The experienced handler has the knack of holding the bird in a way which prevents struggling, and which causes no harm, apart from a slight loss of dignity.

Standard metal swan ring.

Peasant and Gypsy.

4

Food and feeding habits

Myrfyn Owen and Janet Kear

Trumpeter Swan flexing upper jaw.

Swans rely for their food on aquatic vegetation, which they reach by dipping their heads and necks or by tilting like ducks.

The most important part of their feeding apparatus is the bill. This is large and, except in the Coscoroba, is well suited to a number of different feeding actions. The skull is high and wide, providing a strong base for muscle attachment, and the jaws are powerful, allowing the firm grasping action with which most of the food is secured (100). As in most wildfowl, there is some degree of movement in the upper jaw, although not enough to impair the grip.

Scissor-like cutting edges are present along the sides of the bill, but these are relatively coarse, and the vegetation is more often torn than cut. The nails on the tips of the mandibles are large and strong, and the surface of the tongue is spiny, features which are valuable for both grasping and chopping.

58

There are also horny serrations fringing the tongue and bill, which enable the bird to dabble for floating particles of food. The Coscoroba has developed this feeding method much further than the other swans. Its wide bill is lighter and more flexible, and the serrations are fine and well formed, providing an effective strainer for large quantities of muddy water.

The neck, in all species, is long, muscular and extremely mobile. The number of cervical vertebrae is in fact greater than in any other warm-blooded animal: the Mute Swan has 25, and the Black-necked Swan 24, whereas geese have only 18 or 19, and the Giraffe a mere seven. The possession of a long neck is invaluable to the swans, enabling them to feed on submerged vegetation which lies too deep to be reached by the surface-feeding ducks, and not deep enough for exploitation by the diving ducks.

The presence of salt-excreting glands allows the birds to make use of marine and freshwater habitats. They may even be able to drink salt water. The glands are situated just under the skin above the eyes, and are often noticeably swollen in swans which have been feeding on intertidal vegetation. Salt is removed from the blood-stream and excreted in concentrated solution through the nostrils; this then runs to the tip of the bill and is removed by the bird shaking its head.

Feeding Habits

When feeding in shallow water the swan submerges only its head and neck, keeping its body horizontal on the surface. In doing so it is able to lay its chin flat along the bottom, with the neck in an S-shaped posture which few, if any, other waterfowl are able to achieve (100, 139). The Mute Swan adopts this dipping action when the water is between 20 and 45 cm. deep, and normally submerges for just under 10 seconds (68). The Bewick's Swan stays down for 15–20 seconds (1). During this time the bird can swallow continuously, and the head is lifted only to breathe and look round. This does not apply if the swan is eating dry grain on land; in this case it has to raise and jerk its head in order to shake the food into its gullet.

If the water is too deep for dipping, the bird extends its reach by up-ending (PLATE 8). This movement is characteristic of all species except the Coscoroba (164). Mute Swans start tilting at a depth of 45 cm. and can still touch bottom at 90 cm. The Bewick's Swan has the shortest reach at 50–60 cm. (41) and the Trumpeter the longest, at 100–110 cm. Adult Whooper Swans up-end for 10–20 seconds at a time (3) and Bewick's Swans for 20–30 seconds (1). The Mute Swan averages 13 seconds (68). Each of a pair of feeding Trumpeters was seen to up-end about fifteen times in the course of half an hour. The birds acted quite independently and there was no sign of any synchronised system of feeding and guarding (14).

Food is also taken by placing the chin and bill horizontally along the surface and by filtering the water through the fine serrations along the side of the bill and tongue. The water is drawn in at the front of the bill and squirted out sideways leaving the particles of food trapped on the comb-like lamellae.

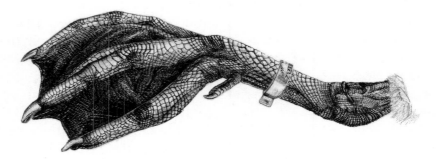

Leg and foot of Mute Swan. *Carol Ogilvie.*

All three of these feeding actions are accompanied by frequent foot-movements. These vary from gentle patting on a muddy surface to a vigorous racking of the bottom vegetation with the large webs and prominent toes (see above). The movement most often seen is combined with dipping and up-ending. The floating swan raises the front of its body, thrusts back with one foot after the other, and then returns to the feeding position (26, 41, 132, 141, 185, 332). This clears the mud from the roots and rhizomes of the aquatic vegetation, and loosens or severs the plants themselves. The food is then pulled to the surface, and shaken or chewed into pieces small enough to swallow. If the water is shallow, large holes, up to 30 cm. deep and more than a metre in diameter, are sometimes excavated in the mud (14, 41, 298). This probably does no harm; it has in fact been suggested that swans may help to improve the habitat by cultivating the marsh and by disseminating seeds and tubers over a wider area (298). Sometimes the holes are made in flooded meadows, and a certain amount of damage is apparent when the water recedes. The grass recovers, but for a while there may be some loss of grazing. Swans, especially of the northern forms, will also go ashore and feed on dry pasture, rather as geese do

(PLATE 21). The habit is more frequent nowadays when improved agriculture provides succulent grazing. Root crops, such as turnips and potatoes, are increasingly, although still rarely, taken. The roots are usually nibbled, or pecked to pieces with the nails on the tip of the bill, but large soft chunks may be gripped sideways and chopped in two with the edge.

The development of feeding patterns in young swans

Initially, the cygnets have most of their food brought within reach by their parents, and at this stage feed only by pecking and, to a lesser extent, by filtering the water surface. By the seventh day, however, a young Mute Swan is able to dip the whole of its head below water, and to hold it there for an average of just under two seconds (68). This increases to 4 seconds at 14 days, 6 seconds at 28 days and 7·5 seconds at 60 days. Up-ending begins at about ten days, but is brief and clumsy; even at seven or eight months a young Whooper Swan up-ends for shorter periods than its parents – a maximum of ten seconds as against twenty (3). At two weeks the babies start pulling and severing their own food, instead of just snapping up single items, and at four to eight weeks a young Trumpeter has been seen to start foot-paddling. Grazing ashore does not usually develop until the bird is fully fledged, or in the case of the migratory swans, until it reaches the wintering grounds.

At first the food is selected mainly by eye. The young bird hatches with an inclination to peck more at one type of object than another. It can see colour, and if presented with a variety of coloured dots will peck most frequently at the greens and yellows (176). Shape, size and brightness are also important, and more especially, movement. A smallish, moving insect is irresistible. The cygnet does not 'know' that the insect is good to eat, but has an innate inclination to try; if the outcome is successful it repeats the action and so learns by experience.

Later on, the young bird will do much of its feeding under water or at night, when selection by eye is impossible. Under these conditions the food is presumably selected by taste and touch. Although there is no direct proof of this, it is known that both bill and tongue are well provided with taste-buds and nerve-endings. As in most birds, the organs of smell are rather poorly developed.

The cygnets' choice of feeding ground is guided largely by the knowledge and tradition of their elders. It seems, however, that families of swans are more adventurous in seeking new feeding areas than groups of immature and non-breeding birds. Families of Whooper Swans quite often stray away from the main wintering flocks, encouraged perhaps by the eagerness of the cygnets to explore (3,332); they are also said to be less wary.

Mute Swans with cygnets. *Robert Gillmor.*

Food requirements

The amount of food required by swans varies, depending on the time of year. The periods of highest intake are before egg-laying and incubation, before the annual moult, before migration and during hard weather. In the first three instances the extra food is taken in anticipation of a period in which heavy demands will be made on the birds' reserves; in the fourth, it is needed to compensate for the additional energy which the bird uses in keeping warm. The variations in the reserves of fat are often substantial. Mute Swans have been found to lose an average of 770 gm. or more than 5% of their weight, during the four-week period of the moult (340). A 5% change in weight has also been noted among the Bewick's Swans wintering at Slimbridge; in this case the birds arrive with only small reserves of fat after their long migration, and gain steadily in weight over the next three months.

Information on the actual amount of food taken is hard to obtain under field conditions, and the results are contradictory. One estimate, based on an autumn study of the Mute Swans in Rhode Island, U.S.A., put the daily consumption of vegetation at 3,850 gm. (8·4 lb.) wet weight. At the time, however, the birds were losing weight, and the intake needed to keep them in good condition must be even higher (340).

PLATE 9 Mute Swans. ABOVE: female at her nest at Slimbridge. Her posture is threatening but less aggressive than in Plate 6 and she will probably not attack. She bears a numbered plastic ring. *E. E. Jackson.* BELOW: female at her nest in Switzerland with newly-hatched cygnets. *Kurt Gloor.*

PLATE 10 Mute Swans. ABOVE: a courting pair face each other with curved and fluffed necks, wings slightly raised. BELOW: family group. The brown-grey juveniles lack bill-knobs. *Philippa Scott.*

PLATE 11 Mute Swans. ABOVE: a cob threatening, or 'busking'. The wings are lifted high, neck feathers fluffed and head laid back, as in Plate 9. *Philippa Scott*. BELOW: a cob in Denmark charging a rival, a stage following the threat seen above. *Niels Preuss*.

PLATE 12 Male Mute Swans in boundary dispute in Switzerland. The 'wrists' of the wings and the beak are used in fighting. *Kurt Gloor*.

Feeding associations with other species

Swans are wasteful feeders and often leave drift lines of severed but uneaten vegetation in their wake. These are utilised by a variety of water birds, which lack the long reach of the swan, and cannot themselves exploit the deeper feeding grounds. Mallard have been seen in company with Bewick's Swans, waiting for the particles of food which the latter were stirring up from the bottom (185). Goldeneyes will close in on Mute Swans to take advantage of the aquatic animals disturbed by the larger birds (48), and flocks of Whoopers have been seen with Goldeneyes, Tufted Ducks and Wigeon gathered downwind (332). Pochard dive around up-ending Whoopers, and both Mute Swans and Whoopers are sometimes accompanied by Wigeon and Little Grebes (90,141). Whistling Swans are likewise followed by a variety of ducks and geese, sometimes several hundred strong. The species involved include Canada Geese, Snow Geese, Mallard, Pintail, Gadwall, Canvasback, Redhead and Bufflehead (298). Gulls parasitise the clam-eating Whistlers in Chesapeake Bay. There is even a report of shoals of small fish, *Leucaspius*, pursuing Mute Swans and feeding on their droppings (98).

These relationships are typical of the wintering, rather than the breeding grounds, and in general the swans show no resentment towards their satellites.

The Food of Swans

The food preferences of several species of wildfowl have been studied in detail by examining the stomach contents of birds shot by hunters in different types of habitat and at different times of year. This is one of the most reliable methods of assessment, but in the case of the swans it is seldom practicable, because in most countries the birds are strictly protected. The majority of studies are therefore based on the more general information obtained by direct observation in the field.

The swans are predominantly vegetarians, although some may take small amounts of animal material, either by accident or as part of their regular diet. The bulk of their food consists of the leaves and stems of submerged aquatic plants, including algae. *Potamogeton* is particularly important, and is taken extensively in many districts. The roots, tubers and stolons of aquatic and marshland plants are also favoured, especially by the North American swans. The stems and leaves of emergent vegetation are not much used, at any rate in winter, but may be more important on the breeding grounds. Seeds are seldom taken, except probably by the Coscoroba, but may provide a useful stop-gap in autumn and winter when other foods are scarce. Animal material is taken regularly by the Mute Swan, and to a lesser extent by the Whistling Swan, but not by other species. Fish and spawn are not an important part of their diet, despite the widespread statements to the contrary.

In recent years several species have been making increasing use of agricultural crops. The Mute Swan, Bewick's Swan and Black Swan graze regularly on cultivated pastures, especially when flooded, and the Whooper, and to a lesser extent the Whistling Swan, have taken to gleaning both cereals and roots. Some even scavenge on rubbish-dumps. Bread is also an important item in the diet of some swans, especially in the neighbourhood of large towns.

The following sections contain a brief account of the principal foods of each species, and further details are included in Appendix 4.

Mute Swan

Several investigations into the food of Mute Swans have been completed during the past fifteen years, notably in south-west England (95), Denmark (307), Sweden (27, 210, 248) and Rhode Island, U.S.A. (340). The results, which are summarised in Table 2, give a good indication of the relative importance of the various types of food in the areas under review, but the picture is by no means complete. In most cases the studies were carried out during the summer, and were confined to salt or brackish waters.

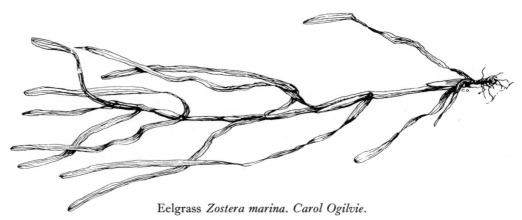

Eelgrass *Zostera marina. Carol Ogilvie.*

The British study was based on field observations on a resident flock of about 200 swans on the estuaries of the Exe and Otter in east Devon. It is of special interest because it reveals a marked change in the feeding pattern during the course of the year. Between April and June the birds graze on the salt-marshes, showing a distinct preference for the succulent plants, such as Sea Arrow-grass *Triglochin maritima*, Sea Plantain *Plantago maritima*, and Sea Aster *Aster tripolium*. The semi-succulent Sea Poa Grass *Puccinellia maritima* is also taken, but other grasses are avoided. Later in the summer the flocks move to the estuary itself, where they feed mainly on *Zostera* and the green algae *Enteromorpha*. During autumn and winter they either graze on the adjoining fresh marshes, or resort to the freshwater stretch of the river at Exeter, where their diet is supplemented by bread and other food provided by the public.

In Sweden, a major study of the Mute Swan was undertaken between 1957 and 1962 in response to accusations that the large flocks of birds along the Baltic coast were having an adverse effect on the stocks of fish. The work included two separate investigations into the birds' food. One took place on the coast around Karlskrona in the extreme south-east of the country, and was based on the examination of fifty-one stomachs obtained at intervals between April and August. The other was carried out on the brackish inlet of Valdermarsviken, some 200 km. further north, and was confined to the period July to October. In this case the study was based partly on an analysis of droppings, and partly on an examination of the drift lines of uprooted vegetation left behind by the feeding birds. Although the latter technique may be subject to errors, it seemed that the swans were taking the various plants in proportion to their availability.

The Danish investigation was also prompted by fears that the large and rapidly increasing population of swans around the coast of Zealand might be in conflict with the fishing interests. The work was based on the analysis of seventy-three stomachs, obtained at intervals between October and June. Here again the birds were found to be almost exclusively vegetarian.

The study of the feral population in Rhode Island was less detailed, relying for the most part on observations in the field. Some stomachs were examined, mostly from birds found dead, but often the contents were not fully identified. Nevertheless the results provide an interesting comparison with those obtained in Europe.

In addition to the foods listed in Table 2, the Mute Swan takes advantage of a wide range of other items which sometimes become available.

This applies particularly to the semi-domesticated birds which live on rivers and lakes in the neighbourhood of towns, and which subsist to a large extent on bread and other titbits provided by the public. In Britain these urban

Table 2. The food of Mute Swans at various sites in Europe and America

FOODS	A	B	C	D	E
			SITES		
Potamogeton spp. leaves		**	***	**	***
Chara spp.		***	**	**	**
Myriophyllum spicatum			***		**
Zostera spp.	**			***	
Ruppia spp.		**		***	
Other submerged aquatic plants		**	*	*	**
Green marine algae, *Enteromorpha* spp., *Ulva* spp.	**	**		*	**
Green algae, *Cladophora*, *Vaucheria*		**	***		
Brown algae, *Pylaiella* sp., *Fucus* sp.		*			
Saltmarsh succulents, *Plantago maritima*, *Aster tripolium*, *Triglochin maritima*, *Spergularia maritima*, *Glaux maritima*	**				
Grasses, *Puccinellia maritima*, *Glyceria maxima*, and unidentified	*		+		*
Emergents, *Scirpus* spp. leaves				*	
Seeds, *Najas marina*, *Scirpus maritimus*, unidentified		*			**
Animal – Mollusca		+		+	
Animal – Crustacea		+		+	

***Major source of food; **Regularly taken in small quantities or seasonally important; *Infrequently taken; +Accidental or trace.

A – Exe estuary and saltmarshes, SW England. Throughout the year.
B – Coast and islands around Karlskrona, SE Sweden. March–August.
C – Brackish inlet, Valdermarsviken, SE Sweden. July–October.
D – Coastal and inland waters, Zealand, Denmark. October–June.
E – Rhode Island, U.S.A. Mainly August.

flocks represent a sizeable proportion of the national population and it may well be that the species relies on this source of food for its present successful status. The birds in rural districts also depend on Man for a good deal of their food. Large flocks, sometimes several hundred strong, are attracted by the waste grain from mills, maltings and distilleries, as for example at Mistley in Essex, Burton-on-Trent, Invergordon and Alloa. Grazing on cultivated land is common in all parts of the country, and in Kent a party of Mute Swans was seen walking into a field of standing oats, to feed off the heads (121).

Despite the evidence of the Scandinavian studies, a certain amount of animal material is taken regularly. Among the items quoted are frogs, toads, tadpoles, worms, freshwater molluscs, and insects and their larvae (345). There are also reports of small fish being caught and eaten, notably in the Lake of Geneva (337). In parts of east Scotland it is normal to find flocks of wintering swans feeding on the refuse from the fishing fleets, and on the effluent from sewers (34). On one occasion a bird was even seen eating dead roach from a pond which had recently been frozen solid; some of the fish were as much as 15 cm. long, and were swallowed with considerable difficulty (145). Mute Swans have also been observed eating chunks of raw meat from the river at Bath (186).

Some of these examples are no doubt exceptional, but they serve to illustrate the adaptability of the species. The Mute Swan is an opportunist, and has learnt that a close association with Man can sometimes have advantages.

Whooper Swan

The Whooper Swan is almost entirely vegetarian, feeding for the most part on aquatic and marshland plants, and on flooded pastures. Coastal and estuarine feeding grounds are also used extensively, and in some districts increasing numbers of birds are resorting to arable land.

Of nine birds examined in Denmark, three had been feeding on *Zostera*, two on *Ruppia* and one on *Potamogeton*; the remainder had been foraging on land (307). *Zostera* is also taken in Ireland and the Hebrides (86, 180). In the lochs of Scotland, Whooper Swans have been observed feeding on *Potamogeton*, *Chara* and the troublesome Canadian Pondweed *Elodea canadensis*; on the Ouse Washes in East Anglia they feed on the leaves, roots and rhizomes of *Glyceria maxima*, *G. fluitans* and other wetland plants, and in Germany make regular use of Clover *Trifolium* sp. (141). Insects, molluscs and worms are eaten occasionally in small quantities, and on one occasion, during hard weather, a bird was seen trying unsuccessfully to swallow a number of fish, some 18 to 20 cm. long (18).

The habit of feeding on agricultural land seems to have developed since the hard winters of the 1940s. Among the items taken are the shoots of winter wheat, gleanings of grain (PLATE 21), waste potatoes and unharvested

Reed-grass *Glyceria maxima. Carol Ogilvie.*

turnips (74, 141, 174). Some Whoopers even take the cut turnips which are put out on the fields for cattle. They have also been known to scavenge on rubbish-dumps, feeding on refuse and waste potatoes (19, 281). Other records refer to them taking acorns and plums (141), but this must be exceptional.

Little is known about the food on the breeding grounds. An adult bird shot in Iceland during summer contained the leaves of Water Crowfoot *Ranunculus trichophyllus* and the seeds of Cotton Grass *Eriophorum* sp. (275). Non-breeding swans on a small lake were seen to make extensive use of the filamentous green algae from the lake and *Empetrum* berries from the surrounding slopes (116). They also burrow for the roots and young shoots of aquatic plants, and for small aquatic animals. The young birds eat insects, larvae and water-weeds on or near the water surface.

Canadian Pondweed *Elodea canadensis. Carol Ogilvie.*

Bewick's Swan

During winter the Bewick's Swan subsists mainly on shallow lakes and flooded grasslands. Coastal habitats are seldom used, except perhaps by birds on passage. The diet appears to be almost entirely vegetarian, although some earlier writers have referred to the taking of fish, worms, insects and larvae (57, 71).

In the Netherlands a study was made of the feeding habits of the large flocks on the Ijsselmeer, shortly after its closure from the sea, the work being based partly on direct observation, and partly on the examination of droppings (210). For the most part the birds were taking the roots and perennating organs of submerged aquatic plants. *Potamogeton* spp. were especially favoured, but extensive use was also made of *Zannichellia, Myriophyllum, Ceratophyllum* and *Chara.* The only animal remains found in the droppings were two Chironomid larvae; these were extremely abundant at the time, and a certain number were no doubt being ingested accidentally. Prior to the closure of the dyke, when the Ijsselmeer was still a tidal basin, the flocks had fed mainly on the roots and rhizomes of *Zostera,* which was then plentiful.

Similar results were obtained from a sample of eight birds shot in Denmark. Of these five had been feeding solely on *Potamogeton,* and three on the roots and rhizomes of *Zostera.*

The Ouse Washes.

In England the great majority of the wintering Bewick's Swans are found on wet or flooded pastureland, the largest concentration being on the Ouse Washes in East Anglia. The birds here usually feed while standing or floating in shallow water. The vegetation available to them at any time depends on the depth and extent of the flood, but they normally graze over stands of *Glyceria maxima* and mixtures of the finer wet pasture grasses *Glyceria fluitans*, *Alopecurus geniculatus* and *Agrostis stolonifera*. One bird, killed by wires, was found to contain quantities of all four of these plants. Two others had been feeding on *G. maxima*, and on the seeds of *Eleocharis palustris* and *Polygonum amphibium* which were plentiful in the area. In both birds the seeds comprised less than 9% of the stomach contents. Two samples of droppings gathered in the same area contained only *G. maxima*. When the Washes are not flooded the swans graze like geese on the pastures, and may come up on to the flood banks in hard weather. In late winter they flight out to the fens to feed on young winter wheat, a habit which has not been reported elsewhere.

During recent years large and increasing numbers of Bewick's Swans have been attracted to the grounds of the Wildfowl Trust at Slimbridge (PLATE 35). In response to daily feeding, mainly with wheat, they have developed a regular flight pattern and appear punctually at the appointed

PLATE 13 Black-necked Swans. ABOVE: a Slimbridge cob carrying a cygnet. *A. Middleton.* BELOW: a family party. *Zoological Society of Philadelphia.*

PLATE 14 Black-necked Swan. ABOVE: swamp nest in Argentina. *M. W. Weller*. BELOW: female sitting on her nest at Slimbridge. *Philippa Scott*.

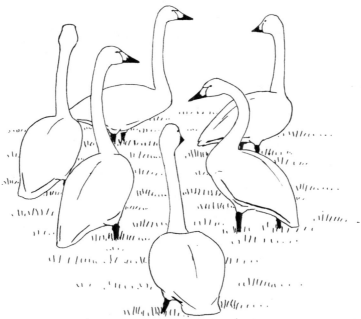

Bewick's Swans on winter wheat. *Dafila Scott.*

time each morning and evening. During the day they either resort to their roost on the estuary or graze on the surrounding pastures. Most of the fields concerned are dry, and contain a high proportion of the grasses *Lolium perenne*, *Poa trivialis* and *Agrostis* spp. There is also a record of Bewick's Swans taking advantage of the maize which was at one time fed to the Canada Geese at Ellesmere in Shropshire (84).

Whistling Swan

The diet of the Whistling Swan varies considerably from district to district, and in some areas includes a substantial amount of animal material. In general, the birds show a marked preference for the roots and tubers of aquatic plants; they also graze extensively along the margins of lakes and ponds.

The local preferences in diet are well illustrated by the studies undertaken on the important passage and winter resorts around Chesapeake Bay, and in the Great Salt Lake Valley in Utah. At Chesapeake Bay forty-nine birds were collected for examination, of which forty-one were taken from brackish waters, four from freshwater ponds and four from the saltwater pools around the estuary (313). The birds from the freshwater habitats had been feeding almost exclusively on Wild Celery *Vallisneria spiralis*. Those on the estuary had been taking a variety of plants, notably *Ruppia* and the stems and roots of *Scirpus*, together with various grasses and a certain amount of *Chara*. In neither case was there any sign of animal material. On the brackish waters, however, nearly one-third of the food consisted of molluscs, chiefly *Macoma baltica* and the Long Clam *Mya arenaria*. The remaining two-thirds was made up of the leaves and roots of *Ruppia* and *Potamogeton*.

Sea Club-rush *Scirpus maritimus. Carol Ogilvie.*

In Utah, a further fifty birds were examined, of which only twelve contained traces of food. In each case they had been feeding exclusively on the tubers and seeds of the Sago Pondweed *Potamogeton pectinatus*. Other food plants, such as *Ruppia* and *Zannichellia* were available but were not found in the stomachs (298).

Other known food plants include *Polygonum, Equisetum* and *Sparganium*.

The tubers of *Sagittaria* are also favoured, and in some districts may form an important part of the diet.

In California part of the wintering swans' food is made up of grain and waste potatoes gleaned from arable land (318). This habit is unusual elsewhere but was recorded in Utah in the severe spring of 1964 when all the usual lake haunts of the birds were frozen (237).

Trumpeter Swan

The food and feeding habits of the Trumpeter Swan are described at some length in the detailed review, which was published by Banko in 1960 (14). This work continues to be the chief source of information on the species, and is quoted extensively in the following account.

The diet of the Trumpeter is similar in several respects to that of the Whistling Swan. Roots and tubers are utilised at all times, especially those of *Sagittaria* spp., a plant which is known locally as 'wapato' or 'duck potato'. The birds uncover the tubers by digging with their feet in the soft bottom mud, and by undermining the banks with their bills. The stems and leaves of submerged aquatic plants are a favourite food during spring and summer; *Potamogeton* spp., *Myriophyllum*, *Elodea* and various aquatic mosses are all used extensively (224). Emergent plants are also a major source of food, especially on the breeding grounds. The most important species are Sedges *Carex* spp., Horsetail *Equisetum fluviatile* and Bur-reed *Sparganium angustifolium*.

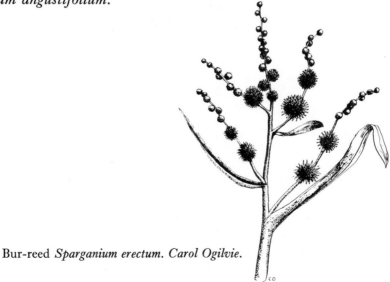

Bur-reed *Sparganium erectum. Carol Ogilvie.*

In late summer and autumn this type of food becomes increasingly scarce, and the swans feed extensively on the seeds of sedges and water lilies *Nuphar* spp. They obtain these in quantity by eating or stripping whole heads, but often fail to digest them efficiently. In one instance, a single dropping was found to contain no fewer than 769 seeds, most of which were intact.

Comparatively little is known about the Trumpeter's food during the critical winter months. Tubers and seeds are presumably the staple diet, especially in areas where the ground is snow-covered for long periods. In some districts in the northern United States the birds are supplied with grain when the lakes are ice-bound. Animal foods, such as fish, molluscs and insects, are taken occasionally, when easily available, but are not a part of the regular adult diet.

During the first three or four weeks after hatching, the cygnets feed mainly on insects and molluscs. They then turn to duckweed and the leaves of aquatic plants, and to the seeds of *Carex* and other emergents. In Alaska they take both vegetable and animal material from an early age, their favourite plant food being the tips of *Equisetum*.

Black Swan

The Black Swan is usually found on large, shallow lakes and swamps (PLATE 5), and is often present in dense concentrations. Its diet is almost exclusively vegetarian, consisting mainly of the leaves and shoots of aquatic and marshland plants. Pasture plants are also taken, especially during times of flood.

A great deal of research into the feeding habits of the species has been undertaken in recent years, notably in New South Wales where more than 600 birds have been collected for examination (88). The most important food in this area is the leaf of the emergent Reedmace *Typha angustifolia*, otherwise known as 'cumbungi'. Submerged aquatic plants, such as algae, *Potamogeton* spp. and Wild Celery *Vallisneria* spp. are also taken in quantity. The diet varies, however, depending on the water level. When the levels are high, the normal food plants are no longer accessible, and the birds spread outwards to the shallows around the edge of the flood. In this situation as much as 90% of their food consists of pasture plants.

Black Swans in Queensland feed primarily on submerged aquatic plants, particularly *Potamogeton* spp., algae, and the Stoneworts, *Chara* and *Nitella* spp. *Myriophyllum*, *Ceratophyllum* and *Vallisneria* spp. are taken on occasion, and in winter substantial use is made of the seeds of Club-rush *Scirpus littoralis* and Spike-rush *Eleocharis dulcis* (198). The moulting swans in Tasmania also take submerged aquatic plants, chiefly *Chara* and *Nitella* spp. (112).

The habitats occupied by the species in New Zealand are similar to those in Australia, and the food plants are presumably much the same. Grazing on land is rather more common here than elsewhere, and there are sometimes reports of damage to pastureland, especially near the water's edge. The swans have also developed the habit of stripping and eating the leaves of willow trees (32).

The cygnets take the same foods as the adults, though they may not be able to reach some of the deeper lying plants. Seeds are often eaten during the first few weeks of life; there is no evidence of animal food being taken at any stage (88).

Black-necked Swan and Coscoroba Swan

The two South American swans have not yet been studied in detail. Both species occur mainly on brackish lakes and swamps and both rely on submerged aquatic plants for the bulk of their food (164). Their habits differ, however, and this probably saves them from undue competition. It also seems that the Coscoroba prefers the coastal districts, while the Black-necked Swan tends to keep further inland.

The Coscoroba, with its broad and flexible bill (PLATE 2), is specially suited to dabbling, and its diet may well include a substantial proportion of seeds and animal material. The birds normally feed while wading in shallow water, and not infrequently come ashore to graze on the marginal vegetation. In some districts they have been seen feeding in company with Magellan Geese, and are in fact referred to as geese by the local people (288).

The Black-necked Swan is clumsy on land, and rarely, if ever, comes ashore to feed. Although predominantly vegetarian in diet, it is said to be not averse to animal matter in the form of aquatic insects, fish spawn and the like. In Tierra del Fuego groups of birds are sometimes seen on the coast feeding on kelp and other algae. The cygnets apparently take the same food as the parents.

Feeding in captivity

Swans do well in captivity, and occasionally live to a great age (Appendix 3). In order to reproduce successfully, each pair needs its own enclosure. All species have bred, although neither the Bewick's Swan nor the Whistling Swan nest readily at the latitude of most Zoological Gardens in Europe and North America.

Feeding is no problem. During most of the year, a diet of wheat, barley or maize with broken biscuit, brown bread and green food is entirely adequate. A high energy diet, with more grain and bread, is required in cold weather. Before egg-laying, the females should be given poultry breeder pellets or similar foods with a higher protein and calcium content, together with plenty of green stuff, such as lettuce, watercress, endive, cabbage or lawn-clippings. Additional protein is also needed before and during the moult. A supply of hard grit should be provided at all times; this is essential to the digestion of coarse foods. As much as 120 gm. has been found in the gizzard of a wild Mute Swan.

The young birds require a diet containing around 18–20% protein, especially the fast-growing northern swans. Chick-starter crumbs are suitable for the first three weeks, then growers pellets. These should be placed around the edge of the water until the cygnets have learnt to come ashore and feed from a dish. If the cygnets are being reared away from their parents, they can be encouraged to feed by scattering sieved egg-yolk or fragments of greenfood over the starter crumbs. Plenty of greenfood is desirable; cygnets love Duckweed *Lemna* not only for the plant itself but for the abundance of animal life which it contains. Beware, however, of keeping cygnets on stagnant pools, where duckweed occurs naturally. In these conditions there is a serious risk of birds becoming infested with various parasites, especially *Acuaria* (page 139). To overcome this difficulty, keep the birds on moving water, and bring the duckweed from elsewhere.

If grain is being fed to the adults, as is usually the case, the young birds will start taking it when they are ready. With Trumpeters, this happens after about five weeks (335). If the cygnets are being hand-reared, the diet of growers pellets should be supplemented with soaked grain when the birds are four to five weeks old. Black-necked cygnets may be given cooked rice or grain after only fourteen days (204). The change to full adult diet is made when the birds are fully feathered.

It is important that young swans should have enough water to enable them to spend most of their time afloat; otherwise, as they put on weight, they are likely to have trouble with their legs and feet. Another difficulty, which sometimes occurs, is that balls of grass become lodged beneath the tongue, creating an obvious bulge under the chin. This can be remedied by opening the bill, lifting the tongue and removing the debris with a pair of tweezers. The bulge probably does no great harm, but may cause some discomfort; in most cases the trouble ceases as the birds become older.

Amphibious bistort *Polygonum amphibium. Carol Ogilvie.*

Mute Swan pair with young. *Robert Gillmor*.

5

Reproduction and family life

Janet Kear

Of all a species' activities, nothing is more important to its survival than successful reproduction. Natural selection therefore acts strongly in maintaining the most efficient breeding systems, and much of the behaviour associated with mating and parental care is inherited and fixed. In courtship displays, nest-building movements and feeding of the young, all the members of a species tend to behave in the same way because, presumably, the individuals that deviate from the most effective course are the least likely to leave offspring. Closely related species, such as the swans, likewise share many patterns of breeding activity. The degree of uniformity depends to some extent on the conditions under which the various species breed; if, for example, the climates and seasons are different, a number of genetic variations will almost certainly have evolved. Short-term changes in environment may also lead to variations in behaviour, in this case as a result of learning. These new traditions, which often develop within a few generations, are particularly noticeable in aspects such as feeding habits, territory-holding, and reaction to predators. The aim of this chapter is to describe these behaviour patterns in the various swans, and to account, so far as possible, for the differences and similarities between them.

Age at first breeding

All swans mature typically in their second or third year. Despite this the northern forms do not usually establish a territory and breed before their fifth or sixth summer (64). Trumpeter Swans, for example, are said to nest first when four to six years old (14), but on occasion they can form pairs at twenty months and begin nesting at only thirty-three months, provided that there is no competition for acceptable nest sites (232). The situation in the other northern swans has not been studied, but is probably similar.

Recent observations on the Mute Swan confirm earlier reports that a few nest successfully when only two years old (75, 143, 239). The majority, like the Trumpeter Swans, form pairs at least one season before laying, and the characteristic breeding age is three or four years, the females being slightly more precocious than the males (230, 256). As with the northern forms, the lack of a territory may prevent nesting in an otherwise mature pair. Captive Black-necked Swans frequently breed at two years old (339); the situation in the wild is probably the same as for the Mute.

The non-territorial Black Swan matures even earlier. It has been shown that some males produce sperm before they attain adult plumage at fifteen to twenty months old (40) and cases are known of captive females laying at one, and one and a half years old (61). This early breeding is probably encouraged by the habit of colonial nesting, and by the ready availability of nest sites, both of which tend to favour successful reproduction in the majority of individuals at two years of age.

Nothing is known about the Coscoroba Swan except that both male and female have bred in captivity at four years old. Maturity is probably reached earlier, perhaps in the second year, judging by the loss of juvenile plumage.

Prolonged immaturity is perhaps an adaptation arising out of the difficulties inherent in breeding which make young, inexperienced birds unsuccessful, and may even endanger their survival (191). This agrees with what is known of the swans: the Black Swan is an irregular migrant, nests in colonies and matures early; the temperate species migrate short distances, hold small territories, and reach breeding age rather later; while the long-distance, northern migrants need large territories and mature the most slowly of all.

Courtship and pair-bond maintenance

In all swans the male participates to a large extent in raising the family, which takes at least six months; it is important therefore that firm bonds should exist between him and the female and to a lesser extent between both parents and the family. Perhaps to ensure this, courtship is slow, and displays (especially the triumph ceremony) have great significance.

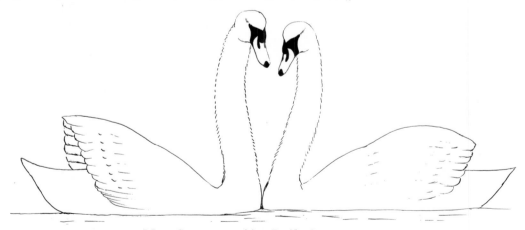

Mute Swan courtship. *Dafila Scott.*

The sexual displays of the Mute Swan have been described by a number of authors (33, 132, 148, 162). Mutual head-turning, the birds' breasts almost touching, is seen frequently from late autumn on, and appears to act as a courtship greeting (PLATE 10). The triumph ceremony, used between adults only after the pair have 'chosen' each other, occurs when an 'enemy' has been repulsed. It is similar to the male's threat posture (PLATE 11 and page 89) of raised wings and fluffed neck feathers but is assumed by both birds and is accompanied by calling (a kind of snoring) and by chin-lifting.

Copulatory display patterns are also important in maintaining the pair-bond, most pairs mating far more often than is necessary to fertilise the clutch (33, 335). Precopulatory behaviour in the Mute Swan consists of both birds alternately dipping their heads beneath the water, and preening or rubbing the back and flanks. Gradually the activities of the two birds become synchronised and, between head-dippings, their necks are held upright and close together for a moment or two. The wings are low, often dragging in the water, and the male pushes his neck and body over the female's until he is on her back grasping her neck feathers in his bill. After mating the cob slips off and both birds give a hoarse muted trumpet, which is often difficult to hear. They rise half out of the water, breast to breast, with necks extended and bills pointing first up, then down and finally from side to side. Both partners then usually bathe, preen and tail-wag.

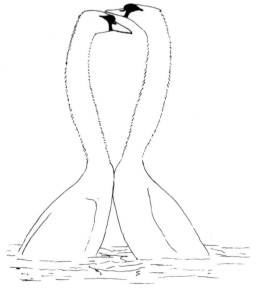

Post-copulatory display of the Mute Swan. *Dafila Scott.*

The Black Swan is closely related to the Mute Swan and the displays of the two species are similar. The triumph ceremony, which is also used in pair formation, consists of raised wings, erect fluffed neck, chin-lifting and calling. The precopulatory display lacks the latter's conspicuous preening movements and, after mating, there is no side to side turning of the head; before bathing the birds often swim in a circle (162).

The Black-necked Swan differs in some respects from the two preceding species but has more behaviour patterns in common with them than with the northern swans. The nuptial display is simple, being limited to a rhythmic dipping and stretching of the neck in both cob and pen. The triumph ceremony has no wing-raising and consists mainly of calling and chin-lifting. The pair continue to call for some minutes with their heads a few inches apart and bills almost touching. Copulatory behaviour is similar to the other swans, the pair repeatedly dipping the head and neck before mating, although, except for bathing, there is no conspicuous display afterwards (204, 280).

The closely related Bewick's, Whistling, Whooper and Trumpeter Swans are essentially alike in their sexual behaviour. Bobbing of the head is the normal greeting (3) and courtship involves the same breast to breast posture as in the Mute Swan (PLATE 21). The triumph ceremony, which is also used in greeting (PLATE 22), consists of the wings being waved in a half-opened and lifted position while the neck is repeatedly bent and extended as the birds call loudly (6, 14, 148, 162). In the Whistling and Bewick's Swans the waving wings are sometimes fully extended. When either bird of a pair of northern swans is calling, the other usually joins in (PLATE 37). The notes are at first alternated with the mate's but are finally synchronised and in the Whooper the display may terminate with the necks rigidly out-stretched. The precopulatory display is limited to head-dipping, with none of the preening, feather rubbing and posturing common in the Mute Swan. The dipping movements closely resemble those of bathing, except that the pair do not thrash their wings in the water, and the synchronised display lasts only a few seconds before the male mounts. After copulation the cob, and sometimes the pen, spread wings and both begin to call, rather more softly than usual. The birds then rise together in the water and turn a partial circle before settling back and starting to bathe, tail-wag and preen (132, 162, 335).

The Coscoroba Swan presents a curious mixture of behaviour patterns. The species has no triumph ceremony and, in greeting, the bill is merely flicked upward while calling. Unlike other swans, copulation occurs while the birds are standing in shallow water, not while swimming. Head-dipping by the male is the only precopulatory display, after which he flies on to the female's back and grasps her nape. After treading, both birds stretch neck and head vertically, and call in concert as the male raises his folded wings (162).

Divorce

It is often said that swans are strictly monogamous, but this is true only of some species. A study of the Mute Swans in central England showed that a number of birds changed to a new partner while the original mate was still alive. The divorce rate over six years amounted to 3% among pairs which had already bred, and 9% among pairs which had failed, or had not yet begun, to breed (230). On the other hand an intensive study of the Bewick's Swans wintering at Slimbridge has revealed not a single case of divorce and remating, even between unsuccessful pairs (289, 339).

A strong pair-bond is, in fact, more important to the northern Bewick's Swan than to the largely non-migratory Mute Swan, the crucial difference between the two being the time available for breeding. Both have the same tasks of nest-building, incubation and rearing to perform, but in the case of the Bewick's Swan all these activities have to be more closely synchronised, rapidly initiated and intensely performed, otherwise the young will not be old enough and strong enough to fly south when autumn comes. In these circumstances a firm pair-bond provides the best background for shared parental care. Divorce would mean the loss of the pair's accumulated experience of wintering and breeding grounds and migration routes, and also of each other's social status and behavioural repertoire. Thus, in the long term, the pair which stays together is likely to be the more productive, even though its earlier attempts at breeding have been unsuccessful. The low divorce rate in the Mute Swan likewise reflects the advantages of fidelity.

If the mate dies or disappears, most swans will form a new pair with another bird (132, 230, 297, 340) and this is obviously to the advantage of the species. Mute Swans normally remate after only a short period although some prefer to remain single (264). A few of the Bewick's Swans at Slimbridge have also remained unpaired after bereavement, although this is not the usual case (page 13).

Sexual aberrations

Captive swans, like many other animals, sometimes show gross abnormalities of behaviour. These are due almost entirely to the artificial conditions under which the birds are kept and are relevant only as examples of the lengths to which deprived creatures will go to satisfy their natural urge to reproduce. Fortunately, the majority of zoos have now abandoned the practice of keeping animals solely for public exhibition, and are becoming increasingly interested in breeding and rearing.

Homosexual partnerships occur quite commonly when male and female swans are separated, especially from an early age (132). They have also been recorded in feral populations, containing a preponderance of males. In the Mute Swan colony at Abbotsbury, two cobs not only associated together, but even built an annual nest, on which they sat in turn (208). Homosexual female pairings, leading to the laying of infertile clutches, occur where the situation allows no other choice. There is, however, no known case of an isolated female producing eggs; a companion is always necessary (67, 222).

The companion may be a bird of a different species. Mute Swans in captivity have mated with Bewick's, Whistling, Whooper, Trumpeter and Black Swans and have produced hybrid offspring with at least the last four (35, 132, 264, 299). Hybridisation has also been recorded between captive swans and various geese, including Swan Geese, Snow Geese, Canada Geese and Greylags (106). The only swans which have not been known to cross with other species are the Black-necked Swan and the Coscoroba. A hybrid bond, once formed, may be very long lasting. At Copenhagen Zoo, where a female Mute Swan and a male Whooper were paired for three years, the female showed no interest in a male of her own species which was later placed in the next enclosure (264).

Cases of polygamy, both casual and sustained, have sometimes been noted among captive and feral Mute Swans, usually while the real mate was occupied with incubation (67, 76, 148, 208, 264). The majority of these relationships are probably brought into being by the continual approach of an unattached female and not, at least initially, by the promiscuous tendencies of the paired cob. In one instance, the male of a captive pair repeatedly drove away a single female from the vicinity of his nest, but once beyond the territorial border started head-dipping with her and finally copulated (141). In another instance, an unattached female was allowed into the territory after the pen had been sitting for fourteen days, and built a second nest only nine metres away, from which she eventually hatched a brood of young. Throughout this time, the male defended only the first of the two nests (262). There is also a record of a Black Swan breeding polygamously with two female Mute Swans which had no mates of their own. The male incubated the eggs of one nest while the two females alternated, and eventually hatched young, on the other (141).

Incestuous matings between brother and sister or between parents and offspring occur commonly in captive swans, usually in the absence of others of their kind; they have also been detected among Mute Swans in the wild (230). It is not yet known whether this is a normal, or merely a chance, occurrence.

Breeding seasons

The dates on which the first and the last of the various swans at Slimbridge can be expected to lay are separated by a period of more than three months (see Table 3).

PLATE 15 Black-necked Swans. ABOVE: flock with other waterfowl in Argentina. *M. W. Weller*. BELOW: adult female and feathering cygnet. *Russ Kinne*.

PLATE 16 Black-necked Swan family at Slimbridge in a severe winter, January 1963. The cygnets, older than that in Plate 15, have black necks but greyish feathering. *Gloucestershire Gazette, Dursley.*

Table 3. Dates of the first egg of the first clutch laid each year at Slimbridge (52° N)

SPECIES	EARLIEST DATE	MEDIAN DATE	NO. OF BREEDING SEASONS	HOURS AND MINUTES BETWEEN SUNRISE AND SUNSET ON MEDIAN DATE
Black Swan	24 Jan.	5 Feb.	17	9·20
Black-necked Swan	2 Feb.	11 Feb.	13	9·50
Coscoroba Swan	24 Feb.	12 Mar.	7	11·40
Mute Swan	26 Mar.	4 Apr.	3	13·10
Whooper Swan	7 Apr.	13 Apr.	3	13·50
Trumpeter Swan	6 Apr.	25 Apr.	12	14·30
Bewick's Swan	30 Apr.	8 May	10	15·20
(Whistling Swan*	16 May	16 May	1	15·50)

*Female died laying single egg.

The low-latitude swans lay early, at a time when the day-length, though increasing, is still short, while the northern species wait until the days are as much as six hours longer. It is evident that day-length is relatively more important than temperature; for example, the Black and the Black-necked Swans lay during February when the weather in England is considerably cooler than in their native habitats, while the northern species, which in the wild start breeding before the ice has disappeared, at Slimbridge defer until the warm spring. This behaviour is almost certainly determined genetically and adapted in the course of evolution to the best 'average' egg-hatching season in their native land. It is noticeable that although the Bewick's Swan nests late she does not need the midnight sun of Arctic Russia to stimulate her into laying. This suggests that it is the increasing day-length at some point on the northward migration which is crucial, not that of the actual breeding ground.

These swans, assembled at Slimbridge from all over the world, not only continue to lay at the time of year appropriate at home, they also spread their nesting seasons over a similar period. The Black-necked Swans have produced their first egg at any time in the thirteen weeks following 2 February. On the other hand, if the Bewick's Swan at Slimbridge fails to lay within the five weeks between 30 April and 6 June, she will not lay at all. The low-latitude swans are much the more adaptable in this respect. The correct short day-length, that means spring at home, brings them into breeding condition; they then stay in condition and breed when the climate warrants it. Indeed the Black Swans can nest at almost any month of the year, both in the wild (40, 112, 197) and in captivity. This is in keeping with their native habitat which is affected not so much by predictable seasonal changes as by variable conditions of rainfall and water level. It is therefore advantageous for the bird to be capable of laying whenever suitable conditions arise. This is well illustrated by the introduced population of Black Swans in New Zealand. On Lake Ellesmere (44° S), both breeding and climate are markedly seasonal, whereas in places nearer the tropics, such as Lake Whangape (37° 30′ S), downy cygnets may be seen in most months of the year (228). At Slimbridge the Black Swans have laid in each month from January to April, and again in August, September and October. A similar pattern has been noted at the London (287) and Zürich Zoos. The Coscoroba Swan is the only other species which breeds twice a year in England, on an increasing and a decreasing day; it is not known whether it does this in the wild.

Territorial behaviour

All the white swans are markedly territorial in their nesting behaviour, that is to say they select a site around which they defend an area of ground and do not usually leave this until the young can fly. The extent of the territory varies considerably. The Trumpeter Swans in Montana defend larger areas on open shorelines than pairs nesting on islands in shallow water; the lowest concentration allows each pair about 60 hectares (150 acres), and the highest about 30 hectares (14). The Whistling Swans in Alaska nest at densities varying between 130 and 320 hectares per pair (200). The Whooper and Bewick's Swans have not been studied in detail, and the size of the true territory has almost certainly been exaggerated. In Iceland, for instance, some twenty pairs of Whooper Swans were found breeding in an area of apparently suitable habitat, which covered a total of 11,400 hectares, about forty-four square miles (293). This gives an average density of one pair per 570 hectares, but there is no evidence that the whole of this area was in fact defended. In Russia, the Bewick's Swan is said to breed at a density of one pair per 2,000 hectares although it may breed more closely on some of the islands (66). The breeding density of the Mute Swan depends on the availability of suitable habitat. A favourable study area in Staffordshire had approximately one pair per 2,000 hectares, but the defended area was normally limited to a length of stream only a few metres wide (230). A stream in Norfolk, with a fairly typical distribution of pairs is shown on page 90. The average distance between nests on the rivers near Oxford is 2·4 km. to 3·2 km., with 90 metres (100 yards) as a minimum (256). On the Alster in Hamburg, the average territory measured 300 × 150 metres (257). Little is known about the territory size of the two South American species, but they certainly nest more closely than the near-Arctic swans (94, 280).

Cob Mute Swan at his territory boundary.

Territorial defence is evoked by other adult swans but not usually by the grey-brown first-year birds. Two male Mute Swans will parade the boundary between their domains with the secondary feathers of the wings raised, necks ruffled and heads laid back (PLATE 11), making themselves as conspicuous as possible. One of the birds will sometimes attack (PLATE 11) and the other withdraw, but if the aggressor goes too far from his own territory he is likely to be counter-attacked and forced to retreat to the boundary. On rare occasions both birds respond with force, and a fight develops, which the territory owner normally wins (96) (PLATE 12).

The conspicuous white plumage of the adults, which Wynne-Edwards has called 'continuous advertisement', may well play an important part in keeping other swans at a distance (178, 346). The Mute Swan in particular has been quoted as an example of a species which, because of the efficacy of its visual advertisement, can dispense with other forms of recognition-signalling and tends therefore to be silent except at close quarters. This visual impact does not, however, suffice for the northern swans, which, although white, are among the noisiest of birds. The defence, in their case, begins with a warning display of half-opened quivering wings, stretched neck and calling by one or both of the resident pair (14, 66, 297). Often the trespasser is spotted in the air some distance away, in which case the warning may be sufficient. If the intruder still approaches, a defender flies up in immediate pursuit, and chases the trespasser well over the boundary before returning for a triumph ceremony with its mate. Opponents seldom come to blows, but fights on land, water and in the air do sometimes occur.

The Trumpeter Swan employs these tactics from before the time that the nest is built until the cygnets are half-grown (14). The demonstrations are commonest during nest-building and early incubation, when other swans are searching for suitable territories. In general, the demonstrations are directed not against neighbouring pairs whose boundaries are respected, but against odd vagrants. A stranger will also be pursued much further than a a bird from the adjoining territory.

So much energy is expended in maintaining the distance between pairs that some real benefit must be assumed. Obviously the territory must con-

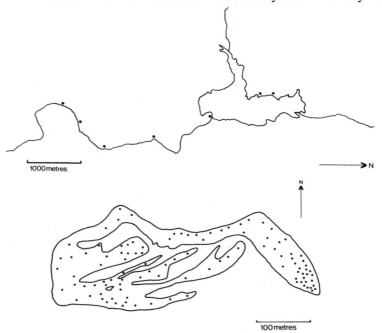

Nesting density of Mute Swans. *Above*, nests near Barton Broad, Norfolk; *below*, nests on the island of Suderø, Denmark, redrawn from Bloch (31). Each dot indicates one nest; the scale of the upper map is ten times that of the lower.

tain at least one suitable nest site, and more especially must be capable of providing the large amounts of food required for the rapid growth of the cygnets. This is particularly important in the case of the northern swans, which have only a short period in which to breed and rear their insectivorous young. It has, in fact, been suggested that Trumpeter Swans vary the size of their territories in accordance with the availability of food (14). They are also known to rear a larger proportion of their cygnets in areas where the density of nests is relatively low. This implies that dispersal may have the additional advantage of reducing the predation of eggs and young. The further the nests are apart, the less likelihood there is of a predator, which has found one nest, being able to find its neighbour.

In contrast to the white swans, the Black Swan is non-territorial, and breeds for the most part in large colonies (PLATE 4), the nests being often no more than a metre apart (112). Paradoxically, the evolution of this nesting habit may also have been influenced by food supply and predator protection. The food is entirely plant material which, to be obtainable, must lie not more than neck and shoulders deep. For successful rearing, a slowly changing water level is essential during most of the pre-fledging period, in order that the young birds may have access to a succession of shallow feeding areas. Because of the climate, which results in very wide variations in water level over the course of the year, these optimum conditions occur only at certain times. The eggs are therefore laid synchronously at a fairly precise moment of the rainy season, before the correct conditions for rearing have actually been reached. As in many other birds which breed colonially, this synchronous laying is probably encouraged by the high level of social stimulation. It may also help to reduce predation: if all the eggs are laid together fewer in total are likely to be stolen than if a steady supply is available over a long period. Predation is not, however, a serious threat to any species of swan in its native habitat. It seems more likely therefore that the presence or absence of territorial behaviour is dependent on differences in the supply of insect or plant food. The northern swans are forced, presumably, to commandeer a large area in order to ensure an adequate supply of animal protein for the rapid growth of the young. The vegetarian Black Swan cygnets grow much more slowly, in an environment where the feeding grounds, though limited by water depth, are constantly changing with the fluctuations in level. A number of families can therefore feed repeatedly on the plants in the same restricted area.

The Mute Swan breeds colonially at two related sites in southern

England. The more important of the two is at Abbotsbury in Dorset, on the tidal Fleet, where a semi-domesticated population was established by monks some 900 years ago. The second, less dense colony is at Radipole Lake, near Weymouth. Similar colonies have been established during recent years in Poland (304), and in Denmark, where in some cases the nests are sited less than two metres apart (31, 52, 159). These colonies are usually on coastal islands (page 90), where the families can spread out after hatching to feed on intertidal vegetation. As at Abbotsbury, the main food plant of the adults is *Zostera* (16). The food of the cygnets is not known, but young Mute Swans are probably less dependent on insect food than the cygnets of other white swans.

There are suggestions that the South American swans have similar colonial tendencies, although solitary nesting is more normal. In Argentina, sixteen Coscoroba nests were found in an area 370 metres square, some only 18 metres apart (94), and in the Falkland Islands a group of six Black-necked Swans' nests (four empty) was found also within 18 metres of each other.

Nesting

In their primitive state swans are probably marshland breeders, building huge semi-floating nests. This presumably helps to discourage predators, but the practice is by no means universal, and all species sometimes nest on dry land. A survey of the Mute Swan in Britain showed that 51% of nests were sited in or near standing water, 46% by running water and 3% in coastal

Black Swans with nest. *Thierry Robyns de Schneidauer.*

areas (43). Those built by running water such as streams, rivers or canals are usually on land. Black Swan colonies are usually sited on islands in lakes or lagoons (PLATE 4) but single pairs often build nests floating in water. In Tasmania they occasionally breed among thickets of Tea-tree *Leptospermum* (113) and, in New Zealand, on the roots of semi-aquatic willows. Bewick's Swans, Whistling Swans and Whoopers frequently arrive on their northern breeding grounds before the snow has melted and at once start building on patches of high ground which are not surrounded by water until incubation is already under way (26, 66). In Alaska, where Whistling Swans and Trumpeters sometimes breed in the same areas, the former choose dry land sites while the latter always build floating nests (187). Further south, Trumpeters frequently nest on the tops of Muskrat houses (14), and Coscoroba nests have been reported on drowned ant-hills (94).

Unlike most other waterfowl, both sexes participate in building the nest (14, 64, 166, 167, 170, 264, 280), and it is often the male that selects the site and lays the foundations. Last year's nest may be used if a brood was hatched successfully, but if the eggs were predated, or failed for some reason, a new site is usually chosen. This is obviously a sensible procedure which in the long run leads to greater success. In Black Swan colonies, nests vacated upon hatching are sometimes occupied by new owners in the same season (228).

A young or newly mated pair of white swans, or an established pair nesting in an unfamiliar place, may take time to settle on a site. In captivity, the male of a young pair will sometimes construct a number of nests before the female 'chooses' one and joins in (220). The nest material consists of sedge, moss, rush, pondweed and any other plant which is readily available. This material is never transported for any distance; direct carrying in the bill while walking, flying or swimming is an activity which waterfowl find difficult. Instead, the bird stands side-on or with its back to the site, reaches forward, grasps a billful of vegetation and drops it over its shoulder in a series of short passes. This results in the gradual accumulation of a mound of material on which the female stands or sits, arranging whatever is passed back by the male. She constructs a rough cup for the eggs at the centre of the pile, using her bill, breast and feet. Softer items, such as grass, form the cup lining, and later she may add feathers and down, although only the Coscoroba Swan uses a substantial amount (PLATE 1). The other species produce a little (PLATES 4, 18 and 26), the low-latitude ones more than the northern forms, but nothing like the quantity common in ducks and geese. The down, even of the Black Swan, is always and proverbially pure white.

Between them the birds construct a large flood-proof mound, often three to four metres across at the base. The material gathered by one captive pair of Black-necked Swans weighed 6,500 gm. or nearly 15 lb. (280). The nests of other species are even larger. In general, the division of labour seems well suited to the job, but a detailed watch has shown that any co-operation between the pair is accidental; at times their actions may even be opposed (264).

Nests built by different species on the same general site and using similar material will not be alike. Black Swans make neat, steep-sided affairs; Black-necked Swans build smaller nests, loosely packed and more haphazard, while the Whooper constructs a huge nest, massive at the base and sometimes with a cup so deep that the back of the sitting female is flush with the rim (170) (PLATES 4, 14 and 18).

Egg-laying

While the cob is constructing and guarding the nest, the female feeds enormously. Green food in bulk seems particularly favoured (14, 220) to build up the reserves needed for egg production and for the period of incubation when she seldom leaves the nest. During the ten days centred on the laying of the first egg, a female captive Trumpeter grazed nearly four times as much as the cob and ate grain nearly one and a half times as often (335).

Captive swans often start nest-building long before the first egg is laid, but in the wild the period is much shorter. The Trumpeter, for example, is said to take only six days (297). In Black Swan colonies on dry land, the first egg is sometimes laid before the nest is even started (112), but this is rare and probably due to a shortage of material. Swans usually lay one egg every forty-eight hours (64, 132, 256, 264, 345). Trumpeters and Coscorobas in captivity have both produced seven eggs in fifteen days (339), and captive Black-necked Swans have taken a week to lay four or five (204, 280). The Black Swan is said to lay at intervals of about thirty-six hours, but after the first three eggs the rate may increase to one a day (112, 228).

Most of the swans at Slimbridge lay in the early morning, although variations occur, especially with the first egg of a clutch. In the wild, it was found that, of 39 Black Swan eggs, 16 were laid between 07·00 and 17·30 hours, and 23 in the remaining $13\frac{1}{2}$ hours, which may indicate an even distribution through the day and night (112).

PLATE 17 Wild Whooper Swans at Hyoko, Japan, in aggressive display with open wings and raised heads. *Kiyoshi Honda.*

PLATE 18 Whooper Swan nesting in the wild. LEFT: a pair in Iceland. *G. K. Yeates.*
BELOW: their small clutch clearly showing the lustrous egg-shells. *G. K. Yeates.* RIGHT:
a larger clutch in Mongolia, *R. Piechocki.*

PLATE 19 Whooper Swans. ABOVE: in Iceland with newly-hatched cygnets. *G. K. Yeates.* BELOW: a pair at Slimbridge with cygnets about two weeks old, one of which is somersaulting. *Philippa Scott.*

PLATE 20 Whooper Swans. ABOVE: birds wintering at Hyoko, Japan, in grey first plumage. *Kiyoshi Honda*. BELOW: wild adult with head and neck feathers impregnated with orange iron oxides. *Philippa Scott*.

Female white swans do not sit constantly until all the eggs are laid (170, 264). The Black-necked Swan does not even cover the incomplete clutch while she is away (54, 170, 204, 280). The Whooper, on the other hand, buries hers under plenty of material, perhaps as a precaution against late frosts (170). Black Swans usually remain on the nest from the moment the first egg is present (64, 170), a sensible precaution in colonies where eggs and nest material are likely to be stolen by neighbouring birds (112, 228).

The egg

Swans' eggs are amongst the largest in the bird world. Only those of the Black-necked Swan approach the conventional 'egg-shape' with one blunt and one pointed pole; the others are almost equally rounded at both ends. Coscoroba Swans' eggs are matt white when fresh, the Black-necked Swans' are cream, and the Mute and Black Swans' pale green with a chalky covering. The four northern swans produce white or yellowish eggs with much less surface bloom and even a slight lustre (PLATE 18). All become scratched and soiled during incubation and are stained a variety of browns, greens and yellows. The shell, which is thinnest in the Coscoroba and Black-necked Swan and thickest in the Trumpeter (286, 327), comprises 11 to 13% of the weight. The yolk forms another 40%, and the white the remainder (193).

Table 4. The approximate size of swans' eggs, based on Schönwetter (286), and the usual clutch size. See Appendix 7 for details and sample sizes.

	LENGTH BREADTH mm.		WEIGHT gm.	EGG WEIGHT AS PERCENTAGE OF FEMALE WEIGHT	CLUTCH SIZE
Mute Swan	112·5 ×	73·5	340	3·8	6
Whooper Swan	112·5 ×	72·5	330	4·1	4, 5 or 6
Trumpeter Swan	111·0 ×	72·0	325	3·5	5
Whistling Swan	107·0 ×	68·0	280	4·5	5
Bewick's Swan	103·0 ×	67·0	260	4·6	4 or 5
Black Swan	105·0 ×	66·0	260	5·1	5 or 6
Black-necked Swan	101·0 ×	66·5	245	6·1	5
Coscoroba Swan	89·0 ×	60·0	185	4·9	7

Table 4 shows the approximate size and weight of swans' eggs in descending order of magnitude, and also the *relative* egg size, that is the weight of the egg expressed as a percentage of the weight of the female laying it. It can be seen that in the smaller species the egg makes up a larger proportion of the body. This is typical of all bird groups (133, 192) and is part of the mechanism which ensures that the young bird will be of optimum size for survival (page 114).

While an average egg weight can be calculated for each species, there are a number of factors which affect the size of individual eggs. The age of the parent may be important: a Black-necked Swan at the Wildfowl Trust produced a clutch when she was two years old which weighed 17% under the average. The following year it was 10% under, and in the third season, normal. The position of the egg in the clutch also affects its size, the first eggs, at any rate in the Black Swan, being somewhat smaller than subsequent ones (62). The eggs in a repeat clutch likewise tend to be small, especially in the northern species which lay again quickly, if at all. At Slimbridge, the second clutch eggs of the Bewick's Swan weigh on average 9·5% less than first clutch eggs, and those of the Trumpeter, 7% less. The reason for this reduction is probably that the female has used up most of her food reserves on the first clutch and cannot build them up to the same level for the second. The southern swans do not produce repeat clutches quite so rapidly, and the egg size varies little between layings.

Although egg size appears to be fixed genetically, there are certain geographical variations, due presumably to differences in the average amount of food available. The Black Swan in Tasmania produces eggs which, at 300 gm. (112), are appreciably larger than those laid elsewhere in Australia and New Zealand. The introduced Mute Swan in Rhode Island is reported to lay an egg weighing on average 295 gm. (114), compared with the usual European weight of 340 gm. The females, however, are noticeably lighter (340), and the relative egg size is the same in both cases. The eggs of the Bewick's Swan vary to the east and west of the Lena river and this is also possibly related to a difference in size in the adult birds (64, 286). The extinct New Zealand Swan *Cygnus sumnerensis* was larger than the very closely related Australian Black Swan and laid a slightly larger egg. The Trumpeter Swan in Alaska also seems to lay a larger egg than those elsewhere (297).

Clutch size

Clutch size, like egg size, is typical of the species and is probably governed by similarly inherited and environmental factors (see Table 4). Lack (192) has

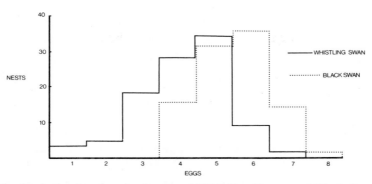

Probable clutch size in a hundred nests of Whistling Swans and Black Swans.

suggested that the average clutch in waterfowl has been evolved in relation to the average availability of food around the time of laying. This may explain why the northern breeders generally produce fewer eggs than the southern ones (Figure above). In the higher latitudes food is often short at the time when the birds arrive; they may also have consumed some of the body fat stored during winter in the course of the migration north. It is also noticeable that the clutch size tends to vary inversely with the relative egg size. For instance, the Mute has a larger clutch but a relatively smaller egg than the Black-necked Swan, and the same comparison is true of the Trumpeter and Bewick's Swan. This inverse relationship holds for other waterfowl groups, and probably indicates that the female has limited reserves which can be used either to form a small number of heavy eggs or a larger number of small ones (192).

The individual's clutch frequently differs from the average, the low-latitude species showing the widest variation. Black Swans may lay as many as 14 eggs (228); Mute Swans, 12 (223, 311); Trumpeters, nine (14, 325); Whoopers, eight (278); Whistling Swans, seven and Bewick's Swans, six. It is often supposed that the younger females lay fewer eggs (66, 75, 159, 189, 311). This is confirmed by the performance of some of the captive birds at Slimbridge. For example, a Black Swan laid over the years, 4 eggs (at five years old), 5, 5, 5, 6, 6; a Bewick's Swan of unknown age, 3, 5, 5, 5, 6, 6; and a Trumpeter of unknown age, 1 (not incubated), 2, 4, 5, ?, 6, 8. There is, however, little evidence of an increase with age among the Mute Swans near Oxford or among the feral flocks in Rhode Island (256, 340). It is possible, therefore, that the special conditions of captivity encourage the laying of small clutches in young individuals which would not normally nest until later.

In the wild swans of Alaska, the clutch size varies with the weather. In warm springs the Whistling Swans normally lay five eggs, but in cold, late springs only three or four (200). The Trumpeters of the Kenai Peninsula show a similar pattern: in 1964, for instance, the average May temperature was 3·5° C and the mean clutch size 4·3, whereas in 1967 when the temperature was 6·3° C the clutch size rose to 5·4 (325). This could be due to a number of factors, in particular the extent of the snow cover, the rate of growth of the food plants, and the amount of energy which the bird consumes while waiting for the higher spots to thaw. The non-migratory Black Swans at Lake Ellesmere, New Zealand, are affected more by winter conditions. If the water levels are high, winter feeding is limited, and clutch sizes the following spring are reduced (228).

The average clutch size sometimes differs consistently in different localities. The Mute Swan has a mean clutch of between 5·7 and 6·2 eggs over a wide range of sites in Europe and North America, but in some colonies the average is only 4·9 to 5·9 (see Appendix 7 for details). Sokolowski (304) has suggested that this may be due to psychological tensions brought about by the density of breeding pairs. Black Swans in Tasmania usually lay five eggs, compared with the six common elsewhere in Australia and New Zealand; the Tasmanian eggs, however, are somewhat heavier. The Whooper Swan in continental Eurasia usually produces six eggs but in Iceland only four (PLATE 18). This variation can scarcely be accounted for by differences in climate, and is more probably due to the condition of the birds on arrival at the breeding grounds. The continental birds are able to migrate the whole way over land, and can therefore make a series of short flights, with stops for rest and food *en route*. The Icelandic Whoopers, on the other hand, have a long sea crossing, and must fly direct to the breeding grounds, where food is often short on first arrival. Thus they may not even have an opportunity to replenish their reserves of protein and energy before commencing to breed.

Repeat clutches are sometimes laid if the first eggs are lost or, more rarely, if the newly hatched young disappear. The chances of the northern swans achieving this in the wild are rather small, because of the shortness of the season (14, 66). Bewick's Swan populations, for instance, require 120–130 days to arrive, lay, incubate, raise their young and depart (66); since the habitat is ice free for very little longer than this, late-hatched young are doomed to starve before they can migrate. In captivity, however, the Bewick's Swan, Whooper and Trumpeter have all produced second clutches, often within two weeks of first eggs being removed for artificial incubation. Wild Mute Swans are known to re-lay after three or four weeks, and captive Black Swans, Black-necked Swans and Coscorobas, after a month to six weeks. The Black Swan, the Black-necked Swan and the Mute have even been known to lay for a second time with a downy cygnet still present from the previous clutch (56, 311, 339).

These repeat clutches frequently contain fewer, as well as smaller, eggs than the first of the season. The second clutches of the Bewick's Swan at Slimbridge have averaged 3·5 eggs (from 10 clutches), instead of 5·1, and those of the Trumpeter 4·7 (3 clutches) instead of 5·2. The Mute Swan also lays a smaller second clutch, on average 4·3 (3 clutches) instead of 6·0 (256). The low-latitude species, which do not renest quite so rapidly, often lay the same number on both occasions in captivity, although this may not be true of the Black Swans in New Zealand (228).

Incubation

Incubation starts usually after the clutch is complete, thus ensuring that the cygnets will all hatch out together. The precise moment of commencement is sometimes difficult to determine, because the adult, especially of the Black Swan, will sit on the eggs without actually warming them. Development begins only when the temperature is raised to about 38° C (100° F). This is achieved by the bird fluffing breast feathers around the eggs and applying the skin direct to their surface. (Body temperature is higher in birds than mammals: the Black Swan's is 40·6° C, the Mute's 41·0° C and Man's 36·9° C.)

Among white swans, only the female incubates, although occasionally the cob may sit on the nest while she is absent. This has been reported for the Mute Swan (264, 304, 340, 345), Bewick's Swan (162), Whooper (339) and Trumpeter (109, 335). It is uncertain whether the cob in fact broods on these occasions; he probably just sits on the eggs while guarding them. There are, however, some reports of male Mute Swans taking over the actual incubation on the death of their mates (311).

In the Black Swan both sexes incubate, the female usually at night (103). In one captive pair, the male relieved his mate at about 08·00 hours and was relieved at 17·00 (170); in another, he sat from 10·00, also until 17·00 (132). The change-over is quite elaborate and not unlike the triumph ceremony. The relieving bird walks forward, greeting its mate and is greeted in turn by a special two-syllabled call, raised wings, head held high and neck feathers fluffed. The newcomer climbs on the nest from behind, still calling and dipping its head over its mate's body. After a minute or two the sitting bird stands up and the other slides under its tail and on to the eggs. As the off-duty swan departs, it passes back two or three beakfuls of nest material (170).

Most swans, both male and female, continue nest-building during the incubation period, especially at the departure or arrival of the sitting bird, and just prior to hatching. In the Whooper (and probably most northern swans) the female leaves daily for about half an hour in the warmest part of the day (170). The Mute pen is more irregular in her feeding (264), and so is the Black-necked Swan (280). The latter sometimes does not leave the nest more than once in every two or three days, mostly in the evening (170) and, at the Wildfowl Trust, females have on one or two occasions died on the nest, apparently because they never fed. The northern swans always cover their eggs with a considerable depth of vegetation before leaving (26, 101, 170, 325), presumably to insulate them from the cold and also to prevent dehydration. The Black-necked Swan does the same in the wild, apparently to protect the eggs from gulls (44), but in captivity may leave them uncovered (204).

As the bird returns to the nest from the water, it carries moisture on its feathers. Some of this is squeezed out with the bill, but some must be transferred to the eggs. The bill is also used to move the eggs around and turn them over in what seems a rather haphazard manner. It is humbling that the bird appears to treat these matters so casually; in artificial incubators, humidity levels and egg-turning are both critical to success.

The usual incubation periods at Slimbridge are given in Table 5. It is clear that the northern forms hatch in a shorter time than the temperate-zone species; the embryo must therefore have a higher metabolic rate and so develop faster at the same temperature. This presumably is a necessary adaptation in birds breeding during the brief polar summer.

Table 5. Normal incubation periods (see Appendix 8 for details)

Black Swan	36	days	Trumpeter Swan	33	days
Black-necked Swan	36	days	Whistling Swan	32	days (15)
Mute Swan	35·5	days	Whooper Swan	31	days
Coscoroba Swan	35	days	Bewick's Swan	29·5	days

The periods can vary appreciably between individuals. Frequent absences of the incubating bird lengthen the time to hatching, but recent work with domestic geese and ducks has shown that metabolism and therefore hatchability are actually improved in eggs cooled periodically for 10–20 minutes (42). The situation in swans has not been investigated, but it is known that incubation can be considerably lengthened without the eggs dying. The longest period on record was attained by a female Black Swan which sat on a completed clutch for 44 to 45 days before hatching it successfully (305). Although she was mated, the cob apparently never sat and the female went through a curiously truncated nest-relief ceremony with herself upon her return to the unattended nest. Unshared and successful incubation by a male Black Swan has also been reported, but only in captivity (229). If the clutch is infertile or dead, the female will sit far beyond the normal period. A Mute Swan at Copenhagen Zoo incubated for 50 days before giving up (264), and another in Scotland for 56 days (33).

Nest defence

Mature swans because of their large size are not much troubled by predators, and do not usually attempt to conceal either themselves, or their nests except when leaving them unguarded. Their reaction to man depends mainly on how familiar they are with him. Captive breeding swans (132, 204, 280) and also feral Mute Swans (141, 230, 255, 304, 340) are likely to stand their ground and respond aggressively to any approach (PLATES 1, 6 and 36); others in their natural habitat seldom attempt to defend their nest or cygnets against humans (but see PLATE 27) (14, 54, 293, 325). Black-necked Swans are said to panic at the sight of man, and to leave their nests without covering their eggs (44). However, all species are vigorous in their use of wings and beak against attack by other mammals or birds.

In the white swans, the male is mainly responsible for nest protection; although the female (at least of the Trumpeter) may be the more aggressive after hatching (335). In the Black Swan, the male stands guard at night and the female during the day. The distance between the defending bird and the nest varies between the species. The male Mute Swan usually stays close, perhaps because the female's voice does not carry far. The Black-necked male invariably sits beside the nest or even on the slope of the structure itself (170, 280), and leaves only for a rare meal, or to chase an intruder with a wild rush across the water. The males of the northern forms swim at a distance unless there is some sign of danger. The broken-wing display which is used by many small ground-nesters to lure predators from the nest or brood is not seen in the swans, although on one occasion in Iceland a male Whooper Swan with cygnets repeatedly took off and walked in front of a party of humans, apparently in an attempt to lead them away (293).

Individuals vary greatly, not only in their fear of man, but in their tolerance of other animals within the territory. Swans in captivity, where space is limited, appear to be more aggressive than in the wild, and are particularly intolerant of other species in their breeding pens. Instances of ducks and ducklings being attacked and drowned by breeding swans are

Whooper Swans in Iceland displaying at a survey plane. *Robert Gillmor*.

well documented but almost certainly atypical in the wild (77, 220, 227, 251, 340). Two classes of intruder are nearly always attacked: other swans and potential thieves of eggs or young. Anything that can be 'confused' with these is likely to provoke threat or assault; for instance, the Trumpeters in Alaska commonly show aggression towards the light aircraft (mainly orange and white) which are used for surveys (297, 325). Often they will rise and

PLATE 21 Whooper Swans. ABOVE: feeding on barley stubble undersown with grass. *Philippa Scott.* BELOW: courting Whoopers do not lift their wings as high as the Mute Swans in Plate 10 and the fluffed neck feathers, being shorter, are less obvious. *Kiyoshi Honda.*

PLATE 22 Whooper Swans. ABOVE: triumph ceremony of a wild pair at Hyoko, Japan. The posture is similar to that of threat. *Kiyoshi Honda*. BELOW: a cob 'ground staring'. This posture frequently ends a threat that is not followed by overt attack. *Sunday Mercury*.

flap their wings as the plane makes low passes over the nest, and will approach in threatening posture as it taxis towards them on the water. On one occasion a female left her nest, flew directly at the wing of the plane and nipped the fabric with her bill. They retreat, however, as soon as the pilot steps from his craft.

White swans in captivity will persecute Snow Geese in preference to other geese, and other large geese in preference to small ducks and coots (63). Wild Whoopers will sometimes chase off families of geese (293) and Trumpeters will attack geese, white pelicans, herons and cranes, although not smaller water birds (14). There are also records of breeding Mute Swans attacking white call-ducks, in one case ignoring brown ducks of a similar size (148, 220). Black-necked Swans show a particular hatred for European Shelduck which possess a similar black head and neck and much white plumage; and Black Swans especially dislike dark-coloured geese (63). Banko (14) told of a harmless Muskrat being killed by a Trumpeter, perhaps because it resembled a dangerous Otter or Mink; Beavers may also be pursued (297), and Mute Swans have made unprovoked attacks on cattle coming to drink (252). Some swans make these 'mistakes' quite often, others manage to live in harmony with all but their real enemies. Delacour (63) suggested that it is merely a question of space and individual temperament. Perhaps, as in human beings, 'temperament' is partly inherited, partly learnt in childhood and partly related to environment.

Egg-retrieval and egg-shell disposal

Sometimes during the female's arrival and departure at the nest the eggs become displaced. These are retrieved, providing that they have not rolled far. The Mute Swan will respond only if the egg lies within reach of the nest (264). The procedure is always the same: the female stands up, extends her neck, hooks her lower mandible over the egg and draws it back into the nest-cup. The wing or foot is never used. The egg is not, in fact, recognised as such, and if rounded wooden blocks of various shapes and sizes are placed on the rim of the nest, these will be rolled in and brooded (264). Swans have also been found incubating stones, bottles and potatoes (141, 285).

The Black Swan is the only species in which both the male and the female behave in this way. The brooding bird skilfully rolls the egg up the sometimes steep sides of the nest and will just as skilfully retrieve an egg which another bird has laid within reach (88). This thieving has been proved conclusively by the use of marked eggs, and it no doubt explains the frequent appearance of fresh eggs in well-incubated clutches (112).

Eggs damaged in the nest will occasionally be carried away. Perrins (255) recorded an instance in which an incubating female Mute Swan attacked him and broke one of her eggs with a badly-aimed blow of her wing. After he had withdrawn, the swan ate the contents and carried three pieces of shell, one at a time, to the river edge – a distance of about four metres – and dropped them in. This behaviour is interesting in view of the difficulty which waterfowl find in carrying material *to* the nest, but is not unknown in other species (163).

Hatching and the imprinting of young on their parents

Hatching in all species tends to coincide with the period in which the food supplies and weather conditions are likely to be most favourable. If there is a sharp peak in such conditions, as in the Arctic, most of the clutches are hatched at about the same time, but elsewhere may be spread over a much longer period.

Hatching is announced by faint clickings from the egg and takes approximately two days. The cygnet uses a thorn-like projection on the tip of the upper mandible, the egg-tooth, to break through the shell. The first opening is small, surrounded by hair-cracks and is close to one end. After a rest of some hours, the bird rotates inside the shell, extending the perforations until a complete circle of holes has been cut. Then with stretching movements of the head and limbs the cap is lifted off and the wet, exhausted cygnet emerges. Its down is at first encased in waxy sheaths which protect it from the moisture within the egg, but after a day spent asleep beneath the parent's wings the wax rubs off, and the cygnet becomes dry and fluffy. It is now an enchanting creature, covered in dense, pale grey down, with bright eyes, a soft voice and apparently no fear of the world (PLATES 4, 9, 13, 26 and 32). The hatching of the complete brood may take 24–48 hours in the low-latitude swans (228), but the northern forms are quicker (349). In the Black Swan the last laid egg is often, although not invariably, the last to hatch (228).

Like all waterfowl, young swans accept as parents the first large moving objects that they see. Normally these are their mother and father; but cygnets will readily accept swans of another species, domestic hens and even human beings as substitutes. This 'imprinting' seems to occur more slowly

Whistling Swan cygnets. *Colleen Nelson.*

in swans than in other birds, most of which rapidly acquire a fear of unfamiliar objects. Although all cygnets follow their parents at once, it takes the northern forms some time to learn to follow them only. On one occasion in Iceland a brood of week-old Whooper cygnets followed the biologists who had just ringed and released them. On the other hand, cygnets aged between two and four and a half weeks feigned death when handled (293). Presumably the territorial swans have less need for precise imprinting than other waterfowl, because no large moving object except a parent is ever allowed near the nest.

Cygnet colour phase

Although the cygnets of the Mute Swan are normally grey, individuals with white down occur from time to time (PLATE 6). These leucistic birds pass straight into a white plumage, similar to that of the adults, instead of the usual grey-brown. They also have pale grey or pinkish feet, instead of black or dark grey, and retain this character into adult life. They were first noted in 1686 on the River Trent near Rugeley (259), and during the hard winter of 1838 a number of examples were shot on the British coast. Yarrell (347) mistook these for a new species, which he called *Cygnus immutabilis*, the Changeless Swan, because the juvenile and adult plumage appeared to be the same. The pale-footed birds were also known as 'Polish' Swans, a name given them by the London poulterers, who used to import them from the Baltic.

The white phase has always been rare in Britain, but elsewhere in Europe has increased considerably over the past 100 years. In the Netherlands it was first recorded near Haarlem in 1840 (310), and is now common throughout the country. On the Lake of Geneva, the first white cygnets were noted in 1868; by 1899 the large adult population contained no less than 28% of birds with the characteristic pale feet (141). Recent reports from Scandinavia show that the white phase occurs in 2% of the cygnets reared along the Danish coast (52); rare instances are also recorded inland in Sweden (322).

The introduced population of Mute Swans in North America likewise contains a large proportion of leucistic birds. In Rhode Island, 10% of 288 males and 26% of 200 females were found to be pale-footed. This uneven ratio prompted a genetic investigation which revealed that the pigment deficiency is due to a gene carried on the sex chromosomes (235). The condition is recessive and dominated by the normal, black-legged/grey plumage phase.

Birds have the usual X–Y mechanism of sex determination but, unlike mammals, the female is heterogametic (X–Y) and the male homogametic (X–X). The small Y chromosome carries no genes, so the female needs only one sex-linked gene (dominant or recessive) to inherit a particular characteristic. This is the reverse of the situation in man where recessive characters, such as haemophilia and colour-blindness, occur mainly in the heterogametic male. Thus a female Mute Swan needs to inherit only a single recessive gene in order to be melanin-deficient, whereas a male must inherit two, one from each parent, for the same to occur. In a male with one black (B) and one pale (b) gene, black will dominate and the bird will be indistinguishable from another with two black genes (BB). The Figure illustrates the result of pairing a 'Polish' cob (bb) with a normal pen (B–). All the female cygnets will be white (b–) and all the males grey (Bb). A cross between two of these offspring will produce equal numbers of grey and white cygnets of either sex.

It is surprising that the white phase has increased, since normal juvenile plumage is supposed to have selective value: note, for example, the excellent camouflage of the grey-brown cygnets in PLATE 8. Juvenile plumage also provides a clear distinction between adult and immature; in this way the young birds avoid hostility, because obviously they present no competition

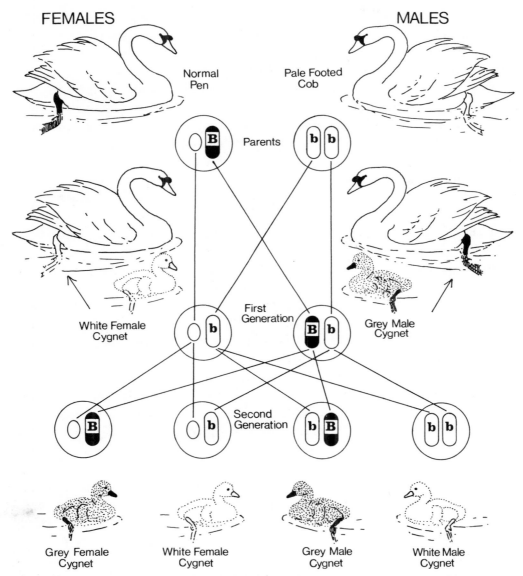

FEMALES

MALES

Normal
Pen

Pale Footed
Cob

Parents

White Female
Cygnet

First
Generation

Grey Male
Cygnet

Second
Generation

Grey Female
Cygnet

White Female
Cygnet

Grey Male
Cygnet

White Male
Cygnet

Sex-linked colour inheritance in Mute Swans. The pairing of a normal (black-footed) pen (–B) with a pale-footed cob (bb). *Colleen Nelson.*

for mates or territory. Cygnets in white plumage lack this safeguard, and there are several records of birds being attacked by their parents, and even killed (13, 141, 220, 221, 304). In each case there were only one or two white cygnets in an otherwise normal brood. Most of the young were half-grown, but one was only eight days old. Both of the parents may be involved, or only one. On one occasion a female was seen trying to drown her white offspring; they reached the shore with difficulty, and were attacked by a Crow. The male then rushed to their defence (141).

The domestication of the Mute Swan has undoubtedly encouraged the spread of the white phase. In the Netherlands it was bred selectively by the swan-farmers who sold juveniles live as ornamental birds, and dead for meat and 'fur'; the normal grey-brown cygnet had hardly any value in either trade. In some other countries, however, the carcases were sold without being skinned, and in this case it was the tender grey-brown birds which were selected for the table. The white cygnets were probably ignored, and allowed to grow on and reproduce. It is odd in view of this that the 'Polish' Swan is so uncommon in England, where the production of swans for food was a minor industry for many centuries.

White instead of grey cygnets are also seen among the wild Trumpeters in Yellowstone National Park. As in the 'Polish' Swan, the downy young pass straight into white plumage instead of the usual brownish-grey, and are distinguished from their parents only by their slightly smaller size, pinkish bill and yellowish legs (14, 64). During the years from 1937 to 1940, it was estimated that 13% of the cygnets in Yellowstone were leucistic. This relatively high ratio was due probably to selective shooting. The hunters wanted only the tender cygnets, and left any bird which was white and therefore presumed to be adult (212).

The mysterious *Cygnus davidi*, described by Swinhoe (316) from a specimen seen in Peking, was possibly a leucistic Bewick's Swan. The bird was almost certainly a juvenile, as the area between the bill and eye was feathered. It was said to be smaller than a Bewick's Swan, with all white plumage and a vermilion bill tipped by a black nail. The legs and feet were orange-yellow. This description is noticeably similar to that of the young leucistic Trumpeters, and is also reminiscent of some of the features of the 'Polish' Swan.

Leucistic Black Swans are likewise recorded from time to time. In this case the lack of pigmentation becomes more, rather than less, obvious with age. Some adults have light brown and fawn plumage, others are white although not true albinos (245, 296). Both types are unusual and, unlike the leucistic Mute Swan and Trumpeter, the birds concerned may find it difficult to obtain a mate and breed successfully. The paler plumage is also subject to considerable abrasion, thus placing the bird at a physical disadvantage. Since more than one white cygnet, with pink legs and bill, is sometimes seen in a brood, the character is probably inherited.

Carrying and brooding of the young

The sight of a swan carrying its cygnets on its back is one of the most appealing aspects of parental care (see PLATES 7 and 13). The behaviour is especially common in the Black-necked Swan and the Mute Swan, but less common in the Black Swan, and almost unknown among the northern forms and Coscoroba (63, 94, 132, 229). The obvious advantages are that the cygnets can sleep warm and dry among the feathers, without having to move ashore, and are also out of reach of most predators.

The cygnets climb on at a point between the tips of the short, folded wings and the tail. They are not helped aboard, except that the adult stays still and perhaps forms a step with the 'heel' of the foot (220). Both parents participate, but the female usually does more carrying than the male, except in the case of the Black-necked Swan where the cob sometimes takes over the duty entirely.

Black-necked Swan with cygnets climbing on to its back. *Robert Gillmor.*

The carrying depends to a large degree on the young themselves. Cygnets of the carrying species show a strong urge to climb which is absent in the others; for example, a small hand-reared Mute Swan is restless sitting in a human lap and must reach the shoulder before settling down, whereas a Trumpeter cygnet is content to remain where it is (163).

The failure of the northern swans to carry their young is probably due to the conditions under which they breed, with fewer underwater predators, and to the structure of the birds themselves. The species which carry migrate only short distances, and have relatively short wings (PLATE 8), which can be arched away from the body to provide a nest-like space for the young to sit in. The northern forms migrate much further, and have long wings which fold closely over the back and tail. It would be difficult, therefore, for the young to climb aboard, and even more difficult for them to find a secure niche in which to rest. Differences in the growth-rate, and in the amount of time spent feeding, may also be relevant. The cygnets of the northern swans have the advantage of long hours of daylight in which to feed, and grow so rapidly that carrying would quickly become impracticable. The small Coscoroba may also find it impracticable to accommodate its rather large brood of seven or more cygnets. It is also noticeable that the carrying species spend more time on the water than the others, but less time up-ending. This is especially true of Black-necked Swans, which rarely come ashore except to nest, and in feeding, when with young, dip only their necks beneath the water.

Coscoroba cygnets and those of the northern swans are brooded on land, usually on the old nest. A female Whooper Swan in captivity took her cygnets back to the nest and brooded them for the first few nights but never by day (170). On the other hand, a captive Trumpeter often retired to the nest with her cygnets for hours together, and continued to do so at night for a long time (29). Wild Trumpeters continue to use the nest for about a month, both for brooding at night and for loafing by day (14).

Calls of the cygnets

Young swans of all species produce rather similar sounds, but in general the four northern forms have deep, slow voices while the cheeps of the Mute, Black and Black-necked Swans are lighter in tone and more goose-like. The Coscoroba has not been studied.

The cygnet's voice is a most important part of its behavioural equipment.

With it, the young bird can indicate that it is lost, cold, sleepy, hurt, threatened or content, and thus elicit appropriate action from its parent. Communication with the mother and the other members of the brood starts when the baby is still in the egg. The first sound, heard about two days before hatching, consists of a regularly repeated 'clicking'. When the warm egg is held to the ear, it sounds as though the bird were tapping at the inside of the shell, but in fact, the clicks are produced not by the egg-tooth but by the cygnet breathing. Some time after clicking starts, and especially if the egg is tapped or cooled, the first cheeps are produced. The female responds by calling softly, and presumably both parents and young become familiar with each other's voices.

During early life a number of simple vocalisations are used. 'Pleasure' calls are the soft sounds heard when cygnets are warm and wide-awake, feeding, preening or exploring in company with each other or their parents. The notes occur in groups of two to five and probably keep the brood in contact. The Figure shows what they look like when turned into visual signals on a sound spectrogram. In greeting another member of the family, a cygnet extends its neck and utters a similar but louder series of notes, usually on a rising and falling cadence, like a question in human speech (177).

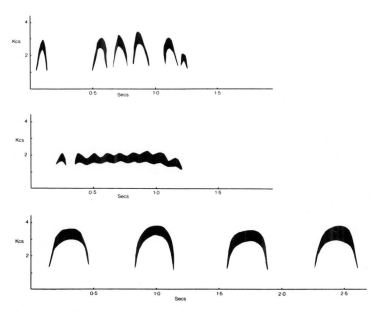

Sonagrams of cygnet calls. *Top*, pleasure call of a Black Swan; *centre*, sleepy call of a Trumpeter Swan; *bottom*, distress call of a Mute Swan.

'Sleepy' calls are given when the cygnets nestle together, with half-shut eyes and bills tucked in each other's down. Sometimes they are heard from a cygnet that is feeding or swimming about, and it can then be predicted that the bird is tired and will soon be on its parent's back, or ashore sitting down. The calls, which occur at longish intervals, are low, soft trills, rather like quiet sighs, and consist of a number of slurred contact notes, rapidly delivered (see the Figure). They probably encourage the youngsters to synchronise their rest periods and may also encourage their mother to brood them.

'Distress' calls are heard when a cygnet is isolated, cold or hungry. A deserted bird holds itself very erect, neck stretched upwards, the down on its head erected, mouth open, uttering one cry to each expiration and making itself as big and noisy as possible. The notes are high and regular, and are given more slowly and over a much longer period than the pleasure notes (see the Figure) (177). Calls of hungry or cold birds are similar but a little harsher. The function of these sounds is to attract the parent; the adult then goes and finds the missing cygnet, leads it back to the group, broods it, and may possibly obtain it food. On one occasion, when attempts were being made to record the voice of the Trumpeter Swan, two cygnets were captured and imprisoned near the microphone. Within ten minutes the parents had found the youngsters, which were calling in distress, and were trying to comfort them. After the sounds of both young and old had been recorded, the cygnets were released from confinement by remote control. The little birds swam busily from one parent to the other, giving greeting calls now, and gradually the united family swam away (189).

A cygnet which is hurt by being stepped on or pecked at by a parent or grasped by a predator, utters a loud, high-pitched shriek. These cries, which are uncommon and very intense, evoke an immediate response from the parents. As the cygnet grows, and becomes more capable of protecting itself, a hiss is added to its repertoire. This is one of the most widespread aggressive or defensive expressions among the vertebrates and one of the easiest to produce. A ten-day-old Mute Swan will stand its ground, even when alone, and threaten an attacker with gaping mouth and raised tongue, and with the head often thrust forward (177). A Trumpeter cygnet first shows this aggressive behaviour at twenty-nine days (335). It is not known precisely when the baby-voice 'breaks', but it happens rather suddenly, probably about the time that the youngsters fly. In the northern forms, where the wind-pipe, or trachea, grows gradually into the breast-bone, the voice of the juvenile lacks resonance and is higher in pitch than the adult's for at least a year.

Feeding of the young

The cygnets are helped to find their food by the parents pulling vegetation from beneath the water, from the bank, or from overhanging branches, and dropping it on the surface. In doing so, they sometimes use the same sideways-passing movement seen in nest-building. This behaviour by the adults may be instinctive (132), but food is, in fact, severed and brought to the surface whether the young are there or not. Another explanation is that the cygnets learn to exploit the usual feeding habits of their parents. During a study of the Trumpeter Swan it was found that the favourite food of the adults was the white understalk of the tule (rush). In pulling up the tender shoots, the parents often dislodged water boatmen and other aquatic insects; these were instantly gobbled up by the cygnets, which were soon leading instead of following their parents about. During the first ten days of their lives, insect food formed the major portion of their diet, but later on they began to pick up more and more of the vegetation loosened by their parents (72).

Nearly all swans pull more vegetation when they have young than when they are alone, and also leave a good deal of what they gather (14, 32, 66, 141). The Black-necked Swan is a possible exception (132); the Coscoroba has not been studied. Another feeding pattern that becomes more common in a breeding pair is foot-trampling. All waterfowl do this occasionally, usually in shallow water, in order to raise small particles of debris to the surface. Parent swans paddle a great deal, and edible items are eagerly taken by the young. The adults seem, in fact, to associate trampling with the presence of food for the cygnets; it is seen, for instance, when a family of Mute Swans is ashore being fed by humans, even before the food arrives. The female, in particular, 'marks time' in what appears to be a highly nervous fashion (220). Heinroth (132) suggested that this movement may have the additional value of attracting the cygnets to their parent's side, thus helping to keep the family together.

The cygnets' weight and growth

Cygnets of all species and of both sexes weigh slightly under two-thirds of the fresh egg at a day old (Table 6). Allowing 11 to 13% for the shell (286), this means that a quarter of the original weight has been used up in metabolism or lost in membranes and moisture at hatching.

Table 6. Approximate body weight at one day old (see Appendix 9 for details)

	gm	PERCENTAGE OF EGG WEIGHT	PERCENTAGE OF FEMALE'S WEIGHT
Mute Swan	220	64·7	2·5
Whooper Swan	210	63·6	2·6
Trumpeter Swan	206	63·4	2·2
Whistling Swan	180	64·3	2·9
Bewick's Swan	178	68·5	3·5
Black Swan	170	65·4	3·3
Black-necked Swan	150	61·2	3·7
Coscoroba Swan	109	58·9	2·9

As one might expect, the larger species produce larger young, but, as with the eggs, the ratio between the weight of the chick and the weight of the parent is higher in the smaller swans than in the large. It is, of course, to the cygnet's advantage to be as large as possible; it is then less vulnerable to cold, less dependent on learning to feed quickly, and better able to escape predators.

The size of the newly hatched bird varies, sometimes, in different parts of the species' range. The weights of young Black Swans from Tasmania, and of Trumpeter cygnets from Alaska are higher than those from elsewhere, and Mute Swan cygnets in Europe are generally heavier than those from Rhode Island. These differences correspond with variations in the size of the eggs (see Appendices 5 and 6), and in the case of the Mute Swan are attributable to differences in the average weight of the adult.

At hatching, the cygnet contains a certain amount of yolk and other food reserves in the liver and fat beneath the skin. These sustain it while it learns to take food for itself. The yolk of a newly hatched Mute Swan amounts to more than 25% of its body weight (134), and it lives on this, probably for a week or more. It has, in fact, been found that the highest mortality (22%) occurs in the second week of life, when the birds are most likely to die of starvation (256). A Mute Swan hatched at Slimbridge lost 25 gm. in the first two days while learning to feed, and it was not until the fifth day that it regained and passed its birth-weight.

The cygnets of some of the northern swans are on the water and feeding only twenty-four hours after hatching (349). Mute cygnets (PLATE 9) often remain in the nest a day longer (304). Black-necked cygnets also stay forty-eight hours (204) and, because of the difficulty they have in moving on land, suffer further delay before reaching the water; one family in captivity took all morning to travel 15 metres (170).

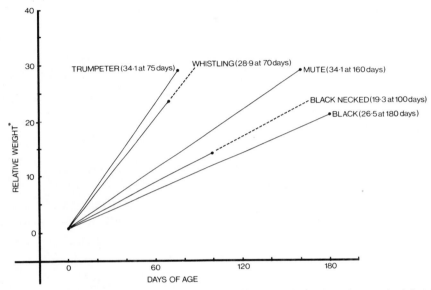

Relative growth rates of five species of swan (hatching weight reduced to 1·0). After Banko (14), Frith (88), Lensink (200), Portmann (263) and Rossi (280).

The northern forms show massive weight gains and steep growth curves compared with other species. The Figure indicates very approximately the rate of increase in the five species for which data are available. The records for the Whistling Swan and Black Swan are based on observations in the wild, the remainder on birds in captivity. The insectivorous Whistling and Trumpeter Swans show a thirty-fold increase in weight in 70–75 days, whereas the vegetarian Black Swan grows to only 27 times its birth-weight in 180 days. The Mute and Black-necked Swans fall midway between the two (14, 88, 200, 263, 280).

Although the size of males and females at hatching is similar, they start to diverge at about two weeks, and an adult pen weighs from 11 to 27% less than the cob (Appendix 2). In general the difference between the sexes is smaller in the northern forms than in the low-latitude ones.

Preening and feather development

During the later stages of incubation the females of many species of water-fowl spend much more time than usual in preening and oiling their feathers. McKinney (218) supposed that this oil was distributed to the young birds but was uncertain of its value. Waterproofing is dependent on the fine structure of the cygnet's dense downy coat and, so long as this is preserved, oil is apparently unnecessary. Nevertheless the cygnet has two sources of oil: one obtained by moving about among its parent's plumage and the other from its own oil gland. This is situated near the tail, on the upper side of 'the parson's nose'. Even at one day old the cygnet makes clumsy efforts to reach the gland and thereafter puts considerable effort into nibbling and oiling. Although the young bird probably spends no more time in preening than the adult, it breaks the performance up into numerous short sessions and tidies itself before and after every nap and every feed (see the cygnet in PLATE 7).

The oiling behaviour is inborn and varies little from individual to individual. The head is first flicked to remove any debris from the bill; the head and tail are turned towards one another; the down around the oil gland is erected; the short wing stub is lowered, and the bird nibbles at the gland and rubs its chin across it. It then rubs its chin over the breast and flanks and nibbles and pulls at the down with its bill.

The timing of the appearance of the various preening, or comfort, movements has been studied only in the Mallard, but is probably similar in all young waterfowl (Table 7). Cygnets are clumsier than most, and have greater difficulty in keeping their balance, but preening is vital and cannot be delayed.

Table 7. The time of appearance of comfort movements in young Mallard (218)

AGE	
1st day	Body-shake, head-shake, shuffling of rudimentary wings, scratching, foot-pecking, jaw-stretch ('yawn'), both-wings-stretch, oiling, nibbling.
1–2 days	Swimming-shake, tail-wag, wing-flap, head-dipping into water, nibbling at down after head-dipping.
3–4 days	Wing-and-leg-stretch (standing on one foot while stretching wing and leg on the other side).
6–7 days	Bill-cleaning ('sneezing' into water).
11–12 days	Washing during bathing.
13–14 days	Wing-thrashing, somersaulting and dashing-and-diving while bathing.

Table 7 lists the complete repertoire of preening movements which the bird uses during the rest of its life (PLATES 28 and 41). Somersaulting and dashing-and-diving are highly infectious, especially on sunny days; if one member of the brood begins, the others will follow suit (PLATE 19). The Coscoroba Swan is the only species which has not been seen to somersault; it seems in fact to do most of its bathing while standing sedately in shallow water (218).

The sequence of feathering is the same for all swans, although the timing varies considerably from species to species. The scapulars (on the shoulders) and the under wing coverts appear first, forming a pocket for the developing wing. In the Black Swan these are seen at 55 days (88), and in wild Trumpeters at about 28 days (297). The tail feathers may start to grow slightly earlier but are not obvious in the field. The feathers on the belly and flanks appear next and then the head feathers. The flight quills emerge later, the primaries after the secondaries. The downy remnants remain longest on the small of the back, on the head and on the underside of the wing – areas which seldom get wet. The Black Swan reaches this stage in 75 to 95 days (88) and the Trumpeter in about 49 days (297). The final number of feathers is enormous: an adult Whistling Swan was found to have a total of 25,216, of which 20,177 were on the head and neck (5). Together they weighed 621 gm. or 10% of the body.

As with incubation periods, there are great differences in the time taken to reach the flying stage. In general, the northern forms develop very rapidly, both before and after hatching. Not much information is available from the Arctic breeding grounds but it is said that the Bewick's Swan is capable of flying at 40–45 days old (326), and the Whooper at 60 days (120). In contrast, the Mute Swan flies in 120 to 150 days and some Black Swans in Tasmania are barely off the ground at six months (112). Indeed, the definition of a downy Black Swan is a bird less than 60 days old (40).

Growth data collected in captivity have only limited value for comparative purposes. In most cases the rates are very much slower, due sometimes to incorrect feeding, but more especially to the effect of the shorter day length. This is crucial to young birds which in nature would experience uninterrupted daylight and would be able to feed and maintain a high metabolic rate throughout the twenty-four hours. For example, the Bewick's Swans at Slimbridge (52° N) take more than twice as long to fledge as those reared in the wild in the Arctic tundra (70° N) – 110 days compared with 40–45. The effect of latitude on growth-rates is also apparent in the wild, among the Trumpeters which breed in widely separated districts of North America. In Kenai, Alaska, at 60° N, the cygnets are able to fly at 84 days (325), whereas those in Wyoming and Montana (44–45° N) take 100–120 days to reach the same stage (14, 301). Captive Trumpeters in Manitoba (50° N) take 91 days.

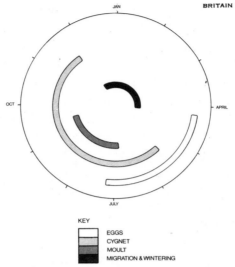

Annual cycle of activity in the Mute Swan.

The moult of the adults

While the cygnets are still young, the adults go through their annual feather moult. This involves the simultaneous loss of all the wing quills and renders the birds flightless and relatively helpless until the new ones have grown. In order that the brood may always have protection, the parents normally moult at different times. Observations on the Whooper Swans in Iceland indicate that the females almost certainly moult first (293); the same has also been noted in the Mute Swan, and in other species in captivity (132). The female Trumpeter usually starts to lose her feathers as soon as the cygnets hatch, and the Whistling Swan when the brood is about two weeks old (15). Most authorities maintain that the males of both species commence to moult after the female has regained her power of flight; it is possible, however, that the male Trumpeter may sometimes moult earlier, while the female is still engaged on incubation. This suggestion has been prompted by the finding of feathers around the nest, and by the absence of moulting males

118

PLATE 23 Whooper Swans in flight. ABOVE: *Shigeo Yoshikawa*. BELOW: *Pamela Harrison*.

PLATE 24 Head of Whooper Swan showing the yellow area extending past the nostril. Compare with Bewick's Swan in Plate 39. *Philippa Scott*.

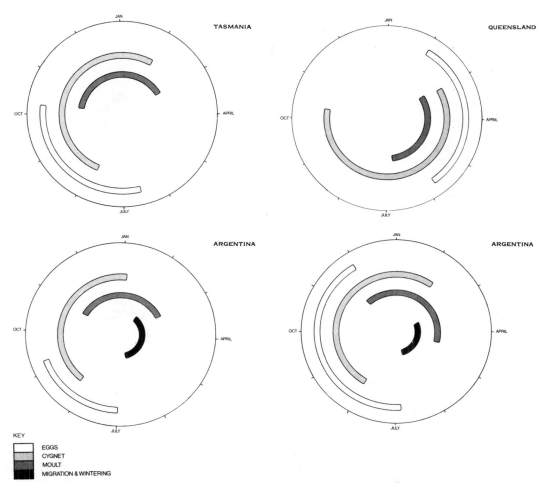

Annual cycles of activity in *upper left* Black Swan in Tasmania, *upper right* Black Swan in Queensland; *lower left* Black-necked Swan (somewhat conjectural); *lower right* Coscoroba Swan (somewhat conjectural).

after hatching (297, 325). The male and female of the Bewick's Swan moult simultaneously (66). The other species have not been studied.

The length of the flightless period varies. The Mute Swans in Denmark are said to be flightless for about seven weeks (283), and in Poland for six weeks (304) but in Rhode Island, U.S.A., for only three to four (340). Wild Trumpeters (15, 297) and Whoopers (66) are grounded for around a month. Bewick's Swans are reported to replace their flight feathers more rapidly than other species but no actual period is given (66). In any species, the moult of the body feathers may continue well into the autumn (3).

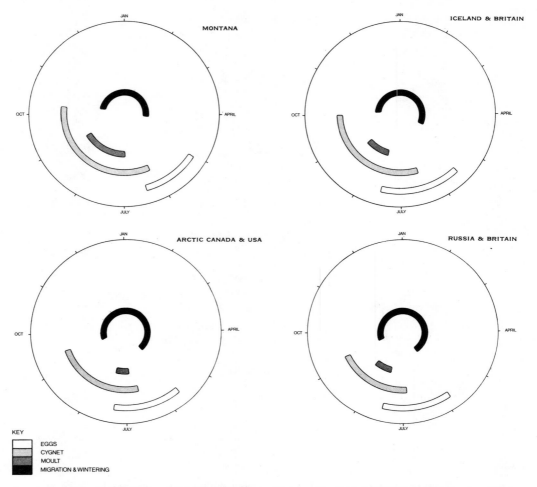

Annual cycles of activity in *upper left* Trumpeter Swan; *upper right* Whooper Swan; *lower left* Whistling Swan; *lower right* Bewick's Swan.

Birds which have failed to breed moult before successful ones, and immature and other non-breeding swans moult earlier still (33, 112, 293, 326). In many species the non-breeding birds congregate during the summer, including the moulting period. For example, large concentrations of Whooper Swans are known to assemble on certain lakes in Iceland. Gatherings of up to 10,000 Mute Swans are also recorded off the coasts of Sweden and Denmark, during the period of the annual moult (283). Black Swans make similar movements to larger and therefore safer waters, but the moulting season in this case extends over a much longer period, and flightless birds can be found at any time of the year (88). The moulting season of the Coscoroba also seems to be extended. In one particular area in Argentina, two flightless females were shot in the middle of November, and another in mid-April (104). The moult in non-breeding Mute Swans and Trumpeters is simultaneous in both sexes and may be more prolonged than in breeding birds (14, 33).

Migration, wintering, and the break-up of family life

Before leaving the breeding grounds, the adults and young of the migratory swans increase their food intake and build up large reserves of fat. They thus anticipate the approach of adverse conditions and in fact migrate before the lakes freeze and food becomes short. For instance, on the Perry River (at 68° N), the Whistling Swans all left by the end of August although there is usually no ice until September (89). The preliminary build-up of fat, and also the migration, must be prompted by some internal rhythm tied to an external cycle. The most obvious external factor is the shortening length of day, which in the first instance induces migratory restlessness and a weakening of the ties to territory; the flight itself is probably triggered off by local events, such as favourable winds and clear skies.

The family flies together, in company with one or two other groups. When travelling long distances, swans fly in V-shaped wedges; this reduces the air-resistance as each bird flies in the expanding wake of the one in front. It has been suggested that, because the leader has the hardest work to do, he is relieved at intervals and drops back to rest (26). It has also been said that the leader is normally an old male (10), but the evidence is inconclusive, and both theories must be regarded as supposition.

The immature birds and unsuccessful pairs leave the summering areas first (27, 297), but the first arrivals on the wintering ground are often family parties (289). Presumably the non-breeding birds, which are mainly one and two year olds, tend to dawdle on the journey while the older birds, remembering where to go, are inclined to travel direct. Many individuals are thought to return year after year to the same area (91, 92); this has certainly been confirmed by the Bewick's Swans which regularly travel over 2,000 miles to winter on the ponds at Slimbridge (289, 292). Swans tend, however, to be much more mobile in winter than in summer, and move about a good deal, depending on the weather and the local food supply.

Once they leave the nesting grounds, the white swans lose their territorial possessiveness and flock together at favourable feeding sites. They now encounter other adults and a great deal of aggressive interaction occurs; after a while this ceases and the group lives together with the minimum of irritation. New arrivals upset the peace, and need to be assimilated into the flock. This is usually achieved with threat displays rather than actual fighting (PLATES 29, 37 and 38). Swan species differ in their aggressive behaviour in much the same way as they do in courtship; indeed many patterns are common to both situations (3, 6, 14, 33, 140). For instance, most species ruffle the neck feathers as a sign both of aggression and of sexual interest (PLATES 6, 10, 11, 17 and 21), while a sleeking of these feathers is an indication of fear or submission (162). The Mute and the Black Swan lift the wings from the back in both threat and in triumph; the Mute also lays its head against its plumes (see page 89). When approaching an enemy on the water, the feet are used simultaneously to thrust the body forward and, on contact, quite fierce blows may be delivered with the wings and beak (96, 132, 220). The Coscoroba Swan also raises its wings in threat and jerks its head and neck backwards and forwards to exaggerate its aggressive mood (PLATE 1).

The Black Swan and the Mute Swan employ vigorous wing flapping and calling as a secondary threat display. The Black-necked Swan differs in keeping its wings close to its body in a head-forward threat. Like the northern swans, it sometimes ends the display by lowering its neck into the water with the bill pointing downwards, in which case the attack is not pressed home. The northern forms sometimes add hissing or vigorous wing shaking, and, on land, terminate this posture by 'ground staring' (PLATES 22 and 34). Before attack, the wings may be spread widely but are not flapped (162). A display which looks very like the triumph ceremony, with partially opened quivering wings, bending and extending of the neck and calling, is also used as threat. A complete analysis of the flock displays of the Bewick's Swan is now being made at Slimbridge, and should help to determine what advantage, if any, a bird obtains by being aggressive.

A group of displaying Bewick's Swans, Whistling Swans, Whoopers or Trumpeters is a clamorous affair (PLATES 37 and 38). The voices are distinctive but the behaviour and postures seem very similar; indeed the first two subspecies are so alike that the birds themselves do not apparently differentiate their race (292). Between the Trumpeter and the Whooper, there are subtle but obvious variations in display, which perhaps indicate a more distant relationship. The Whooper pumps its neck vigorously and throws its head so that the bill points upwards (PLATES 17 and 22). The Trumpeter performs less wildly and seldom raises its bill above the horizontal (PLATE 29).

Although displaying reduces the need for fighting, overt attack seems commoner among the northern swans than others. The Whooper, for example, always gets the better of the Mute in captivity because it 'wastes less time' posturing before using force (132). Family parties do not quarrel nor do close acquaintances. The offspring of previous years may even rejoin their parents on the wintering ground and parties of Bewick's Swans, containing parents, cygnets, yearlings, and two year olds plus their potential mates, sometimes move around together in amicable groups (289).

Swans are believed to recognise one another partly by voice and partly by face. If a swan has had its head beneath the water for a while, it is sometimes attacked from the rear by a friend; when a well-known countenance emerges, the aggressor rapidly withdraws and assumes a submissive attitude as though asking to be excused (132). This often occurs among the Bewick's Swans at Slimbridge. Perhaps the variable black and yellow patterning on their bills has been evolved as an aid to individual recognition. This patterning, which has been noted by several authors (1, 91, 285, 295), is the principal means of differentiating between Bewick's Swans at Slimbridge (289, 292).

It is uncertain to what extent the slow process of pair formation begins on the wintering ground. On several occasions the wild Bewick's Swans at Slimbridge have seemingly established bonds during their second winter but only one of these liaisons was still intact the following year (289). Pair formation in Black Swans probably occurs most frequently in autumn (40). The Mute Swan certainly enters into courtship in autumn and winter

(33, 230), but here again the majority of permanent pairs are formed in the herds of young birds, after the adults have left to nest. In all probability most of the migratory species do likewise.

Throughout the winter, the young birds are defended by their parents, except usually against man, and the family remains close. The exact time of the break up varies, and in some species is uncertain. The migratory Bewick's Swans, Whistling Swans and Whoopers leave the wintering grounds in families but arrive at their nesting territories in pairs. Perhaps the young are left behind at the last large lake while the parents fly on the remaining few miles alone. In the case of the largely non-migratory Trumpeter Swans of Montana and Wyoming, adult pairs start leaving the wintering flocks as early as February. This happens before their territories are clear of ice, and the birds are repeatedly forced back to the spring-fed ponds six or eight miles away. The flights become more frequent as the season advances and the territories are occupied as soon as conditions are suitable, usually some time in April (14).

Family parties of Mute Swans remain together until the end of the year, and sometimes into January. Territorial defence begins in January or February, although occasionally a pair will maintain their territory throughout the winter and remain there to breed (226). More usually, they congregate on to large areas of water. The cygnets seldom attempt to follow their parents out of these winter flocks, and instances of adults having to drive their young away are comparatively rare (33, 148). The cygnets of all species often stay together during the following summer and winter (14, 289, 297).

With the departure of the young birds, parental duties are complete but reproductive activity continues almost without pause. Territories must be reoccupied, a nest constructed or repaired, eggs laid and the next generation raised. The birds are probably twenty or thirty years old before age affects their fertility, but few survive that long (Appendix 3).

6

Mortality

J. V. Beer and M. A. Ogilvie

Old swans die; young ones are reared to take their place. In a stable population these two forces are in balance. At the simplest level a pair of breeding adults needs to produce only two offspring during their whole reproductive life, provided always that those two survive to become breeding adults in their turn.

The reproductive rate of swans is more or less constant. Each pair normally lays one clutch each season, the number of eggs being dependent on the species, and to some extent on the area in which the birds are breeding (see page 98). The clutch size does not apparently alter in response to short-term factors, such as a change in the breeding success or a decline in numbers. Any increase or decrease in the population must therefore be attributed to a change in the rate of mortality.

Intensive studies of the Mute Swan in Britain have provided a fairly accurate indication of the average mortality rates within the different age-groups. The work was done mainly in the West Midlands (230) and around Oxford (256) and in both cases was based on observations of marked birds. Ringing data from other parts of Britain have also been incorporated (242). The results are contained in Table 8, together with an estimate of the mean life expectancy at each stage.

Table 8. Mute Swan mortality rates in various age-groups

AGE	PERIOD OF MORTALITY	MORTALITY RATE PER CENT	MEAN LIFE EXPECTANCY IN YEARS
Eggs	prior to hatching	42·0	
Cygnets	1st week of life	9·0	2·3
	2nd week of life	22·0	
	2nd 2 weeks of life	12·0	
	3rd 2 weeks of life	8·0	
	4th 2 weeks of life	2·0–4·0	
	Each subsequent fortnight	2·0–4·0	
	1st three months	49·5	3·2
Immatures	3–12 months	32·1	4·2
	1–2 years	35·4	4·5
	2–3 years	25·0	4·8
	3–4 years	25·0	4·9
Breeding birds	4 years and over	18·0–20·0 per annum	4·8

PLATE 25 Trumpeter Swan female on her nest with the Centennial Mountains of Montana towering behind. *Winston Banko.*

PLATE 26 Trumpeter Swan. ABOVE: a nest in Montana with newly-hatched cygnet. *Winston Banko.* BELOW: a cygnet in Alaska. *U.S. Dept. of the Interior, Fish and Wildlife Service.*

PLATE 27 Trumpeter Swans. ABOVE: in flight. *U.S. Dept. of the Interior, Fish and Wildlife Service.* BELOW: a pair in Alaska defending their nest (in the centre). Compare with Plate 6. It is unusual for Trumpeters to show this behaviour towards humans in the wild. *Will Troyer.*

PLATE 28 Trumpeter Swans at Slimbridge. ABOVE: in greyish first plumage. *Christopher Stringer*. BELOW: preening. *E. E. Jackson*.

Some of the heaviest losses occur before the cygnets are even hatched. During the Mute Swan study of 1961–1967 a total of 456 nests with eggs were recorded in the West Midlands; of these no less than 192 failed to produce a single cygnet (230). The greater part of the loss, 78%, was due to human interference and more especially to the removal or destruction of eggs by small boys. Other causes included flooding (8%), the death of one or both parents (7%), and desertion (3%). In addition to the clutches which failed completely, a number of eggs was no doubt lost from some of the nests in which cygnets were hatched. A similar study at Radipole Lake near Weymouth in 1969 revealed losses which, although substantial, were noticeably smaller than those in the West Midlands – a reflection perhaps of the warnings against interference made in the local schools. In this instance a total of 141 eggs was laid in 44 nests; of these eight complete clutches, comprising 28 eggs, were lost, together with another four eggs from three other nests.

Mute Swan cygnets, two normal individuals, with a 'Polish' cygnet on the right. *Colleen Nelson.*

The death-rate among cygnets in their first few weeks of life is high, due mainly to starvation and chilling. The losses during the second week are particularly heavy, because by then the young birds have used up the reserves of yolk which sustain them through the first few days (79, 273). In subsequent weeks the main cause of death is adverse weather, but predation may also play a part.

Throughout their first year the young birds are gaining experience the hard way, and accidents are common, especially in the autumn when the cygnets are flying for the first time. The winter is also a time of high mortality, due to cold and shortage of food. Thereafter the mortality rate falls, but there are still noticeable peaks each spring and autumn when the birds are on the move, looking for territories or assembling into flocks for the winter (256). Among adult Mute Swans, the annual mortality rate for both males and females amounts to a constant 18–20%; death from old age is thus comparatively rare.

The life expectancy figures contained in Table 8 are calculated from the observed mortality rates in the various age-groups. Their purpose is to show the number of additional years that an individual is likely to live, having reached its present age. Thus a breeding adult, four years old, will live on average for a further 4·8 years. This fits well with the tentative suggestion that a pair of Mute Swans takes an average of five breeding seasons to produce the two adult replacements required to keep the population at a stable level (256). Some individuals, of course, live much longer than others, especially in captivity (see Appendix 3), but in population studies this potential life-span is much less relevant than the mean.

The following example shows the number of birds surviving to various ages, beginning with 1,000 newly hatched cygnets. It will be seen that although the odd bird may live for nearly twenty years, more than 96% are dead by the age of ten.

> 1,000 eggs hatch (out of *c.* 2400 laid)
> 500 cygnets survive to three months old
> 325   ,,   ,,   ,, twelve   ,,   ,,
> 224 birds   ,,   ,, 2 years
> 125 ,,   ,,   ,, 4 years, and become breeding birds
> 35 ,,   ,,   ,, 10 years old
> 12 ,,   ,,   ,, 15 ,, ,,
> 1 bird survives   ,, 19 ,, ,,

In Denmark, during the 1950s, the annual mortality rate among Mute Swans was estimated at about 20% (251). This included all age-groups from three months onwards, and was thus substantially lower than the present rate in Britain. As might be expected, the population was increasing rapidly at the time (page 39).

The Whooper Swans, which breed in Iceland and winter in Britain, show an annual mortality of about 17% (39). This figure includes the losses of young birds during their first winter; for adults alone the rate might be as low as 10%. The rate among adult Bewick's Swans wintering at Slimbridge is estimated tentatively at 15% (290). The Trumpeter Swan in North America has been studied closely in recent years, and a good deal of information is available on the losses among eggs and cygnets (14). Hatching success varies between 51% and 66%. About 13% of the eggs are lost through flooding or predation; the remainder are mostly deserted, addled or infertile. The losses among unfledged cygnets can be as high as 50%, but in some populations may be substantially lower. The causes of death include predation by various carnivores, and the disruption of family parties by human disturbance. The adult mortality rate has not yet been examined in detail, owing to the lack of adequate ringing data.

Accidental Causes of Death

In the absence of shooting, the main causes of death among swans are accident, starvation, adverse weather and disease. The accidental deaths, which in some species comprise a large part of the annual mortality, are nearly all related to some human activity. Because of this, they tend to be reported more frequently than deaths from natural causes, which in the more remote areas must often pass unnoticed.

Flying accidents

Swans fly at speeds of 30–50 m.p.h., and because of their size, find difficulty in making sudden changes of course. They also seem to have relatively poor forward vision, and may have difficulty in seeing, or fixing the position of, an approaching obstacle. As a result they are frequently in collision with bridges, buildings, and more especially with overhead wires. One even flew into the cliffs at Dover.

Accidents of this nature are the cause of death most commonly reported among Mute Swans in Britain. Of 1,050 birds found dead, no less than 65% had been involved in collisions (242). Two-thirds of these incidents involved overhead wires, and there is no doubt that this has been a major

Mute Swans and power cables. *Robert Gillmor*.

factor in limiting the population in some areas. Wires are particularly lethal when they run across rivers or canals, or pass close to sites holding large concentrations of birds. In Kent no fewer than twenty-one Mute Swans, about 30% of the local flock, were killed in two months along one quarter-mile stretch of power line, which lay midway between the roost and feeding ground (123).

Some birds are killed by impact with the wires, and others by electrocution, but the proportions are not known. Those which survive the collision are often stunned and fall heavily to the ground. In the absence of serious injury, they eventually recover and fly off, but for a while are vulnerable to foxes and other predators.

Contamination by oil

Pollution of the world's waterways by the deliberate or accidental discharge of oil is still a common occurrence, despite the measures taken to prevent it. During recent years there have been several major disasters, resulting in the death of many thousands of birds; minor incidents are reported almost weekly (PLATE 43). The sea birds are particularly vulnerable, but any species which lives on water is likely to be affected.

The effects of oil on birds are varied and complex. Initially it clogs or saturates the feathers, which then lose their properties of waterproofing and insulation. In this condition the bird will spend much of its time attempting to remove the oil, instead of seeking extra food to combat the loss of heat.

Some oil is ingested, and irritates the gut, causing enteritis. Detergents, used to disperse the oil, or to clean the bird, exacerbate its already poor condition. Death usually results from a combination of exposure, emaciation, poisoning and stress (21, 124, 127, 128).

The Mute Swan is the only swan known to have suffered serious casualties, but there is no reason to suppose that the others will escape indefinitely. The involvement of the Mute Swan is a reflection of its association with man; unlike the other species it occurs in substantial numbers close to the main centres of industry, where the danger of pollution is greatest. During the past ten years swans have been killed or contaminated by oil in at least ten counties of Britain (107, 124, 242). At Burton-on-Trent, 85 birds died out of a flock of 100 (242). Incidents involving swans have also been reported from Switzerland and Sweden (38, 196).

The best method of dealing with oiled birds is far from clear, and opinions differ widely (22, 51). The central problem is to restore the plumage to normal, after the bird has recovered from the initial exhaustion and poisoning, so eventually it may be returned to the breeding population. The Mute Swan is one of the less difficult species to rehabilitate, partly because it is easy to find and catch at an early stage, and partly because it responds well to captivity and unaccustomed foods.

Poisoning

The ingestion of lead shot is a common cause of poisoning and death among wildfowl in some districts (246). Each time a gun is fired some 200–300 pellets are scattered over quite a wide area, where they remain almost indefinitely; this happens whether or not the target is hit. If the pellets fall on marshland or in shallow water, they are likely to be picked up by waterfowl in mistake for seeds or grit. Any which are swallowed, are ground down in the gizzard, and the lead is absorbed into the tissues. Poisoning may also result from the traces of lead in mine-washings (49).

Lead is a cumulative poison, and the taking of even a few shotgun pellets is likely to result in death. Concentrations of only ten parts per million in the tissues are enough to cause sickness (49, 205). The symptoms include anaemia, emaciation and progressive weakness; the droppings are often bright green; and the pellets themselves are usually detectable in the gizzard by radiography (150). At autopsy the gizzard is frequently impacted, and the lining and contents may be stained by an excess of bile. Diagnosis may also be aided by the presence of acid-fast intra-nuclear inclusions in the kidney cells (205) and by the levels of lead in liver and bone (12, 55).

Deaths from lead-poisoning have been recorded in all the species of swans, except the Black-necked Swan and Coscoroba (14, 24, 38, 214, 344). The Whistling Swan seems particularly prone, the losses in one wintering area amounting to as much as 3% of the peak population. In one group of 45 affected birds, the average number of pellets in each gizzard amounted to no less than 50; the largest number was 236 (324).

The development of non-toxic pellets is clearly of the utmost importance and urgency; there is no sign, however, of this being achieved (25). Even the palliative measures employed at present are limited in both practicability and effect. Attempts have been made to treat affected swans with injections of calcium versenate, but these were successful only when the bird was still in good condition. The treatment has to be continued until the lead has disappeared from the gizzard and from most of the tissues (276). In some areas the losses have been reduced by paying attention to the positioning of shooting zones and refuges, by stopping shooting over certain areas of shallow water, and by scaring birds away from sectors where the hazard is greatest. The provision of food and grit may also be helpful (97, 171). If a collection of captive waterfowl is being kept in a former shooting area, the banks of the pools should be reinforced to prevent erosion, which would release pellets buried in the soil (24).

Copper and zinc also cause poisoning, but on a much less serious scale. Two Mute Swans which died within seven weeks on the same stretch of stream in central England were found to have numerous fragments of brass in their gizzards (339). Copper sulphate, in relatively large amounts (c. 180 mg.) is believed to have contributed to the death of two Mute Swans in Switzerland (38). In America, some of the Whistling Swans reported dead from lead-poisoning, were also found to contain toxic levels of copper and zinc. The birds concerned had been using a river polluted by mine-washings (49).

Pesticide poisoning is another potential hazard. Only a few cases have so far been confirmed among swans, but several more are suspected. In one recent incident in central Scotland some 30–40 Whooper Swans, which were picked up dead, were found to contain traces of mercury (219). They were thought to have been grazing on young winter wheat and to have pulled not only the leaf but also the seed, which had been treated before sowing. The ground at the time was light and crumbly after frost. Agricultural chemicals may also have been responsible for the unexplained deaths of Whooper Swans in other parts of Scotland. In central Europe a case of nicotine poisoning has been reported in a Mute Swan (38).

Miscellaneous mishaps

The Mute Swan, because of its associations with Man, is more likely to die of unnatural causes than most other species. On several occasions death has resulted from birds swallowing fish-hooks, or becoming entangled in broken lines; they have also landed on wet roads, presumably in mistake for rivers, and been killed or injured by traffic. Others have been crushed between boats, or caught between lock-gates; one hit a plane at London airport, another became impaled on underwater barbed-wire, and a third was sat on by a cow. Whistling Swans also have bizarre mishaps. On one occasion more than a hundred birds were caught in the rapids above Niagara Falls and were swept to death among the rocks and whirlpools below (83).

Disease and Death from Natural Causes

Most of the adult swans which die from natural causes are killed by a combination of bad weather, starvation and disease. Bad weather, by itself, is seldom a killer except, for example, when migrants are met by contrary winds and perish from exhaustion in the sea. Eggs and cygnets are, of course, highly susceptible to chilling, but adult birds are well able to withstand long periods of cold, provided that food is available. In practice, bad weather and starvation often go hand in hand, and together are a major cause of death in some species. As a result of the cold winter of 1963 the Mute Swan population in Britain was reduced by more than a fifth (242); the migrant species were unaffected. Starvation and disease are similarly interrelated, and so are the various diseases. Often a bird which is weakened by one disease will contract, and may even die of, another. For simplicity these interrelations have been largely ignored in the following account.

No comprehensive review of the diseases of swans has yet been compiled, although some species, notably the Mute Swan, have been covered in considerable detail (38). Some aspects have also been studied more fully than others; there are for example a number of reviews and bibliographies covering the taxonomy, occurrence and pathology of the parasites (194, 215, 216). There is still much to be learnt about the general and comparative pathology of the swans, and about the importance of disease as a controlling factor. The present section reviews the more common and interesting conditions, and includes some hitherto unpublished information from the files of the Wildfowl Trust. During the past sixteen years nearly 150 dead swans and cygnets, both wild and captive, have been examined here; the totals per species are as follows: Coscoroba 8, Black Swan 16, Mute Swan 43, Black-necked Swan 38, Whistling Swan 4, Bewick's Swan 26, Whooper Swan 4, Trumpeter Swan 7. The details of these autopsies are available for reference.

VIRAL DISEASE

Viruses are relatively common in birds, but only a few types cause illness. Birds may, however, act as a reservoir for viruses which affect other vertebrates; in such cases the organism is often transmitted by blood-sucking insects (309).

Duck plague is a myxovirus which affects Anseriformes in scattered parts of the world. A Mute Swan has been infected experimentally (73), and a case in a wild Mute Swan has been reported from North America (199). Marek's disease, caused by a herpes virus, is a serious and highly contagious condition in poultry (294), and has been reported in several species of wild birds, including a swan (28).

BACTERIAL DISEASE

Salmonellosis and Colibacillosis

Bacteria form an important part of the micro-flora of birds; only some are harmful. The diseases caused by *Salmonella* normally involve the gut, and

PLATE 29 Trumpeter Swans. ABOVE: wintering flock in Montana. The displaying birds in the centre hold their heads lower than the Whooper Swans in Plates 17 and 22. BELOW: aerial view of a January flock of 80 birds in Montana. *Winston Banko*.

PLATE 30 A pair of the Trumpeter Swans presented to H.M. The Queen by the Canadian government, living at Slimbridge. *The Wildfowl Trust*.

may be serious or mild. In poultry the usual organisms are *S. gallinarum* of fowl typhoid, and *S. pullorum* (294); in wild birds, the commonest is *S. typhimurium* (319). An aquatic environment is ideal for their dissemination, but infection does not necessarily lead to disease. Epidemics are usually attributable to adverse conditions, such as shortage of food, stress of breeding, changes of temperature and overcrowding.

Two cases of salmonellosis have been reported in wild Mute Swans in Britain (183, 343), and in Germany twenty-three Mute Swans died of infections involving *S. typhimurium*, *S. paratyphi B* and *S. stanleyville* (38). A case of paratyphoid occurred in a captive swan in France (328).

Related organisms, such as *Escherichia coli*, are seldom virulent and may be normal inhabitants of the gut. Under certain conditions, however, some strains may cause serious disease, such as coliform septicaemia, endocarditis and fibrinous enteritis, all of which have been reported in the Mute Swan (38).

Pasteurellosis

Fowl cholera, caused by *Pasteurella multocida* (*P. aviseptica*) is known from thirteen species of waterfowl (110). Outbreaks have been reported among the Whistling Swans wintering in California (277) and a case was found in a Mute Swan in Britain (157). Fowl cholera has also been reported in a wild Trumpeter (110).

Staphylococcosis

Most infections involve *Staphylococcus aureus*, a common organism found in many animals, including man. The Anatidae are not, in general, susceptible, although arthritic joints, particularly in the leg, may sometimes become infected. The bacteria usually gain access through cracked or calloused feet and then spread to other parts of the body (38). This has been noted in a Bewick's Swan, and also in a Coscoroba, the latter developing endocarditis of the heart valves. Many strains of *S. aureus* are resistant to penicillin and the tetracycline antibiotics, making the condition difficult to treat (294).

Botulism

Botulism is caused by botulinum type C toxin. This is produced by the bacterium *Clostridium botulinum* in warm, alkaline water or mud, under anaerobic conditions. The shallows in which it occurs are much favoured by wildfowl as feeding grounds, and many epidemics have been recorded among ducks, notably in North America (160). The disease is serious, but the less affected birds may recover if given clean water and allowed to rest undisturbed. Injections of antitoxin have been used successfully in cases where the symptoms were more severe.

Botulism has been recorded in the American swans (14, 250, 265, 298), in European swans (30, 38) and in the Australian Black Swan (111). Other names for the disease are western duck disease, alkaline poisoning and limberneck.

Tuberculosis (Mycobacterium avium)

This was at one time a major disease in poultry (37) and is still endemic in many collections of captive birds, including waterfowl. The persistence of the organism in the environment makes it difficult to eradicate, especially when birds are kept on the same ground for many years. The use of high quality food appears to reduce the incidence of the disease (268).

Tuberculosis has been noted in swans of all species, except the Whooper. In the wild it has been recorded in the Mute Swan (38, 122), the Whistling Swan (87), the Bewick's Swan (339) and the Trumpeter (14). The typical lesions in wildfowl are hard caseous nodules from 1 to 10 mm. in diameter, and are found most frequently in the spleen and liver. The gut is often affected, but rarely the lungs.

FUNGAL DISEASE

Only four genera of fungi have been known to cause disease in waterfowl: *Aspergillus, Candida, Mucor* and *Rhinosporidium* (23, 80). By far the most important species is *A. fumigatus*.

There are records of fungi in swans dating back to 1816 (152), but it is not always clear which species were involved. *A. fumigatus* was first described in detail in 1853 (267), and over the next sixty years there were several accounts of mycoses in swans (50). A general review of aspergillosis in birds appeared in 1938 (329). Since then the disease has been reported on numerous occasions in swans of all species (14, 20, 126, 138, 154, 269, 341).

A. fumigatus causes a severe and usually fatal respiratory disease. The inhaled conidia, being only 2–3 μ in diameter, pass through the upper respiratory tract, and become lodged in the finer passages of the lung, giving rise to small white nodules. Those which reach the air-sacs cause lesions, which start as small plaques, but eventually involve the whole structure. If sporulation occurs the lesions turn green. Fragments of hyphae may lodge in the capilliaries and form nodules, for instance in the membranes of the thoracric cavity. Conidia which settle in the larger air passages may cause broncho-pneumonia. Sometimes the passages become blocked by the lesion, and death occurs suddenly through asphyxiation.

The disease is characteristic of young birds, and of those which have undergone some form of stress (20). On Lake Ellesmere, in New Zealand, aspergillosis has caused heavy losses of Black Swans. The contributory factors in this case were probably overcrowding, social stresses and shortage of food due to abnormal water levels (341).

PROTOZOAL DISEASE

Certain species of protozoa are found in the blood and viscera of many groups of birds, and sometimes cause illness or death. Only a few instances have been recorded in swans (137, 201, 213).

Avian malaria

Plasmodium, which causes malaria in man, has been reported in both the Black Swan and the Black-necked Swan (53). The genus is transmitted by culicine mosquitoes, and birds are apparently infected for life. *Haemoproteus* has been recorded in the Whistling Swan (136). It is a genus found only in birds, and is their commonest malarial parasite (144). In ducks, it is transmitted by biting midges (81).

Trypanosomiasis

Certain *Trypanosoma* are highly pathogenic in man, but appear to have little effect on birds (137). The parasites have been found in the Whistling Swan (69); they are transmitted by mites, mosquitoes, hippoboscids and blackflies.

Coccidiosis

Coccidia are found in a wide range of animal hosts. Some are highly virulent and result in heavy losses, for instance among poultry (213). *Eimeria truncata*, a species normally occurring in the kidneys of geese, is said to have been found in a Mute Swan (47). *Tyzerria anseris* has been noted in the intestine of a Whistling Swan (118), and two other cases of coccidiosis, one fatal, have occurred in this species (276, 298).

ENDOPARASITES (HELMINTHS)

Trematodes

The endoparasitic Trematoda or flukes are flat, non-segmented worms. Some, such as bilharzia in man and liver fluke in sheep, cause serious disease. A total of twenty-five genera have been recorded from the swans, mostly in the Black Swan, Mute Swan and Whooper (215, 216). The majority occur in the gut, in the duodenum, small intestine, caecae or rectum, depending on the species. Others invade the respiratory system or the blood vessels. The effects on the host are generally slight, but some species are dangerous, especially if the infestation is heavy (158, 306).

The life-cycles of these parasites depend on one or more intermediate hosts, usually snails. Infestations can be controlled by eliminating the snails with chemicals, but this is likely to result in ecological imbalance and pollution. If the density of wildfowl is high enough, the intermediate hosts are eaten out, thus breaking the cycle. This is the situation at the Wildfowl Trust, where trematode infestations are unusual, except in newly imported birds and in individuals which have been fed on water-weed brought in from snail-infested waters (11).

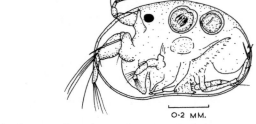

0·2 MM.

An ostracod, the intermediate host of swan cestodes, with two spherical tapeworm larvae in its body cavity. *Roger Avery.*

Cestodes

The Cestoda, or tapeworms, are common segmented parasites. Seven genera are known from the swans (215, 216); by far the commonest is *Hymenolepis*

138

which has been recorded in all except the Bewick's Swan. Although their numbers are sometimes large, they seldom cause serious disease unless the host is weakened by other adversities. An example of this occurred in a group of 350 Mute Swans, which as usual had assembled to moult on a reservoir in south-east England. The summer had been wet, and the water level was unusually high; as a result the birds were unable to reach enough food, and because of the wing moult were prevented from moving elsewhere. Many died, and were found to contain large numbers of parasites, including *Hymenolepsis*. This infestation undoubtedly contributed to the heavy losses (158). A case of multiple parasitism has also occurred in a Trumpeter Swan (59).

Nematodes

The Nematoda or round-worms are a fairly frequent cause of disease in wildfowl. A few are often present in apparently healthy birds, but if the numbers increase they may lead to emaciation, enteritis or pneumonia. Juvenile birds are the most susceptible, although severe cases often occur in older individuals, concurrently with other diseases. Fifteen genera are known in swans (215, 216).

Echinuria (*Acuaria*) *uncinata* is common in young wildfowl, especially those reared in captivity. The intermediate host is the freshwater crustacean, *Daphnia*, which is frequently taken by the birds as food. The larval form, after being carried in the body cavity of *Daphnia*, invades the proventricular glands of the bird, causing extensive ulceration. In severe infestations there is stunting and enteritis, followed by emaciation and death. Drugs are of little avail, but with captive birds the cycle of infection can be broken by

The water flea, *Daphnia*, with worms of *Acuaria* in its body cavity. *Dafila Scott*.

using an alternative source of water, which is free from *Daphnia*, or by increasing the flow to discourage the crustaceans from multiplying (333). Infestations of *Echinuria* have been found in a wild Mute Swan (158) and in captive Black-necked Swans, Bewick's Swans and Trumpeters (58, 339).

The gizzard worms, *Amidostomum*, *Epomidiostomum* and *Paramidostomum* are a common cause of disease in the Anatidae, especially in young geese. They are found in small numbers in all the swans, but appear to do little damage.

Cyathostoma bronchialis, one of the gape-worms, occurs in the respiratory tract and can cause heavy mortality in young wildfowl, through pneumonia. If present in sufficient numbers they may also cause asphyxia. Infestations have been recorded in the Coscoroba and Black-necked Swan (215, 216). Another genus, *Syngamus*, has been reported in the European swans (274).

A further group of nematodes, the filarial worms, are located in the blood-stream and heart. The taxonomy of these parasites is obscure, and *Sarconema* and *Splendidofilaria* may be synonyms. *Sarconema euryurea* has been recorded in the Mute Swan (36), Whistling Swan (142) and Trumpeter (59), in each case in America. *Splendidofilaria* has been found regularly in the wild Mute Swans and Bewick's Swans which frequent the pens of the Wildfowl Trust. Some birds had up to four parasites in the coronary blood vessels, but with no sign of damage to the myocardium. In some of the American cases, however, the heart muscle was damaged, and death was due to cardiac arrest (188). One Whistling Swan, which had failed to migrate in the spring, had no fewer than thirty-six parasites in its heart (142).

Acanthocephala

The Acanthocephala, or thorny-headed worms, are common parasites of the small intestine, especially in water birds. Two genera, *Polymorphus* and *Fillicollis*, are known from the Mute Swan, Bewick's Swan and Whooper (215, 216). *P. boschadis* is a small, bright reddish-orange worm, which in large numbers may cause anaemia, wasting and death. *F. anatis* is a little larger and causes similar debility. Both species spend part of their life-cycle in crustacea, on which wildfowl often feed.

Hirudinea

The Hirudinea or leeches, which feed on the blood of other animals, are a group of the true segmented worms, the Annelida. *Theromyzon* has been found on both the Mute and the Black Swan (215, 216). It is a small leech, about 2 cm. long, which attaches itself to the nostrils or invades the sinuses. In large numbers they cause anaemia, and also a swelling of the tissues, which may sometimes block the respiratory tract.

ECTOPARASITES

Wildfowl are affected by feather-lice, Mallophaga, and by feather-mites, Sarcoptiformes. Each species of bird tends to have its own particular parasites, which live in balance with the host and normally cause little damage.

The Mallophaga are flat in profile, enabling them to lie neatly between the feathers; they can also move rapidly and thus avoid removal by preening. A few are found in the plumage of nearly all birds, but if an individual becomes ill, the numbers may greatly increase. The insects feed on skin and feather debris and in large numbers cause severe irritation which worsens the already poor condition of the feathers, and further affects the health of the bird. The Coscoroba is the only swan in which they have not been reported, but there is no reason to suppose that they do not occur. A list of the species recorded in the other swans is provided by Lapage (194); the most wide-spread genera are *Anatoeccus*, *Docophorus*, *Lipeurus*, *Ornithobius* and *Trinoton*. *T. anserinum* takes blood as well as debris (38). The only feather-mite recorded on swans is *Freyana anserina* (266).

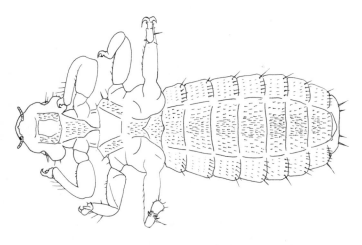

A feather-louse from a Bewick's Swan. *Dafila Scott.*

ATHEROSCLEROSIS

This degenerative disease involves a thickening and hardening of the arterial wall in association with fatty deposits. The condition occurs mainly in captive animals and is common in the Anseriformes. Probable factors include incorrect feeding, social stresses and the advanced age reached by some birds in captivity (203, 270). The lesions in the Anatidae vary from a few small foci to hard yellow plaques with massive involvement of the artery and calcification. The disease has been noted in all species of swans except the Trumpeter (82, 115). Several instances, involving six species, have been examined at the Wildfowl Trust; in each case the bird had died of another disease. One, a Bewick's Swan, had advanced lesions, but in general the condition appeared to be of minor significance. The nearest approach to a case in the wild was noted in three Mute Swans from the outskirts of a small English town; their diet may therefore have been abnormal.

NEOPLASTIC DISEASE

Tumours, although relatively common in poultry (294), are unusual in captive birds (206, 294, 312), and rare in the wild (38, 156, 342). A tumour in the liver of a captive Coscoroba is the only case known from a swan (155). Since tumours in other birds are normally found among the older individuals it is somewhat surprising that they occur so rarely in the swans, with their long potential life-span. Perhaps they are resistant to tumour development, just as some orders of birds seem particularly prone (206).

7

The Swan in mythology and art

Mary Evans and Andrew Dawnay

Since time immemorial Man has been strongly attracted to swans, but his admiration has expressed itself in many different ways: the poet and artist have often given to its beauty an almost mystical significance; the trader has pursued it with relentless greed; the hunter has delighted to destroy it. On balance the swan has come off badly from this ambivalent relationship, but today, at last, it is beginning to receive a proper consideration. The next three chapters look, first, at the swan's influence over a long succession of cultures; secondly, at the various ways in which Man has exploited it, or come into conflict with it; and, lastly, at the change of approach which is necessary if the several swans are to be sure of a place in the modern world.

There is an old Norse legend in which the sanctuary of the gods is said to be a great ash-tree, supported by three outspreading roots. The third root is in the sky, and under it there is a sacred spring, called the Spring of Urd. Here dwell the three Norns, the Norse Fates, whose names are Past, Present and Future. The water of the Spring of Urd is so sacred that everything which comes into contact with it becomes 'as white as the film that lies within an eggshell'. On the water live two swans, and it is from them that the whole race of swans has sprung (350).

It seems that to these Norse story-tellers the swan was the only creature lovely enough to grace the waters of perfection: for them the original swans came out of the very heart of purity. In this they are only conforming to an almost universal tradition, for the swan's striking beauty has given it, perhaps more than any other bird, a powerful grip upon Man's imagination, which must often have been strengthened by the mystery of watching such birds vanish with haunting cries into the unknown, to return again at a new season as inexplicably as they went. Drawings of swan-like birds go back to the Old Stone Age. There are legends, too, out of the deep past, legends of swan-maidens and swan-knights, of transformations and magic. These beliefs do not stand in isolation, for there are many elements of folklore which reappear again and again in the cultures of Europe and Asia, passed on by trade and conquest, altered, perhaps, by the demands of different social patterns, but still recognisably growing from the same roots.

One of the earliest and most insistent of these recurring themes associates the swan with the pagan cult of sun-worship. In this context one sometimes cannot distinguish between swans and geese; both were linked to the sun, but their roles varied at different times and in different places. In Egypt the Chaos Goose or Great Cackler was believed to lay an egg daily which was

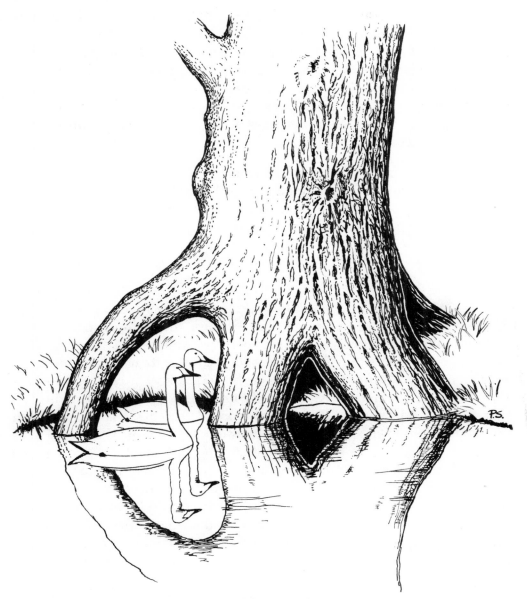

The Spring of Urd.

the sun. In Indian mythology, too, the sun was represented as a goose. Brahma rode upon the One Goose or Swan, and swans towed his chariot which was swifter than thought (179).

Apollo, the Greek sun-god, had a swan-chariot in which he travelled to and from the land of the Hyperboreans, that paradise 'at the back of the North Wind' where men lived for a thousand years. He also rode on a swan when he took Cyrene to Africa, and when he journeyed to the Helicon to visit the Muses. Swans were present at his birth and shared with him his gift for prophecy.

> O Isle of Leto,* isle of pain and love:
> The orbed water and the spell thereof;
> Where still the Swan, minstrel of things to be,
>   Doth serve the Muse and sing!

> Euripides: *Iphigenia in Tauris*,
> trans. Gilbert Murray

Swans were sacred, not only to Apollo but to his mother Leto, or Leda, 'because of their white plumage, and because the V-formation of their flight was a female symbol' (105). This perhaps explains why Zeus, Apollo's father, took on that form for his second and more famous, or infamous, seduction of Leda. After this encounter she laid an egg, or eggs, from which came Helen, Clytemnestra, Castor and Polydeuces. Since she had also lain that night with her mortal husband, the precise parentage is disputed, but one, at least, of the children, and usually two, were accredited to Zeus. Leda was then deified as the goddess Nemesis, the early pastoral nymph who carried an apple-bough in one hand and a wheel in the other (105).

Early myths of Neolithic Europe featured a divine hierarchy, which, unlike the later Greek Pantheon, was dominated by a mother-goddess. Although the rites of the cult are obscure and changed with the passage of time, at one stage the king, as consort to the Goddess, was sacrificed annually and a new one chosen. When the wheel of Nemesis, the solar year, had turned half-circle the king was fated to die, but in practice a boy inter-rex often represented him for that day, and was sacrificed in his stead. The apples which Nemesis carried in her other hand were his passport to

---

* When Leto was about to give birth to Apollo and Artemis and no land would receive her, the little rock of Delos pitied her and gave her a resting-place.

146

Leda and the Swan. *Keith Shackleton*.

147

paradise, which was traditionally an orchard. It was believed that the ghost of the sacred king was personified by Apollo (whose name is possibly derived from *abol* meaning 'apple'). In this way Apollo's annual journey in his swan-chariot to the land of the Hyperboreans could easily be seen as the departure of the dead king's soul. Since Apollo was the god of music and since the Hyperborean paradise lay 'at the back of the North Wind', it seems more than likely that the 'singing' swans, which also went north each year, were especially linked with him. It has, in fact, been claimed that swans were sacred because 'they flew north to unknown breeding grounds, supposedly taking the dead king's soul with them'* (105). This theory is strengthened by the belief that Apollo's visits to the Hyperboreans were never for less than three months (7). It would need little imagination to believe that the wild, fading cries of the migrating swans mourned the dead king as they disappeared into the north.

One mourner in Greek mythology was, in fact, turned into a swan. He was one of the several characters called Cycnus, and he mourned his dear friend, Phaethon. Phaethon had long been plaguing his father, Helios, to let him drive the sun-chariot. At last he was allowed to try, but he found himself quite unable to control it, and came so close to the earth that it burned. Even the swans 'which had been wont to throng the Maeonian streams in tuneful company, were scorched'. Zeus, furious, hurled a thunderbolt at Phaethon, and he fell into the River Po.†

Cycnus was heart-broken and abandoned his kingdom of Liguria to wander, grieving and lamenting the loss of his friend, beside the river. Then 'his human voice became shrill, and grey feathers concealed his hair. A long neck, too, extended from his breast, and a membrane joined his reddening toes; plumage clothed his sides, and his mouth became a blunt bill' (Ovid). Thus Cycnus became a swan, but one that avoided the air for he remembered how his friend had been struck down. It is said that he was later set among the stars, and this is one explanation of the constellation Cygnus the Swan, which is otherwise said to be a trophy chalked in the sky by Zeus to commemorate his success with Leda. Cycnus, whose father was

---

* Graves (105) places the sacrifice at midsummer, when swans are not migrating. The sacrifice was, however, a fertility rite with a highly complex history, and may well have absorbed the swan element from an equivalent festival in the spring.

† Phaethon may be seen as an inter-rex, enjoying the power of kingship for one day before being struck down. In Corinth and elsewhere the sacred king was sacrificed by being dragged at the tail of a sun-chariot drawn by maddened horses (105).

The Transformation of Cycnus. *Hargreaves*.

149

Stheneleus, is further remembered in the scientific name which was once given to the Mute Swan, *Sthenelides olor* – 'the swan of the son of Stheneleus'.

Perhaps it was their association with death that led to the belief that swans only sing before they die. Another, and simpler, explanation that has sometimes been put forward is that the swan could not both *look* and *sound* beautiful. The nightingale's beauty is all in its voice; the peacock makes a horrible screech. So the swan's first song must be its last (130).

> *The Silver Swan, who living had no note,*
> *When death approached unlocked her silent throat,*
> *Leaning her breast against the reedy shore,*
> *Thus sung her first and last, and sung no more,*
> *Farewell all joys, O death come close mine eyes,*
> *More Geese than Swans now live, more fools than wise.*

No. 1 in Orlando Gibbons' set of
Madrigals & Motets of 5 parts (1612)

One of the earliest factual accounts of the swan's death song was made by Aristotle. Swans, he said, 'are musical, and sing chiefly at the approach of death; at this time they fly out to sea and men, when sailing past the coast of Libya, have fallen in with many of them out at sea singing in mournful strains and have actually seen some of them dying'. More than two thousand years later swans were still heard to die in music. In 1898 a reliable naturalist gave this description of a totally unfamiliar song of a Whistling Swan shot in flight and falling towards water: 'Most plaintive in character and musical in tone, it sounded at times like the soft running of the notes in an octave, and as the sound was borne to us, mellowed by the distance, we stood astonished and could only exclaim, "we have heard the song of a dying swan" ' (189).

Perhaps because of this link with death, perhaps because of their prophetic reputation, swans have often been held to be ominous birds. It was said that the *sight* of a swan in a sick man's dream signified an early recovery, but the *sound* of it meant death (253). A vivid illustration of the foreboding powers of the swan was the curse of the Fitzpatricks in the seventeenth century. A Fitzpatrick of Closeburn Castle shot a swan to see if it died in music. After that, whenever a swan with a red stain upon its breast flew into the castle grounds, a member of the family died. Within fifty years the castle and all its heirlooms had been burned to the ground (314).

PLATE 31 Heads of Whistling Swans. Note the varying amounts of yellow on the bill. *Russ Kinne* and *Philippa Scott*.

PLATE 32 Whistling Swan. ABOVE: a nest in Alaska. BELOW: newly-hatched cygnets. *U.S. Dept. of the Interior, Fish and Wildlife Service.*

Death, on the other hand, has not always been considered a misfortune – even philosophical swans have rejoiced at it. Aesop's Fables of the sixth century B.C. contain one of the earliest references to the swan's death song:

> A stork that was present at the song of a dying swan told her it was contrary to nature to sing so much out of season, and asked her the reason for it. Why, said the swan, I am now entering into a state where I shall no longer be in danger of either snares, guns, or hunger; and who would not joy at such a deliverance?

Socrates also realised that the dying swan anticipated the delights of heaven in its song (Plato); and there is a story of that more tangible 'other world', the moon, that swans sang joyously as they carried plaques bearing the names of noble people into a temple (253).

Death or no death, the swan has always enjoyed a musical reputation far more remarkable than its merits. Perhaps being such a beautiful bird, it was awarded an 'honorary' voice to match. Pausanias, the Greek traveller, attributed its renown to Cycnus, the friend of Phaethon, who had been a musician before becoming the King of the Ligurians. A more likely explanation, however, would be that, as Apollo's bird, it came to share his talents for music and prophecy. It was an extension of the idea that swans sang with foreknowledge that led to the belief that the souls of all good poets passed into them. Virgil, for instance, was the Mantuan Swan, Homer the Swan of Meander, and Shakespeare the Swan of Avon. The concept appears most dramatically in the story of Socrates' dream, in which a cygnet on his lap suddenly sprouted wings and soared up with a melodious cry. The next day he met Plato, the prince of philosophers (85).

There have, of course, been many who have brought the cold eye of science to bear upon the dying swan's song; and their final analysis has demanded the sacrifice of the myth to the dull truth that swans do not sing before they die. Such a verdict was given as early as the first century A.D. by the naturalist Alexander the Myndian (253). Some observers have questioned whether swans 'sing' at all, even when in the best of spirits. But to Lucian's accusation that their note is 'a harsh feeble croak', Virgil replies that 'a goose cackles among melodious swans'. The differences between the Mute Swan on the one hand, and the Whooper and Bewick's Swans on the other, have no doubt led to much of the confusion. Perhaps the swans themselves should be allowed the last word on the matter. In another of Aesop's fables a family of swallows asked some swans if they sang only in the loneliness of the countryside because they were ashamed of their singing. They received in reply this stern rebuke: 'swans do not confuse music with noise, which is all that swallows make.'

The legends of Celtic and Teutonic mythology have much in common. Both abound in swans, and there is strong evidence that both derive, perhaps by way of Greece and Rome, from the earlier Bronze Age cultures, in which sun-worship was a dominant feature. The swan was a key figure in these early cults, and was the subject of many representations. Often the birds were shown linked by chains, and sometimes they were further linked to an image of the sun (279). This chain motif recurs repeatedly in Celtic mythology, and it usually indicates that the bird concerned is a fairy, or god, in transformation. The swan, it seems, was the usual link between the natural and the supernatural worlds (272), and was the form taken by the gods when they wished to make contact with mortals, especially when their quest was erotic (279).

The Irish legend *The Dream of Angus* is not quite typical of this theme because neither of the lovers was mortal, but it shows very strongly the magical significance of the swan-shape as an alternative to human form. Angus Mac Oc, who was one of the fairy people, the Tuatha de Danaan, saw in a dream the most beautiful girl in Erin and at once fell in love with her. With the help of his brother, Bove, the fairy chieftain of Munster, he learnt that her name was Caer, and that she lived by Lough bel Dracon in the province of Connacht. When the two brothers came there they 'saw 150 young maidens and they saw the maiden among them. The maidens did not reach her to the shoulder. A silvery chain between every two maidens. A silvery necklace about their neck itself and a chain of burnished gold' (234). It transpired, however, that she spent alternate years as a girl and as a swan, and it was only as a swan that she could be won. So Angus went away and returned next summer to find '150 white birds with their silvery chains and golden caps around their heads' (234). He called Caer to him, and changing himself into a swan, he joined her. They then flew off together, first circling the lough three times (234).

There are similar references to silver chains and transformations in several other Irish legends, notably in the *Wooing of Etain*, and in the *Wasting Sickness of Cu Chulainn*. Most of these old stories were first written down during the twelfth century in manuscripts such as the Book of Leinster and the Book of the Dun Cow, but many originated at least two or three hundred years earlier. Another legend of particular beauty and interest is the story of *The Children of Lir*, which Thomas Moore made famous in his ballad *The Song of Fionuala*:

> *Silent, O Moyle, be the roar of thy water;*
> *Break not, ye breezes, your chain of repose;*
> *While murmuring mournfully, Lir's lonely daughter*
> *Tells to the night-star the tale of her woes . . .*

Although the story is sometimes decried as an eighteenth-century invention, it undoubtedly stems from much older material. It is known as one of 'the three most sorrowful tales of story-telling' (173).

Lir was one of the Tuatha de Danaan. He had four children, a twin daughter and son, Fionuala and Aedh, followed by twin sons, Fiachra and Conn. At the second birth their mother died, and Lir married her sister Eva. The children were beautiful and gentle and loved by everyone – so much so that Eva grew jealous and at last resolved to kill them. Her attendants refused in horror, and she herself when she grasped the sword could not bring herself to strike. She then took them down to Lough Darvra to bathe, and, as they entered the water, touched them with a druidical wand, turning them into four snow-white swans. Fionuala asked how long they were to remain so, and was told: 'Three hundred years on smooth

Lough Darvra, three hundred years on the Sea of Moyle twixt Erin and Alba, three hundred years at Irros Domnann and at Inis Glora on the Western Sea. Until the union of Lairgnen, the prince from the north, with Deoch, the princess from the south; until the Tailkenn (St. Patrick) shall come to Erin bringing the light of a pure faith, and until ye hear the voice of the Christian bell. And neither by your own power, nor by mine, nor by the power of your friends can ye be freed till the time comes.'

Eva was then sorry for what she had done, and allowed them to keep their Gaelic speech: 'and ye shall be able to sing sweet plaintive fairy music, which shall excel all the music of the world, and which will lull to sleep all that listen to it'.

For three hundred years the four swans remained on the peaceful waters of Lough Darvra, conversing by day with the men of Erin, who encamped on the shore to be near them, and chanting by night slow sweet fairy music, 'the most delightful that ever was heard by men.' They then took wing for the gloomy tempestuous Sea of Moyle, off the coast of Kintyre, and the men of Erin in their grief proclaimed it throughout the land that no one should kill a swan from that time forth. On the waters of Moyle, and later at Irros Domnann, their life was lonely, and full of hardship and fear. Worst of all was the night when the sea froze from Irros to Achill. Fionuala lamented their misery: 'Sad is the cry of the swans tonight. It is an ebb or a drought that has caused it; no cool water beneath them, their bodies waste from thirst. No firm supporting water, no wave washes their sides. . . . O God, who made heaven and earth and delivered the six hosts, save, too, this flock. Even the strong become weak through suffering' (70).

At last the time came for them to fly off to Inis Glora, where they settled on a small quiet lough. There they remained until holy Patrick came to Ireland, and Saint Caemhoc came from him to bring the faith to Inis Glora. On the first morning the swans listened in wonder to the ringing of his bell at matins, and when he had finished they sang their own sweet music. Realising that they were the Children of Lir, the Saint welcomed them to live with him, and forged two silver chains which he set between them. Each day they joined in his devotions, and they lived so happily that the memory of their misery was as nothing.

Meanwhile Deoch, the daughter of the King of Munster, had heard of these wonderful speaking swans and asked her husband, Lairgnen, King of Connacht, to bring them to her. When Caemhoc would not give them, Lairgnen tried to take them by force; but as he dragged on the silver chains the feathery robes fell away, and there stood a wizened old woman and three feeble old men. The spell was broken. Caemhoc baptised them, and in that moment they died (173).

Caemhoc was not the only Irish saint to be linked with swans. In Killarney they were said to come at the call of Saint Cainnech, and on Lough Foyle to the call of Comgall; Columba of Terryglass was carried by them from island to island, and they sang to Colman Ela and his monks to console them in their work (260). Eva also had her counterpart. A story from the Island of Skye describes how a baby girl, abandoned by her stepmother, was rescued by swans, who made for her a shawl of feathers, and carried her in a hammock of twisted nettles. For two years they cared for her, until her father returned from the war; they then flew in and gently laid the hammock at his feet (317).

To this day swans are regarded as birds of omen in the Hebrides (279), an echo, perhaps, of their prophetic powers in Greek mythology; and in both Scotland and Ireland they are often thought to embody the souls of the dead: it is therefore unlucky to harm them. In County Mayo the belief applies specifically to the souls of virgins remarkable for their purity (315). This is reflected in a Gaelic name for the swan, 'The Maid of the White Breast', and in the frequent use of 'swan' as a metaphor for 'girl' in Irish – as in Greek – literature (272). The swan is also associated with Saint Brigid, or Saint Bride, who is identifiable indirectly with Leto, and has sometimes been called the 'Mary of the Gael'. Another variation of the same theme comes in a Welsh legend about the court of King Arthur in which a swan, led by a chain, was used as a chastity test, for it would accept food only from the hand of a virtuous wife (249).

The Arthurian legends provide one of the many bridges between the literatures of the Celtic and Teutonic races. These cultures probably stemmed in the first place from a common ancestor. Then, in the Dark Ages, when the successive tribes of barbarian invaders had almost stamped out the fires of civilisation in Europe, it was the scholar-saints of Ireland, secure from their destructive reach, who rekindled the dying spark of learning. As a result of these exchanges, both direct and indirect, there are certain stories which are common to most of the countries of northern Europe.

One story, which is particularly widespread, is the tale of the eleven princes who were changed into swans by their wicked stepmother. To break the spell their sister was required to weave for them eleven shirts of nettles, and to speak not a single word till the task was done. A king found her, fell in love with her, and married her, and still she remained silent. Later she was maliciously accused of murdering her children, and sentenced to be burnt at the stake, but still she kept silent. Even on the way to the pyre she kept silently stitching, until at last all eleven shirts were finished except for the last sleeve. As the crowds pressed round her, down from the sky swept eleven swans and drove them back with furious wings (see PLATE 47). Quickly the princess threw the shirts over their heads, and there stood eleven handsome princes – but one had a swan's wing instead of an arm.

The variations on this story are endless. At the start of one version the queen had eleven sons and longed for a daughter. One day she saw a dead raven lying in the snow. 'If only', she exclaimed, 'I had a daughter whose hair was as black as the raven, and whose lips were as red as blood, and whose skin was as white as snow, I would exchange all my eleven sons for her.' The wish was granted and the sons were turned into swans. In Norway the tale refers to twelve wild ducks, and in an Irish, as well as a Finnish version, the shirts were woven out of cotton-grass instead of nettles. In Grimm's *The Six Swans* it was star-flowers (108). Hans Anderson, in the *Eleven Wild Swans*, tells the story in a long, beautifully detailed narrative, while Grimm is typically leaner and more realistic. Grimm also tells a story in which the eleven princes were changed unwittingly by their sister into crows (108).

These variations, and many more, stem from the very early tale of swan-children which, at the start, has obvious affinities with the beginning of the *Children of Lir*. In medieval times this became welded on to quite a separate legend, the legend of the swan-knight. One version of the composite myth is the story of *Helyas: Knight of the Swanne* (17). It tells how King Oriant met a girl wandering in the forest, and, to the indignation of his mother, Matabrune, made her his queen. In due course she bore him, at one massive childbirth, six sons and a daughter, all of whom had silver chains about their necks. The king was away at the wars, and Matabrune, quickly replacing the children with seven squashed puppies, whisked them away and ordered her squire to drown them. Instead he wrapped them in a cloak and left them in the forest, where a hermit found them and brought them up. One of the sons, Helyas, became his constant companion.

When Matabrune heard that the children were still alive, she again ordered her servant to kill them, but he merely snatched away their silver chains – and at that they were turned into swans. Helyas, who was away with the hermit and so escaped the transformation, eventually recovered the chains; but one of them had been melted down to mend the handle of a cup, and so one of the children had to remain forever a swan.

Some time later the swan-brother appeared on the river leading a boat, and Helyas, taking this as a sign, stepped in and was borne away. Meanwhile Clarissa, Duchess of Bouillon, was in dispute with the Count of Frankfurt, who claimed her lands. The argument was to be settled in the lists, but on the day appointed the duchess waited in vain for a champion. All at once a swan appeared on the river drawing a boat in which sat an unknown knight. The knight was Helyas, who fought and won the day. He also won the hand of the duchess's daughter – but warned her that she must never ask him who he was or from where he came. So Helyas became Duke of Bouillon, and grandfather, so the story goes, of Godfrey de Bouillon, King of Jerusalem and hero of the First Crusade. Then, one night, his wife forgot the warning and asked him who he was. At once the swan reappeared on the river and called to his brother, who rose from his bed, stepped into the boat and vanished forever.

The legend appears in many different settings and with many different heroes: Helyas, Gerard Swan, Salvius, Lohengrin – these are some of the names under which the swan-knight sailed (17). The origins of the story are obscure, but there are strong suggestions that its roots derive, through the folklore of France, from Celtic origins in Brittany, Wales and Ireland. There is, for example, a close resemblance between the vow of secrecy imposed on Helyas and the similar vow imposed on King Arthur's Knights of the Grail. This connection is made even more directly in the story of Lohengrin whose father, Percival, was one of King Arthur's knights. Another parallel has been drawn between the swan knight's arrival and Apollo's journeys in a chariot drawn by swans. It may be, also, that the name Helyas is a corruption of Helios, the Greek sun-god, who sailed across the heavens in a golden boat (207); in the Dark Ages only the Irish monks would have been familiar with Greek traditions. Alternatively, the name may have derived from the celtic word for swan – eala or ealadh (17).

Whatever its origins, the legend of the swan-knight, rising out of the mists of mythology, flows on into history. Many of the ruling families of the Lower Rhineland claimed descent from him, notably de Bouillon, Brabant and Cleves. Cleves was particularly proud of the connection, using models of swans as prizes at tournaments and as centrepieces at banquets. The ducal castle was the Schwanenburg, and there is also said to have been a knighthood of the swan, although no evidence of it remains. In Brandenburg there was an authentic Order of the Swan from 1443 to 1525, but its connection with the swan-knight is uncertain (336).

The swan came into English chivalry mainly by way of the de Bouillon family, one of whom was Maud, Stephen's queen. The Earls of Hereford and Essex were also descended from the de Bouillons, and they, by marriage, passed the emblem on to the Earls of Buckingham, and to the Earl of Derby, who later became Henry IV. He, in turn, passed it on to his son Humphrey, Duke of Gloucester, and to Henry V, who bore the swan on his pennon at Agincourt. The Dukes of Buckingham also bore the swan, and to this day it is the county crest (336).

The importance of the swan in English heraldry is reflected in the number of inns which bear its name. Many of those which date from Tudor times were named after Anne of Cleves, Henry VIII's fourth wife, an ironically graceful compliment to the lady whom her husband described as 'The Flanders Mare'. In some cases the signboards still depict the swan wearing the symbolic collar and chain of the swan-knight (see PLATE 44). The origin of the 'Black Swans' is less obvious. Many were named before the discovery of Australia, when the bird was still a mythical figure, usually associated with evil. Since innkeepers would hardly have put a sign of evil upon their houses, it seems probable that the adjective was used to distinguish the inn from others near by of the same name. York, for example, has a Swan, a White Swan, an Old White Swan, a Black Swan and a Cygnet. The Swan with Two Necks, which is not uncommon, is a corruption of the 'two nicks' which form the swan-mark of the Vintners' Company (page 173).

HARGREAVES

158

PLATE 33 Whistling Swans. ABOVE: in flight in California. *Jim Moffitt*. BELOW: in flight near Chesapeake Bay, Maryland. *Philippa Scott*.

PLATE 34 Whistling Swans at Slimbridge. ABOVE: 'ground staring'. Compare with Plate 22. *Peter Scott.* BELOW: a pair. *E. E. Jackson.*

PLATE 35 The wild Bewick's Swans at Slimbridge. ABOVE: seen from the studio window. *Philippa Scott*. BELOW: a general view of 'Swan Lake'. *E. E. Jackson*.

PLATE 36 The only Bewick's Swan female to have bred in captivity. She is defending her cygnets with slightly lifted wings and open bill. *J. V. Beer*.

The concept of the swan-maiden is another motif which appears in many different countries throughout the northern world. *The Dream of Angus* (page 152) is a famous swan-maiden story, although it contains only some of the usual elements. Typically the maiden is a semi-supernatural being who can change her form at will, so long as she has in her possession some essential garment, usually a feather robe. In its simplest form the story tells how a young man hides the robe and persuades the maiden to become his wife; they live happily together until eventually she finds the lost garment, or until her husband asks about her origin or breaks some other taboo. She is then compelled by an overwhelming urge to change back into a swan, and flies away into the unknown.

There is some doubt as to where this motif originated. Some authorities suggest that it came from north-west India in about the tenth century B.C.; it seems more likely, however, that it stemmed from much further north in Europe or Asia. This supposition is based partly on the parallel between the maiden's urge to leave and the swans' equally compulsive urge to migrate, but more especially on the parallel between the loss of the robe and the casting of the swans' feathers during the summer moult. The following version is a fairly typical example of the basic tale, except for the final twist.

The scene is set on Islay in the Inner Hebrides. One spring day a swan-maiden, having shed her feather robe, was wandering carefree by a burn. A young man who was also strolling by, found the robe and hid it, and on meeting the maiden fell in love with her. They were married and had three children, and all was blissful, until one day the children found a beautiful feathered garment hidden in a cave. Triumphantly they took it home to show to their mother, who, instead of being delighted, 'gave an awful cry, and, burying her face in her hands, wept as though her heart were broken.' Then, unable to resist her fate, she put on the robe and, changing into a swan, flew off to join her kind. The children were adopted by another couple, and the father lived on, alone and lonely.

In due course the season came for the swans to return to Islay and there, in the midst of the flock, was a group of birds bearing a feather mantle. This they carried to the cottage, and the swan-maiden, slipping off her own robe, went in to her husband. Helped by her, he put on the mantle which the swans had brought, and they both flew off – but not, as one might expect, forever. Two hundred years later the man returned to Islay. It was Sunday, and he thought that he had been away only for a day; but when he heard the church bells he crumbled into dust (317). As in *The Children of Lir*, the presence of Christianity signified the end of magic.

In countries where there are no swans the maiden takes the form of a goose or some other animal. There is, for example, a story from West Africa of a hunter who married a fairy in the shape of a forest rat, but lost her when he broke a vow. Sometimes the 'animal' element is not even defined. In one of the Noh plays in Japan a young fisherman steals the feather robe of a spirit, and refuses to return it until she has shown him the heavenly dance 'that can turn the palace of the moon'. She does so, saying 'for the sorrows of the world I will leave this new dancing with you for sorrowing people.' She then fades away in mist, while the chorus unfolds that the steps of the dance are the moon's phases, and the whole a spell of great potency (209).

The swan-maiden motif reappears in an altered, but still recognisable, form in some of the Norse tales about the Valkyries. By no means all Valkyries were swan-maidens, but the two traditions certainly overlap from time to time. The Valkyries were the hand-maidens of Odin, and had the task of selecting from the warriors destined to die in battle those that might enter Valhalla. They would also take part in the battles, and sometimes formed attachments to particular warriors (195). One such story tells how Kara became guardian-mistress of Helgi, and flew above him in battle singing a charmed song, so that the enemy lost all wish to defend themselves. When Helgi was fighting for the Swedes against the Danes, Kara was as usual hovering above his head in the form of a swan. In the fury of the battle Helgi swung his sword high to deal a mighty blow – so high that he struck off Kara's leg and she fell to the ground dead. Within minutes Helgi also fell, and the army was routed (182).

A different type of battle-maiden appears in the legends of the Minusinian Tatars from Central Asia. They were demons of the air who lived among raven black rocks, scourged themselves with swords, drank the blood of the dead and flew replete on it for forty years. They numbered forty, but at times appeared as one; at other times the sky was overcast with their many wings (17).

The wings of the devil-maidens spread across the sky like thunderclouds; but in ancient India swans were identified with clouds of a gentler sort. The Apsarases of the Vedic heaven were something between Valkyries and true swan-maidens. They gathered the souls of heroes into their arms, but were not warlike; and sometimes they would come down to earth to become the wives of mortals, although it was never long before their true nature reasserted itself. The Indians, looking up at the fluffy white clouds sailing across the blue sky, saw them as swans gliding across water, and wove a legend of a heavenly lake in which the Apsarases bathed (17).

Clouds have no doubt played a considerable part in the making of swan legends; not least, in the widespread belief that they towed the chariots of the gods. This, also, was a tradition of the Indian gods, especially of Brahma. The swan, indeed, is conspicuous in the folklore of India, where it is nearly always given a high-minded and noble character. Perhaps it was a reflection of this spiritual translucence that encouraged the strange belief that swans fed upon pearls. From India comes what is perhaps the kindest association for the swan in all mythology. When Buddha was a young man a swan shot with an arrow fell wounded at his feet. Buddha took out the

arrow and refused to surrender the swan to the hunter, on the grounds that a life belongs to him who saves it, not to him who takes it (8). The swan thus became the symbol for a great moral principle, and one of the signposts which directed Buddha towards the good life and away from a life of material power.

In contrast, the Black Swan was regarded in European mythology as a symbol of evil. Before the discovery of Australia it was a truly mythical creature. At first, following Juvenal's famous line

Rara avis in terris nigroque simillima cygno

it was, like the blue moon, a symbol of impossible rarity – 'a bird as rare in this world as a black swan' – but on the few occasions when it appeared in folk-tales it almost always wore the cloak of hell. There is for instance, an old Irish story which tells of 'three wonderful streams, namely, a stream of otters, a stream of eels, and a stream of black swans. Great flocks of birds arose from these streams and flew past the voyagers; and the black swans followed close after, tearing and tormenting them.' The birds, the story explains, were the souls of people suffering punishment for their crimes, and the black swans were the devils who tormented them (173). Similarly, in Tchaikovsky's ballet, Swan Lake, Odile in the evil role is in black, while Odette is in white.

The true Black Swan of Australian folklore was known as Byahmul, the bird of Byamee, the Great One, who is a central deity of Australian legend. Thus the Black Swan like the white swans was closely associated with the Spirit of Creation.

Many of the aboriginal legends are explanations of the physical properties of birds and animals. One story describes how the swan got its neck. The fire-bird had brought back a live coal from the sun, and a corroboree was arranged in his honour. When the day came no one could find him, and someone had to take his place. Many of the birds painted themselves red to look like him, and others went to be painted by the midget owl who lived in a hollow tree in the mangrove swamp. The black duck was one of those who came to watch. Just at that moment there was a shower of rain, and the duck, being a 'sticky beak', poked his head into the hollow – and it stuck. The tide went out and left him hanging; and when at last the others pulled him free his neck was stretched and his head was bleeding. Now he is a swan, and his beak is still red from the blood (153).

Another story explains, not only why the bill is red, but also why the plumage is black. Wurrunnah, who was skilled in magic, had turned two of his brothers into handsome snow-white swans, in order that they might create a diversion while their kinsmen raided the camp of a neighbouring tribe, composed solely of women. The women had never seen swans before and would try to capture them, leaving the camp unguarded. The plan was a success, but only just, and in the excitement of escaping, Wurrunnah forgot about his brothers. Now Mullyan, the Eagle, was flying by on his way to deliver a message for the Spirits, and when he and his brothers saw the swans, they attacked them, wounding them viciously and ripping out their feathers. As the tufts of white feathers floated away in the wind they spread over the desert like a storm of snow, and wherever a feather settled it turned into a soft white flower. Suddenly the eagles remembered their message and soared away, leaving their victims to die of cold. But, just when the swans had lost all hope, they felt a warm, soft, black shower drifting down from the sky. Looking up, they saw Wahn the Crow and a flock of his brothers pulling the feathers from their breasts and letting them fall. From that day swans in Australia have been black, except for the patch of white wing-feathers which the eagles had not pulled out; and their bills are still red from the blood from their wounds (217).

The interesting point of this story is why the aborigines should have thought that swans ought to be white. One would like to regard it as the echo of some deep atavistic memory, but it seems more likely that the white man told them, and that the story-teller wove it into the pattern of traditional legend.

Many of the legends of the South American Indians are also explanatory. One, told by a Chilean story-teller, finds the swan in a prominent role, and, once again, in close association with the sun-god. Indeed both South American swans apparently come into this story, for the Black-necked Swan, which carries its young on its back, is the hero, while the escort with pink bills and legs, and black wing-tips, must surely be Coscorobas.

Ollal, whose father was the sun, had come down in a vain attempt to civilise the savage Araucanians, and had gone away disappointed. He had promised, however, to return later as a holy child. Meanwhile the Araucanians were being punished by a plague of cannibalistic giants. Now if clouds touch the earth they become people, and one cloud which came too close changed into a maiden and was at once seized and ravished by a giant. She then prophesied that the child she would bear would kill him, at which the giant cut the baby from her womb, and began to eat her. Meanwhile a rat ran off with the baby and nursed it. When the child was grown into a boy the rat made plans for escape, and chose four strong animals to help: the Ostrich, the Swan, the Flamingo and the Puma. Because of the treachery of the Skunk, who still stinks, only the Swan was able to fulfil her task. She arrived, whistling gently, and moving with care to avoid being seen; the Steamer-duck lifted the holy child on to her back, and away she went, first swimming across the lake, then flying on to Patagonia. During the journey an escort of other birds kept guard, and as a reward they were given black tips to their wings, and flesh-pink bills and legs. The Swan, so the story-teller says, is serenely happy, but serious and proud too, for she never forgets that she saved the divine child. Now she carries her own young on her back, like no other bird (190).

Swan legends alone could fill a book; we have but dipped here and there like a swallow on the surface of a pond. Yet this is only one corner of the

imaginative landscape. The inspiration of the swan's beauty, and of the legends themselves, re-echoes down the corridors of poetry and art and music: on the walls of every gallery there is a picture of *Leda and the Swan*; the swan-knight lives on in Wagner's *Lohengrin* and *Parsifal*; Tchaikovsky set the corner-stone of the ballerina's repertoire when he wrote *Swan Lake*; Sibelius took his theme for the *Swan of Tuonela*, from the old Finnish epic, the *Kalevala*, in which the bird swims on the river which separates the living from the dead. One could give a long catalogue of artists who have celebrated the swan, but it would serve no purpose; nor is there space for an anthology of swan poetry. Swans without number, magic and mystical, float through the complex fancies of the creative mind, now rising powerfully in strength and fury, now gliding serene and lovely upon still waters; for ever tantalising man to capture and crystallise their elusive spirit (see PLATES 45 to 48).

The craftsman and his patrons have also paid their tribute. An interesting example is the small gold brooch, known as The Dunstable Swan Jewel, which is now in the British Museum. The bird it portrays is enamelled in white, with the eyes picked out in black, and about its neck there is a gold coronet with a chain and ring attached. It was probably made in France in the early fifteenth century, and may well have belonged to one of the families which traced their descent from the swan-knight. Another, more grandiose, curio, dating from the eighteenth century, is to be found in the Bowes Museum at Barnard Castle. It takes the form of a life-sized silver swan, which sails by clockwork over a silver pool in pursuit of a shoal of silvery fish (PLATE 44). At one time it was enthroned in a 'temple' eighteen foot high, with mirrors, and a rock of crystal, and a dome crowned by the rising sun, whose rays seemed to spread from an inner body of fire. An even more remarkable work of art was commissioned by Count Heinrich von Bruehl, after the King of Poland had appointed him Director of the Meissen porcelain factory. One of his perquisites was the right to order, free of charge, as much porcelain as he wished, and he determined to indulge himself with a table service more sumptuous than any in the royal household. The result of this ambition was the 'Swan Service', made between 1737 and 1741, and comprising in all more than two thousand pieces. It remained in the possession of the family until the Second World War, when most of it was destroyed and the remainder dispersed (PLATE 44).

The reputation of the swan for grace and innocence has even been turned to political ends. In 1715, an anonymous Jacobite published a highly diverting satire, entitled 'A Tale concerning a Swan'. In it the English scene is portrayed in terms of birds, the Phoenix, Queen Anne, being succeeded by the Eagle, George I. The Swan is the Duke of Ormond who replaced the strutting Jackdaw, Marlborough, as Commander in Chief, when the latter fell from grace. 'Leave to the unlucky Jack-Daw, says the heavenly female Swan to her dear Mate, leave to him, and his airy Consort, the little Arts of hiding in every hole Bushels of stolen Trinkets. We, nobly born, are above those waggish monky Cheats, which please the laughing vulgar, and make them admire the subtle devices of the crafty Birds.'

Another satirist saw the swan as an imposter, using it as a symbol with which to castigate his fellow poets for trying to conceal the shallowness of their thinking behind the elegance of their style. How much better, he said, to emulate the wise and observant old owl, the classicist, bird of Minerva, and avoid the delusions of external grace.

> *Wring the swan's curved neck; that bird of false display*
> *Bestows its note of whiteness on the fountain's blue;*
> *Though it parades its grace, it never felt or knew*
> *The soul of things, nor heard what nature's voices say.*

E. G. Martinez 1871–1952 (165)

That is one point of view, but it is out of sympathy with the general feeling. Down the years writers and storytellers have been almost unanimous in singing the swan's praise. It has become the symbol of purity and innocence, the personification of the unspoiled virgin. A story from Canada tells of a young Indian boy who fell in love with an English girl. He called her 'The White Swan' because she was so perfect. One day, as he went down the river to visit his traps, she was not there, but the noise of great wings rushing through the air made him look up, and he saw a swan flying away to the east. He never saw the girl again. This is a perfect example of swan symbolism: pure, innocent, beautiful – but remote and unattainable, with a touch of mystery that often spills over into magic. Some sad, fine lines by an Australian poetess catch all the yearning beauty of wild swans flying. Although they were written about the Black Swan, they might equally well apply to any of the white swans that ride the long currents of the cold North Wind.

> *Whither ye wanderers in the heights your wings still dare,*
> *Crying as though forgotten things mourned in your keening?*
> *Our hearts are broken as we hear you go,*
> > *So few in flight, so slow.*
>
> *Lone, in the lonely verge, scarce can the ear ensnare*
> *The thin sad notes that downward fall; that leaning*
> *On the shouldering air seem but a breath*
> > *Of sound, haunted by death!*
>
> *Out of the land long swept away, from woods laid bare,*
> *Surely the wonder of our youth went with them there.*

Mary Gilmore: 'Three Swans went by'

166

PLATE 37 Wild Bewick's Swans calling aggressively to others in the flock. *Philippa Scott*.

PLATE 38 A family of wild Bewick's Swans (the Kontikis) displaying aggressively, and a pair in triumph ceremony. *Philippa Scott*.

8

Exploitation

Andrew Dawnay

Despite their magic and beauty, the swans have long been exploited for food and trade and sport. This is now changing, but the civilised world still imposes problems, even on creatures as handsome as these. New pressures and new conflicts are constantly arising, and could prove disastrous unless action is taken to avert them. In many ways the new dangers are more insidious than the earlier exploitations, because they stem from activities which appear at first sight to have little or nothing to do with the lives of swans, and are wholly disinterested in their survival.

It is only during the past fifty years that most of the swans have won some measure of protection. Before that they were harried in summer and winter alike. The sporting chronicles of the eighteenth and nineteenth century are riddled with dead swans. One account of Whoopers in Kent in 1778 goes: 'We had the pleasure to see thirty of these graceful majestic birds alight in the water . . . Their continuance was but short, as the loud and shrill cry they made attracted at least fifty men to pursue them, who scarcely gave them time to wet their beaks' (202). Half a century later a notable fowler entered this in his diary: 'Saw seven splendid hoopers! – gave up everything for them' (131). The situation in America was the same; here, too, the sight of a swan at any time of year was 'the signal for every man with a gun to pursue it' (189). Apparently the challenge of sending these great birds crashing from the sky was more than our forebears could resist. Some species, because of their behaviour and distribution, were more vulnerable than others. For example, the Trumpeter's habit of migrating in small parties along the coastline caused it to suffer much more severely than the Whistling Swan which moves in larger flocks and stays over open water (189).

The exploitation on and around the breeding grounds was even heavier. All swans, when they moult in summer, are flightless for several weeks, and can then be rounded up and caught in large numbers. Many of the northern communities relied on this method of hunting for their stocks of meat; they also took eggs, and no doubt still do so in some districts. In Iceland they used to chase Whoopers 'on small, but active horses', either riding them down, or more often setting their dogs to catch and hold them till the rider came up (169). The Whistling Swans in Arctic Canada were pursued and speared by Eskimos in kayaks and canoes, and the young men would compete for the honour of running down and capturing a bird single-handed (189). The swan drives in Russia were more elaborate; using sail-boats and nets, they often captured as many as 300 Whoopers in a day. Large numbers of Whooper Swans were also netted on the wintering grounds in Iran (66).

In Denmark the shooting of flightless Mute Swans was a royal prerogative. For several days beforehand the birds were driven along the coast by fishermen, while farmers on horseback prevented them from escaping inland. The resulting massacres yielded bags of between 200 and 500 (285). A contemporary wit commented: 'this morning the flock of swans ought to sing with gay and delicate tongue (if swans can sing); for it is a comfort to die knowing you were killed by such a brave and noble hand!' (285). This royal hunt was first described in 1557 and continued until about 1750, but on the Swedish shore of the same moulting area the slaughter went on till much later.

Exploits of this sort have several times banished a species from part of its range. The Whooper Swan, for example, no longer breeds regularly in Greenland, the Orkneys and parts of Finland, and the Whistling Swan has deserted the Perry River in Arctic Canada (26, 119, 285, 345). It also seems likely that hunting was one of the factors responsible for the extinction of the New Zealand Swan, *Cygnus sumnerensis*. The evidence for this lies in the numbers of swan bones found in the middens of the Polynesian Moa-hunters, who came to New Zealand in about the tenth century. The Moas became extinct probably in the seventeenth century, and the swan a hundred years earlier.

The Trumpeter Swan, too, was brought to the brink of extinction, this time by trade. In the sixty years between 1820 and 1880 the Hudson's Bay Company sold 108,000 swan skins on the London market, and most of these were Trumpeters (15). The trade apparently began in the 1770s and continued until about 1900, when the scarcity of birds brought it to an end. Several of the other swans were also hunted extensively for their skins. On one occasion an observer from one of the American museums found 'hundreds of thousands' of Black-necked Swan skins awaiting shipment in an Argentine warehouse (45). They were destined to be made into powder

puffs. This trade was certainly flourishing in 1899, when the price was quoted at twenty-five cents, or about fivepence, a pelt (94). The Bewick's Swan was equally in demand on account of 'the great thickness of very beautiful snow-white down, which, when properly dressed by a London furrier, makes boas and other articles of ladies' dress of unrivalled beauty' (102). In the U.S.S.R. Bewick's Swans were still being hunted commercially in the 1940s, their tough skin and warm soft pelt being used for things such as wallets, jackets and caps (66). Swan quills were at one time prized as pens, windpipes were made into flutes, and, in Iceland, the feet with the nails left on were fashioned into purses. The bones were once used for tools.

These exploitations are in striking contrast to the careful husbandry of the Mute Swan in medieval England. Exactly when it was domesticated is not known; it may even be that it was never a truly wild bird in this country. It seems likely, however, that some occurred, at least in East Anglia, and that these were rounded up, either as cygnets or flightless adults, and brought into captivity. Suggestions that the Mute Swan was introduced into Britain by the Romans (75), or brought back from Cyprus by Richard I (348), are apparently without foundation. The first was a guess, and the second is refuted at length by Ticehurst, who argues that the bird's status in the early

thirteenth century was far too secure for such a recent introduction (323). To illustrate his point he quotes the contemporary story of St. Hugh, Bishop of Lincoln. On the day of his enthronement, 29 September 1186, a swan arrived 'such as had never before been seen there. Who, within the space of a few days, overwhelmed with his great bulk and slew all the swans that he found there in great numbers; one, however, of the female sex he saved alive, not for the increase of her fertility, but for the comfort of her society. He was in truth quite as much larger than a swan as a swan is than a goose; he was nevertheless in all things very like a swan, especially in colour and whiteness; in addition to his size he was also unlike them in this, that he did not exhibit the knob and black colour on the bill after the manner of swans, but had in truth the same part of the bill flat and, together with the head and upper part of the neck, becomingly adorned with yellow.' This aggressive bird at once attached itself to the bishop, fed from his hand, welcomed him vociferously and allowed no one else to come near him. Obviously this was a Whooper arriving stained from migration. It is obvious, too, that the writer was familiar with the Mute Swan, and that Mute Swans were commonplace in Lincoln six years before King Richard's return from Cyprus (323).

St. Hugh of Lincoln. *John Secrett.*

The story of St. Hugh also contains a reference to the Mute Swan being a royal bird, a distinction which it still holds. This meant that, although anyone might keep swans on his own property, and pursue them if they escaped 'provided that the pursuit was continuous', all swans on open or common land belonged to the Crown. Ownership could be extended by privilege to swans on public waters, but in that case the owner was responsible for pinioning and marking his birds. All unmarked swans remained the property of the Crown (323). From this arose an elaborate system of controls, wrapped in reams of medieval red tape – ordinances and proclamations, laws and statutes, courts of swan-mote, and swan-rolls bearing the marks which distinguished ownership: all the paraphernalia of ponderous legality, and all emphasising the solemn esteem in which the swan was held. Today (in 1971) the royal status of the Mute Swan is exactly as it was in medieval times.

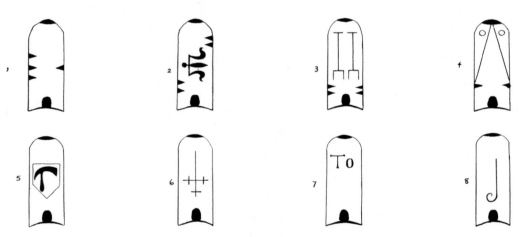

Swan Marks. Redrawn from Ticehurst (323). 1. Mark of Bishop of Norwich used until 1843. 2. Mark of Robert Flower of Ely from his Armorial Bearing, a fleur-de-lys, 1553. 3. 'Ye firging forkes' (oven forks), the mark of Thomas Clapthorne of Whittlesey, Cambs., 1619, with its colloquial name. 4. The original swan-mark of the Vintners Company which was later modified in 1863. 5. Mark of Abbot of Thornley, Cambs., depicting the mason's hammer of St. Botolph, patron of Thornley Abbey. 6. Mark of Thomas Howard, Duke of Norfolk (d. 1554), derived from his Armorial Bearing. 7. Mark of Thomas Orpwood, Mayor of Abingdon, Berks. 8. Mark of Abbot of Cirencester, Glos., derived from his calling.

The usual form of swan-mark was a pattern of notches cut into the upper mandible of the bill. This was done at the annual ceremony of swan-upping when the local owners went out with the representative of the royal swanherd to round up the cygnets. When the parent birds belonged to different owners they chose the cygnets alternately, the owner of the cob having first choice. The third cygnet belonged to the owner of the grass where the nest was, to pay for their keep, but he had to pay the King twelve pence for it. Marking at any other time was illegal, except by special arrangement (323).

The ceremony of swan-upping is still performed on the Thames, where two of the City companies, the Dyers and the Vintners, have kept their traditional rights (PLATE 48). Both maintain swanherds, and these, in company with the royal swanherd, are responsible for the swans as far upstream as Henley. In the third week of July the annual Voyage of Swan-upping sets out in colourful style from Blackfriars, rounding up all swans, and marking the cygnets with one notch on the bill for the Dyers, and two for the Vintners, leaving the Royal birds unmarked.

In medieval times the ownership of swans was a mark of social standing, and a gift of them, whether to adorn the moat or the table, lent distinction to both the giver and the recipient. By an Act of Edward IV no one was allowed to own swans unless he owned land to the value of five marks. A later Act put the punishment for stealing their eggs at imprisonment for a year and a day (323). This was not such an apt penalty as the fine for stealing the swan itself. The bird was hung up by its beak with its feet just touching the floor, and the thief had to pour wheat over it until the tip of the beak was covered. The wheat was then paid to the owner (57).

Swan-farming in those days was a profitable business. In 1553 Sir William Cecil reared ninety cygnets, of which he kept fifty-one to increase his flock; the other thirty-nine were sold for £4 17s. 8d. His expenses were 9s. for food and 6s. 8d. for wages, leaving a profit of £4 2s. – no mean sum at that time, and certainly an excellent return on the outlay. In 1274 the City of London set the price at which a swan might be sold for food at 3s., compared with $2\frac{1}{2}d$. for a best capon, 5d. for a goose, and 4d. for a pheasant. The swan was thus pre-eminent as a table bird. It was usually the set-piece at banquets, and until the introduction of the turkey from America in the sixteenth century, it was the customary Christmas dinner (323).

The swan's reputation as a delicacy has been decried in more modern times. One author, writing in 1738, described its flesh as being 'blacker, harder and tougher (than that of a goose), having grosser Fibres hard of Digestion, of a bad melancholic Juice; yet for its Rarity serves as a Dish to adorn great Men's Tables at Feasts and Entertainments, being else no desirable Dainty' (4). The secret of eating swan is that it must be young. Like so many gastronomic expressions, the word 'cygnet' came from France, and originally it referred only to birds that were tender enough for the table (238). In the days when swan-farming was a serious business, the cygnets were caught up and kept in a swan-pit, where they were fattened on malt and barley. They were at their best in October and November; after that the flesh became gradually coarser and stronger. At the famous swan-pit belonging to St. Helen's Hospital in Norwich eighty to a hundred cygnets were being fattened each year as late as the 1880s (323). Both the Dyers and the Vintners still have an annual 'feast of cygnets', and pronounce them delicious. Here is a typical old Norfolk recipe:

'Mince finely 3 lbs. of rump steak with 3 shallots, and season liberally with salt, pepper and grated nutmeg. Truss the bird like a goose, stuffing it with the rump steak, etc., sewing it up to prevent the stuffing escaping. Wrap it in well greased or buttered paper, and cook for about 2 hours, basting very liberally. When cooked, remove the coverings and froth it with a little flour and butter, and dish up with brown gravy round it, and port wine sauce.'
From *Birds and their Eggs*, compiled by André Simon.

Swan-farming was no prerogative of the English; in the Netherlands, for instance, the tradition continued until the Second World War. Most of the birds produced were of the pale 'Polish' form, and were sold either as ornamental birds or for 'fur' and food. As in England, this organised cropping of the Mute Swan was one of the best possible means of conserving a species which might otherwise have been exterminated by excessive hunting. By taking only cygnets, the swan-farmers were able to maintain the breeding population at the required level; they thus avoided the error made by the communities who 'harvested' wild swans indiscriminately and sometimes depleted the breeding stock so much that it never recovered.

The Black Swan is another species which is managed on a massive scale. During the past hundred years the population in New Zealand has increased to such an extent that the numbers now have to be controlled. In Christchurch alone some 10,000 birds are shot each year, mostly on organised swan drives. Eggs are also collected, strictly under permit, the quota varying from year to year. One of the largest collections was in 1966, when 43,200 eggs were taken. They are sold at a dollar (50 new pence) a dozen and at one time went mainly to the making of a malt chocolate drink. This was stopped by

'to feed racehorses'. *Giles*.

175

pressure from the poultry farmers, and the eggs are now used either in Christmas baking, or more especially to feed race-horses. In spite of all this the numbers remain high; at Lake Ellesmere a population of 40,000–50,000 is considered reasonable, and it may rise as high as 100,000. In south-east Australia, where the Black Swan population is also large, the State of Victoria sometimes allows the numbers to be reduced (88).

Complaints of agricultural damage are not uncommon in other countries, but seldom warrant drastic action. The damage is almost invariably local and, tiresome though it may be to the individual farmer, it does not amount to a serious economic problem. An investigation into the harm done by the Whooper Swan in Iceland brought a number of complaints but no real indictment. Three farmers complained that their sheep were attacked by nesting birds; this was likely to cause panic, and a sheep might be lost or drowned, though none had so far suffered this fate. Other farmers claimed that the birds were taking valuable summer grazing on pastures leading down to the water's edge (175). In Scotland they occasionally develop a taste for turnips during spells of hard weather; they also graze on young winter wheat, but this seldom affects the yield. The Mute Swan presents a more serious problem, especially in England where substantial numbers of birds remain in the same areas for quite some time. They are chiefly accused of taking the early spring grazing, which the farmer can least afford to lose. Even so, the sums involved are relatively small. After one particularly severe attack, the damage was assessed at £75 (78); but this was quite exceptional. In such cases, the Protection of Birds Act, 1954*, permits the farmer to kill Mute Swans in defence of his property, but the onus lies on him to prove that the action was necessary to prevent serious damage. Whooper and Bewick's Swans are afforded special protection, and may not be shot, except under licence; they can, however, be discouraged. Low voltage electric fencing will prevent swans from walking ashore to graze; and dogs are often effective, especially against Whoopers. Fluorescent scarecrows, and acetylene bangers have also been used with success, but they need to be moved at frequent intervals. If placed in position as soon as the birds start to assemble, they will help to prevent excessive concentrations.

*If a Mute Swan is living in a wild state it is protected by the Protection of Birds Act, 1954, and if in a tame and domestic state, by the Protection of Animals Act, 1911. It is larceny to steal a tame and domestic swan, and an offence under the Malicious Damage Act, 1861, to kill, maim or wound it.

Damage to fisheries is another crime of which swans are often accused, but here again the charges are usually unjustified. At most it is a local problem, and there is certainly no call for widespread action. In Sweden an extensive survey was recently undertaken to assess the effect on the commercial fisheries of the very large concentrations of Mute Swans which assemble in summer on parts of the Baltic coast. The results were entirely in the swans' favour: they were not taking spawn or fry, except perhaps occasionally by accident, nor were they spoiling the spawning grounds by uprooting large areas of the bottom vegetation. Even in places where the number of birds was large, they were consuming only a small fraction of the total growth (27). In England, and also in Iceland, it is claimed that large flocks of swans can do considerable damage to the vegetation in rivers and lakes, but in England at any rate this is a potential, rather than an actual, problem (78). The complaint that they foul the water with their droppings is also unfounded: if anything, they enrich it for both plant and animal life. Swans can, of course, be a nuisance to fishermen, eating their ground-bait and tangling their lines. The hardship, however, is not all on one side: swans are often found with ugly wounds from these disputes, and also from swallowing hooks. Usually the trouble can be avoided by a little common sense. 'To cast thy bread upon the waters' is asking for trouble when swans are about.

Wildfowlers sometimes take exception to Mute Swans on the grounds that they are strongly territorial and drive away other nesting wildfowl. This may be true of individuals, usually old birds, but in general they are aggressive only to their own species. Ducks have often been found nesting within a few feet of a swan's nest, and have brought off their young without interference (78). It is also untrue that the wintering flocks consume a disproportionate amount of the available food; for the most part they feed at depths which cannot be exploited by either dabbling or diving ducks (page 63).

The situation is more worrying when swans become a hazard to the instruments of civilisation. Reference has already been made to collisions with overhead cables (page 130). These accidents are not only disastrous to the birds concerned, but often result in power failures. In some districts these faults must seem to occur with exasperating frequency. Even so the number of failures attributable to swans is small compared with those from other causes. One solution, for the engineer but not for the swan, would be to insulate the cables along certain stretches (78).

The possibility of collisions between birds and aircraft is another hazard which is causing much concern, especially in North America. Even small birds cause massive damage when struck at a speed of 500 m.p.h.; with a bird the size of a swan the result can be catastrophic. It is easy, therefore, to take alarm at the prospect of 50,000 Whistling Swans migrating across the busy air-lanes of the eastern seaboard on their way from north-west Canada to the wintering grounds along the Atlantic coast. There have, in fact, been very few authenticated cases of collision. The worst incident was in 1962 when a Viscount airliner hit a flock of Whistling Swans at 6,000 feet over Maryland; one side of the tail plane was ripped off, and the aircraft dived vertically to the ground, killing all seventeen people aboard (308). Despite the horror of this disaster, the problem is not so serious as it might appear. The dangerous migration period is limited to a few weeks only in autumn and spring; the routes followed by the birds can mostly be defined, and the height at which they fly is well below the cruising height of high speed civil aircraft. Since the hazard is predictable, it ought to be avoidable. The time of greatest risk is during the five or ten minutes before landing or after take-off, when the aircraft is below 7,000 feet; it might be wise, therefore, to consider closing some airports temporarily during the period of peak migration.

Except in the rare instances when swans endanger human life, their conflict with Man's interests can seldom be described as more than a minor annoyance. New Zealand is probably the only country in which they might cause significant economic losses, and even there they are tolerated in surprisingly large numbers. This tolerance is typical of their present relationship with Man; people enjoy seeing swans, and for the most part wish them well. What is needed now is an understanding of the problems which confront them in the years ahead, and of the compromises which will have to be made to safeguard their future.

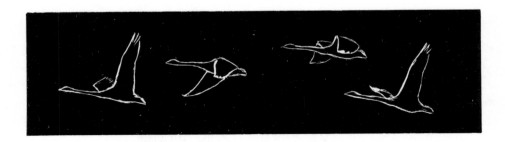

In days gone by I haunted the lakes.
In days gone by I was beautiful when I was a swan.
Ah! me. Ah! me – now I am black and roundly roasted.

I was whiter than snow
More lovely than any bird.
Now I am blacker than a raven.

The fire burns me freely,
The cook turns and twists me on the spit,
The steward serves me for the banquet.

I would like rather to live on the waters
Under an even, clear sky
Than to be swamped in this pepper.

Now I lie on a charger
And can no longer fly.
I can see the teeth of the feasters champing.

Trans. by Mr. James Street from the *Carmina Burana* manuscript (thirteenth century). '*Olim lacus . . .*'

9
Conservation

G. V. T. Matthews

'The Last Trumpeter'. *Raymond Sheppard.*

Conservation is no longer the preserve of the ageing, desperate to retain something of the good earth they have known. There has been an upsurge of interest among the young, urgent to prevent the destruction of the natural world before they have had time to enjoy it. Education has at last become a more powerful force than experience. In my own case the dilemmas of conservation were first thrust home, in my early teens, by Elmer Ransom's story called 'The Last Trumpeter', published in the old *Zoo* magazine. In this tale the last breeding pair of Trumpeter Swans was migrating south with their three young. Ambushed by shooters, the young were destroyed but the parents flew on. Trapped on their roosting lake by a sudden overnight freeze-up, the male struggled free but the female was

PLATE 39 Head of Bewick's Swan (Shieldy) showing the highly variable yellow area that never extends beyond the nostril. Compare with Plates 24 and 31. *Philippa Scott*.

PLATE 40 Wild Bewick's Swans. ABOVE: head of juvenile, feathered between eye and bill, unlike the adult. BELOW: adults (Peasant and Gypsy) and immature, the latter showing greyish plumage. *Philippa Scott.*

held in an icy grip and was about to be devoured by a ravening wolf. A field-biologist, who happened to be studying the decline of the Trumpeter Swan towards extinction, appeared on the scene and drove off the wolf. He himself was faint with hunger and exposure. However he cut her free, she rejoined her mate and the species' continuity was ensured. The story ended with the biologist drifting into numbing death.

For all its crudity this little parable sets out the essential problems. Conservation is concerned with Man, his demands on the environment and on the creatures which share it with him. Conservation is of men, by men and for men. It would not be necessary were it not for Man, especially now that he is equipped with the godlike powers of modern technology. Certainly the concept of conservation has developed late in human evolution. Only when much has been destroyed does an appreciation develop for the little that remains. Hopefully, however, the countries now emerging into the techno-logical age will avoid the mistakes of those that reached this stage too early.

Man can bring catastrophe to swans in several ways; by direct slaughter, by accidental killing, by denial of food resources, and by restriction or degradation of living space. For much of his time on Earth, Man was not a very efficient predator. Massive slaughter occurred only where moulting concentrations could be attacked during the weeks of flightlessness. Then came the development of firearms; and swans present large, slow-manoeuvring targets. When the incentive of commercial gain was added to the individual desire for meat and warming feathers, the outlook became bleak. The concept of a natural 'harvest' is a misleading one when we reap what we do not sow and thoughtlessly add to the losses without increasing the production. Small wonder that in 1932 there were only sixty-nine Trumpeter Swans left in the forty-eight United States.

The control of direct exploitation is, nevertheless, one of the easier elements of conservation, provided that the need for it is recognised early enough and provided that society is sufficiently organised to pass laws and enforce them. Such measures should obviously be taken before numbers are reduced to a mere handful. Some species seem to need the stimulus of sheer numbers to reproduce successfully, perhaps through the media of complex social systems. This was probably so in the case of the Passenger Pigeon, whose fantastic hordes absorbed an outrageous slaughter for a while and then collapsed abruptly into oblivion. Further, if there are deleterious genes within a species, they are more likely to make their effect felt in small populations which enforce the mating of closely related individuals. This is not always the case, witness the present flourishing stock of the Laysan Teal, which at one time was reduced to only seven birds by a museum collector. Nevertheless small populations are terribly vulnerable.

The requirement is for a regular monitoring of the population and its reproductive success. This is particularly difficult in the case of migratory populations, international co-operation being required as well as a corps of trained observers within each country. Nevertheless considerable success has been achieved (pages 53 and 54).

It is a relatively simple decision to ban completely the hunting of a species which is clearly at a low ebb. It is much less easy to decide how much exploitation should be allowed where a species is apparently in no immediate danger of disappearing. A pair of swans produce in the course of their lives many more than the two birds needed to replace them. Thus, in a relatively stable population there must be a great natural 'wastage'. There is good evidence, in some cases at least, that a part of this surplus can be removed by man without increasing the total loss. As the losses through shooting increase, those due to natural causes, such as starvation, may become correspondingly lower. Another consideration is that selection by shooting favours behavioural and other characteristics different from those imposed by natural selection. So the species may be subtly changed, perhaps reducing its ability to cope with natural hazards. The exploitation equation is a tricky one to balance, especially with regard to waterfowl, which congregate in relatively few places and are rather easily over-exploited. In North America much time and money has been spent for decades in attempts to match the kill of ducks and geese against breeding success, by an elaborate array of varying season lengths and 'bag limits'.

In 1962 the State of Utah introduced, despite opposition, a 90-day open season on Whistling Swans (298). In 1969, 2,500 sportsmen were issued permits to kill one swan each during a period of 86 days. As a result 1,290 swans were bagged and a further 1,217 were hit but not retrieved (225). These figures will undoubtedly cause raised eyebrows in the 23 countries of Europe, in which all swans are protected, often with special penalties. The thought of a conservation-minded country like the U.S.A. permitting the killing of swans for sport is at first sight surprising, but this is only a measure of the effect that mythology and tradition have upon us. Once the killing of any bird for sport is accepted, then, biologically speaking, the decision as to which species can be shot rests solely on the ability of its population to absorb the imposed shooting pressure. In particular, the population must produce a regular 'surplus' of young birds on which shooters can prey without affecting the replacement of the breeding stock. This requirement eliminates as a game bird a high-Arctic nesting species which, like the Dark-bellied Brent Goose, frequently experiences seasons of almost complete breeding failure (244). Unsuitable, too, are the species like flamingos which have evolved, presumably in the absence of effective natural predators, a slow and erratic reproduction. They produce but one egg per pair and often go several years without breeding. In the case of abundant species, producing many young each year, the distinction between game and non-game birds is often far from logical. Anglo-Saxons are in general disgusted by the Latin prediliction for shooting thrushes and the like and seek to argue that such small birds cannot be considered as game; yet a thrush weighs more than a snipe. If size alone were the criterion then swans would head the list.

Dark-bellied Brent Geese.

However much repugnance one may feel at the shooting of Whistling Swans – and some Nevada hunters are known to have obtained permits solely to prevent them being shot (225) – if the population does not decline from its present level of some 50,000 in the western states, then the limited take is acceptable biologically and opposition must rest on other arguments. A very practical one is that another, by no means plentiful species, the Trumpeter Swan, is practically indistinguishable from the Whistling Swan, certainly in flight. Indeed at the Trumpeter's nadir the shooting of Snow Geese was banned in its range (14).

There is, of course, the view that killing any animal for sport is morally wrong. A shooter, however, has more of a vested and practical interest in the survival of his quarry species, and of the countryside in general, than has a city-bound 'anti-blood-sport' protagonist. Moreover, if some species were

185

not hunted their numbers could rise to 'pest' proportions. This is because Man has already interfered with the natural scheme by removing predators or other forms of population control. It is ironic, incidentally, that nowadays the hero of our opening parable would have yet another dilemma, for the Wolf is at present in greater danger of extinction than the Trumpeter Swan.

While no one can reasonably object to the hunter eating or sharing what he kills, most countries, advanced in conservation, agree that commercial exploitation of wildfowl should not be permitted. In Britain legislation banning the sale of dead wild geese was recently enacted at the insistence of the wildfowlers themselves. The commercial exploitation of migratory species is particularly undesirable. In the case of sedentary species a carefully controlled cull may sometimes be necessary. If so, it is certainly preferable that the meat and other products be sold through a government agency, than that the carcases be left to rot, especially in protein-hungry countries.

Sometimes Man upsets the natural balance deliberately and then restores it inadvertently. In the 1950s, for instance, the Mute Swan numbers in Britain soared upwards. A possible reason is that public interest in natural history had been roused particularly by television programmes; in consequence, the feeding of swans and other birds during the winter became widespread, thus reducing the mortality, especially among immature birds. Be that as it may, if the upsurge had continued, the Mute Swan would have become more than a local nuisance. Control measures were discussed by the government departments concerned but, such was the climate of British opinion, an open season on swans was hardly considered. The destruction of eggs was favoured as causing the least distress to swans and public alike. The only snag to this method is the slowness with which it takes effect, and its ineffectiveness in relation to the effort involved. Most of the embryos destroyed would die in any case within the next few weeks, and only a very few would reach maturity, even in an expanding population (page 128). If the expansion had continued the unpleasant but effective solution would have been for licensed 'pest officers' to kill breeding birds. But, surprisingly, the increase slowed and eventually the population fell to a more or less steady level well below the peak numbers. This was not just a case of Nature being helpful. There had concurrently been a vast increase in the overhead wire-scape of Britain, and collisions with wires were now accounting for half the known deaths of full-grown swans. So, the swans were increased by Man's liberality with 'waste' food, and cut back by the wires needed to carry his electricity – both facets of the affluent society. Indeed the interaction is even closer, for without electricity there would be no television.

Wirescapes are a distressing intrusion into the natural environment, tolerated because we are not prepared to pay the price for placing the cables underground. This is but one aspect of the way in which modern technology degrades the environment as a by-product of its efforts to ensure an easy life for us all. Waters and wetlands are particularly prone to such damage. Some pollution is obvious, like the oil spills which cause considerable mortality among swans (PLATE 43). Other pollutions are more insidious in their effects. For instance, persistent organochemicals render egg-shells fragile; sewage effluents deoxygenate rivers; artificial fertilisers encourage choking algal 'blooms' in lakes. Wetlands are also particularly liable to be regarded as wastelands, useful only as dumping places for industrial waste or, when 'reclaimed', as sites for noxious factories, for dangerous power stations, for noisy airports or for marginal agriculture. This whole process of corruption and destruction has been speeded up by new engineering techniques. Along with the vanishing wetlands will go their dependent waterfowl, for, as Shakespeare put it in the Merchant of Venice, 'You take my life when you do take the means whereby I live'.

Strenuous efforts are being made by conservationists to slow down the loss of wetland habitat on both the national and international plane. The International Wildfowl Research Bureau and the International Union for the Conservation of Nature, with the financial assistance of the World Wildlife Fund, have developed Project MAR (149). This programme (named for the first three letters of the word for marsh in many languages) pinpoints and assesses the major wetlands throughout Eurasia and Africa and is seeking to have them conserved through the operation of an International Convention between governments. Each country should also make itself responsible for the host of smaller waters and wetlands within its boundaries which in the aggregate are as important as the great delta marshes.

Despite this activity it is only realistic to fear that the future area of wetlands available to waterfowl will be strongly reduced even from the remnant we have today. This is so despite the fortunate chance that the affluent society's increasing needs for water and for concrete have led to the creation of new wetlands – reservoirs and gravel-pits. But the same society's increasing leisure time and mobility produce pressure to use such areas for water-based sports – many, like water-skiing, inimicable to the continuing presence of waterfowl. So, if waterfowl populations are not to diminish in proportion, the birds will have to use the remaining available wetlands more intensively, and the sites will have to be managed to exploit to the full such natural adaptability as the birds possess. Fortunately the swans, at least, are relatively long-lived and have a prolonged family life. These are essential requirements for the establishment of traditional attachments and habits, passed on from generation to generation by social learning rather than as inherited 'instincts'. The way in which a new wintering tradition can be established in a few years is illustrated by the rapid build-up of the Bewick's Swan flock at Slimbridge. Swans, like most other wildfowl, are naturally gregarious during the winter months. All that is needed to attract them to a given site is a suitable area of water and marsh, a 'lead' of a few wild or captive birds, an extensive disturbance-free zone and a supplementary supply of food, especially in hard weather. Artificial feeding, either by the provision of standing forage crops or by the scattering of grain, will increase in importance as the habitat dwindles. This may be regretted by the purist but will probably be unavoidable. Conservation should not refuse to take advantage of the recent advances in agricultural technology. Despite intensive planting of natural food species round the margins of a large gravel pit, the actual yield was only the equivalent of what could be produced by one-twentieth acre of barley (261). This is not to say that the natural way was not preferable for other reasons, only that artificiality is likely to be forced upon us and may have to be accepted as the only solution.

Some species of swans are already adapting themselves to feeding on agricultural land, mainly on the gleanings of harvested crops. At present their impact on growing crops is marginal and of local consequence, but with the shortage of wetlands this will increase and farmers may be faced with an unacceptable weight of swans. There are several ways in which damage to crops can be prevented, either by the use of various scaring

Bulrush *Schœnoplectus* a species
planted for waterfowl food.
Carol Ogilvie.

devices, or perhaps in the last resort by shooting, if the law permits. By far
the best solution would be to provide extensive refuge areas from which the
swans did not have to emerge in search of food. This technique has been
widely accepted in North America. It costs money. However, there is a net
gain, for expensive scaring activities are unnecessary and the undisturbed
birds will utilise completely the crops set aside for them instead of spoiling
larger areas as they are driven from pillar to post. Support from government
sources can be justified therefore and the public could be encouraged to
contribute directly to refuges which provided the incomparable spectacle of
myriads of waterfowl. None should grudge paying an entrance or member-
ship fee to get close to these wonderful birds along a system of concealed
approaches and comfortable observation posts. Indeed, as at Slimbridge, the
enthusiasts might be persuaded to pay quite substantial sums to become the
'Supporters' of individual swans.

Leo and Stella, two of the 'supported' Bewick's Swans at Slimbridge.

The conservation of swans during the breeding season is beset with more intractable difficulties. The Bewick's, Whistling and Whooper Swans breed in the Arctic tundra where, until recently, they seemed safe enough. Now Man is reaching into these northern areas in search of oil and mineral wealth. The fragile ecosystem is crumbling under the impact of his machines and of the waste-products of his technicians. Even events far away may bring ruin without invasion. Soviet plans to reverse the northward flow of the great rivers Yenesi and Ob, to water the central deserts, are a case in point. In the face of such technological enormities the setting aside of reserves would be a useless gesture. Besides, most swans nest far apart, pair from pair, and in order to safeguard a reasonable proportion of the breeding population, one would have to keep vast areas free from disturbance and exploitation – far greater than at present seems practicable.

The problem would be much simpler if all swans nested in colonies like the Black Swan and some populations of the Mute Swan. Indeed useful research could be done to discover why some Mute Swans give up their aggressive territoriality and nest in compact and easily protected groups. Food supplies are probably the ultimate factor in which case the necessary richness is likely to be reached only in certain places in the temperate regions. Here again something might be achieved by the artificial propagation of food plants. It should be noted, however, that, although nesting colonies are more easily protected, they are much more vulnerable to changes than a scattered population. In Iceland, for instance, a new hydro-electric

PLATE 41 Wild Bewick's Swans (Cressida and Lancelot) preening. *Philippa Scott*.

PLATE 43 ABOVE: oiled Bewick's Swan (Sahara, with mate Gobi) which arrived at Slimbridge and recovered without assistance. *Philippa Scott*. BELOW: officials of the R.S.P.C.A. cleaning Mute Swans after an oil spillage on the River Stour. *Richard Burn*.

OPPOSITE
PLATE 42 Bewick's Swans. ABOVE: in flight. *E. E. Jackson*. BELOW: flying between 'Swan Lake' and the River Severn. *Philippa Scott*.

PLATE 44 ABOVE: inn sign at Piffs Elm, near Cheltenham. *Edwin C. Peckham.* RIGHT: dish and cover from the Meissen Swan Service. *Newman & Newman (Antiques) Ltd.* BELOW: mechanical silver swan from the Bowes Museum, Durham. *The Bowes Museum.*

scheme is threatening to flood the whole fifty square miles of the Thjorsarver oasis; in this area nest about three-quarters of the Pink-footed Geese which winter in Britain.

Pink-footed Goose.

Aviculture is often suggested as a solution to the problem of diminishing populations, particularly since it pulled back the Hawaiian Goose from the verge of extinction. Some species, however, are difficult to breed in captivity. At Slimbridge we have had no success with Whistling Swans, and little with Coscorobas, Bewick's Swans and Whoopers. Trumpeter Swans have bred more freely, Black Swans and Black-necked Swans do so regularly, and Mute Swans have to be restrained. The conditions here are probably not ideal, and other breeders have had success with some of the difficult species. Even so, it hardly seems practicable to undertake swan-farming on a scale large enough to contribute significantly to the natural populations. Moreover, breeding in captivity carries with it the seeds of further difficulties, such as the risks of in-breeding, and the need for frequent introductions of 'fresh blood'. By its very success, artificial rearing tends to keep alive more birds than would survive to maturity in the wild. In other words, the impact of natural selection is dulled and undesirable characteristics are preserved. If such stock is returned to the wild, there is a risk of it being cut back severely when faced with normal adversities. Finally, it is much more difficult to introduce hand-reared birds into a migratory population than it is to restock a marsh or an island with a species which is, or can be, more or less sedentary, such as the Mallard, Greylag and Hawaiian Goose.

C H Nelson - 1970

Trumpeter Swan cygnets hatched at Slimbridge. *Colleen Nelson.*

This is one of the problems confronting the American Fish and Wildlife Service in their effort to reinstate the Whooping Crane, whose population in the wild is now reduced to about fifty individuals. Their plan is to release the captive-reared birds in the wintering grounds on the Mexican Gulf in the hope that they will join the wild birds and migrate with them to the isolated breeding area in Alberta. Wild Whooping Cranes seldom rear more than one young from the clutch of two eggs, so the captive stock can be obtained, without detriment to the population, by taking one egg from each clutch. This is one step removed from aviculture proper, in that the eggs are laid by wild birds. The objection that the stock is not tempered by normal selection is thus partly removed.

A further step from artificiality is to catch up young birds hatched and reared by their parents in the wild. The young are then transplanted and held for varying periods in the area which is to be repopulated. If the wing feathers are clipped, the birds are grounded until the following moult; if the feathers are completely removed, new ones grow within six weeks. The results with geese have not been altogether encouraging. In the south-east of the United States a transplant programme involving 20,734 Canada Geese resulted in only one case, and that a doubtful one, of a new migratory

Canada Geese.

population being established (117). The complicated and expensive logistics of such an operation can well be imagined. With the relatively less migratory Trumpeter Swan rather more was achieved. In the 1968 survey 214 out of the 799 birds seen in the contiguous United States were transplants or the offspring of transplants. However, the strength lay in Alaska where 2,842 birds were seen and transplanting had not been used.

Whichever way we turn, whichever method we use, conservation is time-consuming and expensive. Is it really necessary? In many ways the environmental pollution and degradation which threatens the survival of swans and other animals is also of immediate consequence to Man himself. It is easy, therefore, to make the point that we must keep our environment habitable, as much for our own sake as for other creatures. The reasons for striving to save certain species of animals from extinction are less immediately obvious. Species have been dying since Life began, indeed extinction is an integral part of evolution. The recent, frightening development is the way in which technological Man has telescoped the time-scale so that species, especially those adapted to specialised habits and habitats, are disappearing with sickening speed. It is mainly Man who now decides, often indifferently, which species shall vanish next. The arguments against letting this happen are manifold. In the first place we have no moral right thoughtlessly to destroy something we cannot replace, the more so if our descendants might utilise and enjoy it. Secondly, it is becoming abundantly clear that Man's cities and monocultures, be they animal or plant, are not in themselves sufficient for a wholesome life. We need a variety of sensation and experience whether or not one uses that oft-derided word, aesthetics. There is no need to stress this point when dealing with creatures as lovely as swans; the

illustrations throughout this book are an argument in themselves. It is not enough just to maintain a selection of these exquisite birds in parks and collections, rather like living museum pieces. They must be allowed to remain in the wild state and must be seen in a wild habitat, however much Man's helping hand is needed to maintain it. Few experiences can compare with first hearing the bugling of wild swans and with the sight of them sweeping down out of the northern sky.

The need to conserve wild species can be argued further on scientific and educational grounds. They provide working material for scientific investigations of immediate relevance to Man. They also subserve that pure search for simple truth which is one of the highlights of human endeavour. Education without an ecological background will, in future, be unthinkable, and animals and their habitats must be readily available for study by the schools and universities.

Finally there are the economic arguments, that nature in general and birds in particular have a value in hard cash. Although the trade in migratory wild birds for food or clothing is no longer acceptable, they can and ought to be exploited as a profitable amenity. Watching and studying wildlife is an increasingly popular leisure activity; shooting is also a legitimate pastime, when subject to careful control, though only one shooter can kill a bird whereas many people can enjoy its flight. Wildlife and wild places can be as much of a tourist attraction as stately homes and seaside piers, and will bring prosperity to the district in which they lie.

All these arguments, except the moral one, are basically selfish in that they involve benefit to Man. This brings us back to our initial statement that Man made conservation necessary. And it is the present failure of Man to control his own rocketing populations that lies behind all the present threats of pollution, degradation and extinction. It must be remembered, too, that a child born in an advanced technological country will consume and pollute something like fifty times as much as will a child born elsewhere.

It may seem strange to end a book on swans with a plea for universal, rational birth control. But without it all conservation efforts will be in vain.

Appendices

Appendix 1

Body weights of swans, in kilograms.

| | MALE | | | FEMALE | | | |
	Mean Wt.	*Range*	*No. in Sample*	*Mean Wt.*	*Range*	*No. in Sample*	*Reference*
Coscoroba Swan	4·6	3·8–5·4	2	3·8	3·2–4·5	3	(60, 133, 338, 339)
Black-necked Swan	5·4	4·5–6·7	8	4·0	3·5–4·4	7	(133, 147, 280, 339)
Black Swan	6·2	4·6–8·7	270	5·1	3·7–7·2	243	(88, 197)
Bewick's Swan							
Adult	6·4	4·9–7·8	96	5·7	3·4–7·2	95	(339)
1st winter	5·4	4·5–6·7	15	5·0	3·3–6·4	29	(339)
Whistling Swan							
Adult	7·1	4·7–9·6	76	6·2	4·3–8·2	86	W. J. L. Sladen, pers. com.; (189)
1st winter	5·7	4·3–8·1	25	5·1	4·1–7·2	25	W. J. L. Sladen, pers. com.
Whooper Swan	10·8	8·5–12·7	6	8·1	7·5–8·7	4	(66, 120, 146, 285, 339)
Trumpeter Swan	11·9	9·1–12·5*	10	9·4	7·3–10·2	7	(14, 189, 339)
Mute Swan	12·2	8·4–15·0*	33	8·9	6·6–12·0	30	C. M. Reynolds, pers. com.; (339)

*These means do not include exceptional records of 17·2 kg. in the case of the Trumpeter (10) and 22·5 kg. for the Mute Swan (284).

PLATE 45 ABOVE: 'The Threatened Swan' by Jan Asselyn (1615-1652). An allegorical painting in which the bird (the State Councillor) defends its egg (Holland). *Rijksmuseum, Amsterdam.* BELOW: 'Swans in Flight' by David Wynne at the new Civic Centre, Newcastle upon Tyne. Here the swans symbolise the five Scandinavian states with which the North East of England has cultural and trading links. *City and County of Newcastle upon Tyne.*

PLATE 46 Chinese painting on silk of Whooper Swans. Probably from the sixteenth century but possibly later. Collection R. Soame Jenyns. *E. E. Jackson.*

Appendix 2

Linear measurements of swans in millimetres

	BILL (CULMEN)*			HEAD (BILL TIP TO BACK OF SKULL)			TARSUS			WING (STANDARD CHORD)		
	Mean	*Range*	*No.*	*Mean*	*Range*	*No.*	*Mean*	*Range*	*No.*	*Mean*	*Range*	*No.*
BEWICK'S SWAN												
Adult male	94·7	81·5–108·0	94	163	148–175	93	106	93–119	93	531	485–573	93
Adult female	90·9	75·0–100·0	94	157	144–167	89	102	87–111	94	510	478–543	92
1st winter male	76·7	64·6–98·0	17	160	147–175	17	106	95–115	17	505	458–552	17
1st winter female	75·5	67·7–88·0	31	154	135–165	31	102	85–111	31	487	445–525	31

All these birds were measured by the Wildfowl Trust at Slimbridge (339).

*This measurement, from bill tip to the feather-line, is not invariable in the same individual, since the feathers recede, especially during the first winter.

Dafila Scott.

	BILL			TARSUS			WING			
	Mean	*Range*	*No.*	*Mean*	*Range*	*No.*	*Mean*	*Range*	*No.*	*Reference*
WHISTLING SWAN										
Adult male	102·6	97–107	8	111·9	105–117·5	8	538	501–569	8	(14)
Adult female	99·9	92·5–106	15	107·2	99·5–115	15	531·6	505–561	15	(14)
WHOOPER SWAN										
Adult male	109·1	102–116	10	124·1	120·5–130	10	615·6	590–640	10	(339)
Adult female	103·6	97–112	6	116·0	104–132	6	597·2	581–609	6	(339)
1st winter male	94·3	88–102	3	123·7	121–126	3	599·7	593–605	3	(339)
1st winter female	83·5	82–85	2	108·5	105–112	2	555	535–575	2	(339)
TRUMPETER SWAN										
Adult male	112·5	104–119·5	5	122·9	121·5–126	5	618·6	545–680	5	(14)
Adult female	107	101·5–112·5	3	121·7	113–128·5	3	623·3	604–636	3	(14)
BLACK-NECKED SWAN										
Adult male	74·8	82–86	1	91·9	85–88	1	436	435–450	1	(339) (64)
Adult female	64·3	71–73	1	77·9	78–80	1	418	400–415	1	(339) (64)
BLACK SWAN										
Adult male	69	57–79	247		90–105		489	434–543	247	(88) (64)
Adult female	63	56–72	219		85–100		461	416–499	219	(88) (64)
MUTE SWAN										
Adult male	80·2	76–85	5	112·8	107–120	5	608·4	589–622	5	(285)
1st winter male	79·7	78–81	3	102·3	101–104	3	541·6	517–568	3	(285)
Adult female	76·3	74–80	6	104·8	100–113	6	566·8	540–596	6	(285)
COSCOROBA SWAN										
Adult male				89		1	480		1	(310)
Adult female	64·8	63–68	4	92·9	92–93·8	4	444	427–458	4	(339)

Appendix 3

Life expectancy of swans in captivity. From data collected at the London Zoo (see also 231).

	SAMPLE SIZE	AVERAGE CAPTIVE LIFE EXPECTANCY IN YEARS	MAXIMUM NUMBER OF YEARS IN CAPTIVITY
Black-necked Swan	31	6·8	20
Coscoroba Swan	12	7·3	20
Black Swan	56	7·6	33
Whooper Swan	26	8·3	25
Whistling Swan	4	10·5	15
Mute Swan	27	11·0	21
Bewick's Swan	5	13·6	24
Trumpeter Swan	6	15·6	29

Some of these birds may actually have been older at death since their age on being brought into captivity was not always known. In addition, Kortright (189) recorded a captive Trumpeter Swan at 32½ years and a Whistling Swan of 19 years.

Black Swan. *Valerie Shirley*.

Appendix 4

The food of adult swans

PLANTS	MUTE SWAN	WHOOPER SWAN	BEWICK'S SWAN	WHISTLING SWAN	TRUMPETER SWAN	BLACK SWAN	BLACK-NECKED SWAN	COSCOROBA SWAN
LEAVES AND STEMS OF SUBMERGED AND FLOATING AQUATIC PLANTS							***	***
Potamogeton spp. Pondweeds	***	***	***	***	***	***	—	—
Characeae Stoneworts	***	**	*	*	*	***	—	—
Zostera spp. Eelgrass	***	**	—	—	—	*	—	—
Myriophyllum spp. Milfoil	**	—	*	—	*	**	—	—
Ruppia spp. Wigeongrass	**	+	—	*	—	*	—	—
Vallisneria spp. Wild Celery	+	—	—	**	—	**	—	—
Elodea spp. Canadian Pondweed	+	**	—	—	—	—	—	—
Zannichellia spp. Horned Pondweed	**	—	*	—	—	—	—	—
Ranunculus spp. Crowfoot	—	+	—	—	**	—	—	—
Ceratophyllum demersum Hornwort	+	—	—	—	—	*	—	—
Najas graminea Naiad	—	—	—	—	—	*	—	—
Azolla sp. Water Fern	—	—	—	—	—	*	—	—
ALGAE							**?	?
Enteromorpha spp.	***	—	—	—	—	—	—	—
Vaucheria sp.	*	—	—	—	—	—	—	—
Others	+	—	—	—	—	—	—	—
Unspecified	—	*	—	—	—	*	—	—

APPENDIX FOUR

PLANTS	MUTE SWAN	WHOOPER SWAN	BEWICK'S SWAN	WHISTLING SWAN	TRUMPETER SWAN	BLACK SWAN	BLACK-NECKED SWAN	COSCOROBA SWAN
LEAVES OF EMERGENT PLANTS							*?	*?
Typha spp. Reedmace	+	—	—	*	—	**	—	—
Scirpus spp. Club-rush	+	—	—	*	*	—	—	—
Equisetum spp. Horsetail	—	—	—	*	*	—	—	—
Polygonum spp. Persicaria	+	—	—	*	—	—	—	—
Sparganium spp. Bur-reed	—	—	—	—	*	—	—	—
Sagittaria spp. Arrowhead	—	—	—	—	*	—	—	—
Carex spp. Sedge	—	—	—	—	*	—	—	—
GRASS LEAVES								***?
Pasture grasses	*	***	***	—	—	***	—	—
Glyceria maxima Reed Grass	—	*	**	—	—	—	—	—
Glyceria fluitans Flote-grass	—	+	*	—	—	—	—	—
Puccinellia maritima Saltmarsh Grass	*	—	+	—	—	—	—	—
Paspalum spp. Water Couch Grass	—	—	—	—	—	*	—	—
LEAVES OF OTHER LAND PLANTS								
Saltmarsh succulents	*	—	—	—	—	+	—	—
Trifolium spp. Clover	+	+	+	—	—	—	—	—
TUBERS, STOLONS, RHIZOMES, ROOTS								
Potamogeton spp. Pondweeds	—	—	*	**	**	—	—	—
Sagitarria spp. Arrowhead	—	—	—	*	**	—	—	—

APPENDIX FOUR

PLANTS	MUTE SWAN	WHOOPER SWAN	BEWICK'S SWAN	WHISTLING SWAN	TRUMPETER SWAN	BLACK SWAN	BLACK-NECKED S.WAN	COSCOROBA SWAN
Zostera spp.	—	—	**	—	—	—	—	—
Scirpus spp.	—	—	+	*	—	—	—	—
Glyceria maxima	+	+	+	—	—	—	—	—
Trifolium repens White Clover	—	—	+	—	—	—	—	—
Agropyron repens Couch Grass	+	—	—	—	—	—	—	—
SEEDS AND FRUITS							?	**?
Scirpus spp.	+	—	—	—	—	*	—	—
Eleocharis spp. Spike-rush	—	—	+	—	—	*	—	—
Nuphar lutea Yellow Water-lily	—	—	—	—	*	—	—	—
Empetrum sp. Crowberry	—	*	—	—	—	—	—	—
Carex spp.	—	—	—	—	*	—	—	—
Potamogeton pectinatus Fennel Pondweed	—	—	—	*	—	—	—	—
Others	+	+	+	—	—	—	—	—
ANIMAL MATERIAL							*?	**?
Mollusca	+	—	—	**	*	—	—	—
Insecta	—	—	+	+	*	+	—	—
Crustacea	+	—	—	—	+	—	—	—
MISCELLANEOUS								
Waste grain	**	**	—	*	—	*	—	—
Hand-fed grain, bread, etc.	**	—	*	—	*	—	—	—
Potatoes/turnips	—	*	—	+	—	—	—	—
Refuse	*	—	—	—	—	—	—	—

***Important food source.
**Regular in small quantities or seasonally important.
*Occasionally used.
+ Rarely taken or accidental.
—Not known to be used.

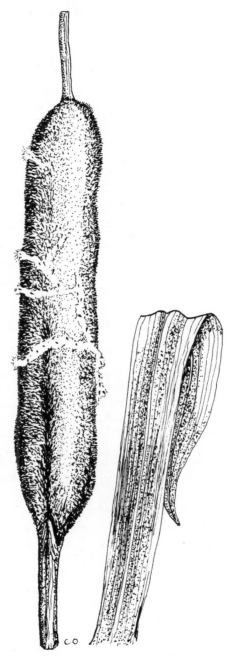

Reedmace *Typha. Carol Ogilvie.*

Appendix 5

Egg dimensions of swans

SPECIES	AVERAGE IN mm.	RANGE	NO. IN SAMPLE	SOURCE OF MATERIAL	REFERENCE
Coscoroba	88·9 × 59·9	87·6–91·4 × 52·9–61·9	14	wild	(99)
	89·1 × 60·2	82·0–94·5 × 56·0–62·0	26		(286)
	89·7 × 61·8	87·0–93·0 × 59·0–67·0	10	captivity	J. A. Griswold, pers. com.
Mute	103·0 × 75·0			Rhode Island	(114)
	108·6 × 73·4	97·1–115·8 × 68·6–76·9	41	semi-wild	(18)
	112·5 × 73·5	100·0–122·0 × 70·0–80·0	88		(286)
	114·5 × 73·1	105·0–122·0 × 70·0–80·0	50		(135)
	114·0 × 73·7	105·0–122·0 × 70·0–80·0	25	wild	(18)
	115·0 × 74·1	105·0–124·3 × 70·0–80·0	68		(346)
Black	104·0 × 67·0	96·0–115·0 × 60·0–73·0	353	near Canberra	(88)
	104·1 × 67·2	87·2–114·0 × 58·0–71·2	147	New Zealand	(62)
	105·0 × 66·3	99·0–113·0 × 63·5–70·0	64		(286)
	106·9 × 69·8	98·0–118·2 × 65·2–79·2	201	Tasmania	(112)
N.Z. Swan (extinct)	106·0 × 72·0		1	in sandhills	R. J. Scarlett, pers. com.
Black-necked	101·0 × 66·5	93·0–109·0 × 63·0–69·5	40		(286)
	101·4 × 65·9	96·8–106·2 × 63·6–68·1	6	wild	(99)
	101·1 × 66·6	95·0–106·0 × 64·0–69·5	13	captivity	(204, 280)

SPECIES	AVERAGE IN mm.	RANGE	NO. IN SAMPLE	SOURCE OF MATERIAL	REFERENCE
Bewick's	102·4 × 67·6	94·5–108·0 × 64·6–71·0	25		(346)
	103·0 × 67·0	96·0–110·5 × 64·8–70·5	35	west of Lena	(286)
	103·2 × 67·1	96·6–108·5 × 64·3–71·7	34		(135)
	105·7 × 70·5	101·8–107·9 × 69·9–71·1	5	captivity	(339)
	108·1 × 71·0	104·0–112·0 × 69·0–73·0	6	east of Lena	(286)
	110·2 × 70·9		4	Okhotsk, east of Lena	(172)
Whistling	106·9 × 68·2	90·0–115·7 × 58·7–68·5	94	wild	(26, 286)
Whooper	111·8 × 82·3	104·5–126·0 × 68·1–75·5	26	Iceland	(286)
	112·5 × 72·6	105·0–126·3 × 68·0–77·0	83	Europe, excluding Iceland	(286)
	112·8 × 73·7	105·2–126·3 × 68·1–77·4	75	Europe	(135)
	113·4 × 72·2	105·2–126·3 × 68·1–76·0	48	Iceland	(346)
Trumpeter	110·0 × 71·1	101·0–119·5 × 62·8–76·5	25		(26)
	111·0 × 71·1	104·1–121·0 × 69·5–72·5	11	captivity	J. A. Griswold, pers. com.; (339)
	110·9–72·4	104·0–123·0 × 68·0–77·5	109	Montana, U.S.A.	(14)
	111·0–71·8	101·0–120·0 × 67·0–76·0	30		(286)
	117·4 × 75·0	109·8–125·0 × 69·8–81·0	146	Copper River, Alaska	(297)

Appendix 6

Fresh egg weights of swans

SPECIES	AVERAGE gm.	RANGE gm.	NO. IN SAMPLE	SOURCE OF MATERIAL	REFERENCE
Coscoroba	159	143–177	4	captivity	(339)
	165			captivity?	(133)
	183	129–203	13	captivity	J. A. Griswold, pers. com.
	185		26	calculated	(286)
Mute	295	258–365		Rhode Island	(114)
	332	366–374	41?	N. Germany	(18)
	337	292–371·5	16	semi-captivity	(339)
	340		88	calculated	(286)
	344	311–355	9	Germany	(141)
	345	294–385	80	Lithuania	(233, 330)
Black	258		64	calculated	(286)
	272	217–298·5	34	captivity	(339)
	290			captivity	(133)
	300	262–347	49	Tasmania	(112)
Black-necked	210			captivity	(133)
	225	172·5 –273·5	57	captivity	(339)
	247		40	calculated	(286)
	271	270–274	5	captivity	(204)
Bewick's	260		35	west of Lena calculated	(286)
	291	253–325·6	29	captivity (bird wild – caught in Holland)	(339)
	300			?	(133)
	306		6	east of Lena calculated	(286)
Whistling	280		94	calculated	(286)

SPECIES	AVERAGE gm.	RANGE gm.	NO. IN SAMPLE	SOURCE OF MATERIAL	REFERENCE
Whooper	328		26	Iceland, calculated	(286)
	330			captivity?	(133)
	331		83	Europe, calculated	(286)
Trumpeter	324		30	calculated	(286)
	329	308–341	4	captivity	(109)
	342	292–394·5	41	captivity, ex British Columbia	(339)

Nesting Whooper Swan. *Valerie Shirley*.

Appendix 7

Clutch sizes of swans

SPECIES	MEAN CLUTCH SIZE	MODE	RANGE	NO. CLUTCHES IN SAMPLE	SOURCE OF MATERIAL	YEAR	REFERENCE
Coscoroba	6·8	7	5–9	17	Argentina	before 1913	(93, 94)
Mute	4·9	5	1–10	181 (colonial)	Bognaes, Denmark	1958–66	(159)
	5·7	5	3–10	49	Lithuania	1960	(330)
	5·7	5	3–8	23 (colonial)	Radipole, England	1969	C. M. Perrins and M. A. Ogilvie, pers. com.
	5·8	5 & 7	1–10	40	Denmark	1954	(251)
	5·9	6	2–7	42 (colonial)	Guldborgsund, Denmark	1966	(52)
	5·9	6	3–10	48	Britain	1955–56	(43)
	5·9	7	3–9	24	Rhode Island, U.S.A.	1967	C. H. Willey, pers. com.; (340)
	6·0	6	3–10	57	Britain	1961	(77)
	6·0	6	1–11	102	Oxford, England	1964–66	(256)
	6·2	6	2–10	153	Hamburg, Germany	1931–35	(141)
Black	4·5	5	1–11	10,365	Tasmania	1960–67	E. R. Guiler, pers. com.; (113)
	4·5	6	1–8	187	Townsville, Queensland	1962–63	H. J. Lavery, pers. com.; (197)
	5·0	5	3–6	30	captivity	1954–69	(339)
	5·4	5	1–14	1,790	Lake Ellesmere, New Zealand	1960–61	(228)
	5·5	6	4–10	407	lakes near Canberra	1963–67	(88)
	5·9	6	1–13	225	Lake Ellesmere, New Zealand	1963	(62)

SPECIES	MEAN CLUTCH SIZE	MODE	RANGE	NO. CLUTCHES IN SAMPLE	SOURCE OF MATERIAL	YEAR	REFERENCE
Black-necked		4 & 5	3–6		Argentina	before 1913	(93, 94)
			5–7		Falkland Islands		(44)
	4·0	3 & 5		2			C. Martell, pers. com.
	4·6	5	3–7	45	captivity	1952–70	(339)
	5·0			1	Argentina		M. W. Weller, pers. com.
Bewick's		4	3–5				(345)
			2–3, occasionally 4–5				(66, 326)
	5·1	5	3–6	11	captivity	1956–69	(339)
Whistling	4·3	5	1–7	297	Yukon–Kuskokwim Delta, Alaska	1963–69	C. J. Lensink, pers. com.; (200)
Whooper	4·0	4	4	2	Scotland	1919 & 1921	(101, 258)
	4·1	4	3–5	9	Iceland	1951–70	(339)
	5·0	5	5	3	captivity	1964–66	(339)
	5·0			1	Norway	1960	(236)
	5·7	6	4–7	7	Continental Europe		(16, 66 and Plate 18)
Trumpeter	4·8	5	2–7	40	Copper River, Alaska	1957–59	(297)
	5·1	5	2–9	74	Montana, U.S.A.	1949–55	W. E. Banko, pers. com.; (14)
	5·2	5 & 6	2–8	9	captivity	1960–69	(339); J. P. Williams, pers. com.
	5·2	5	1–9	146	Kenai Peninsula, Alaska	1963–68	W. Troyer, pers. com.

Appendix 8

Incubation periods of swans

SPECIES	PERIOD IN DAYS	NO. CLUTCHES IN SAMPLES	SOURCE OF MATERIAL	REFERENCE
Coscoroba	35			(64)
	35	1	captivity	(166)
Mute	35			(66)
	35·5			(134)
	35–36			(27, 257)
	35–38			(64)
	39		Rhode Island	(340)
	41		Rhode Island	(114)
Black	36·4 (32–43)	495	New Zealand	(228)
	35		captivity	(133)
	34–37		captivity	(64)
	33–39		Japan	(184)
	39 ± 2		wild	(112)
	39·7 (35–45)	44	wild	(88)
	42 ± 1		wild	(112)
Black-necked	34–36		captivity	(64)
	35		captivity	(133)
	36	1	captivity	(204)
	35–36	2	captivity	(280)
Bewick's	29–30		wild	(326)
	29–30	1	captivity	(167)
Whistling	32		wild	(15)
Whooper	31	1	captivity	(181)
Trumpeter	32–33		wild	(15)
	33	1	captivity	(168)
	33–37		wild and captivity	(14)
	33–35	6	wild	(297)

Appendix 9

Cygnet weights at one day old

SPECIES	AVERAGE gm.	RANGE gm.	NO. IN SAMPLE	SOURCE OF MATERIAL	REFERENCE
Coscoroba	109	99–119	2	captivity	J. A. Griswold,
Mute	220	180–248	17	semi-captivity	(339)
	211	205–213	6	feral, Rhode Island and Michigan	C. Nelson, pers. com.
Black	140	128–156	6	Queensland	H. J. Lavery, pers. com.; (197)
	171	125–215			(88)
	187	155–227	84	Tasmania	E. R. Guiler, pers. com.; (112)
	205		1	captivity	(339)
Black-necked	150		3	captivity	(280)
	148	129–184	16	captivity	(339)
Bewick's	184·5	175–192	5	captivity	(339)
Whistling	179	170·5–189·5	8	captivity, hatched from wild eggs taken at Hazen Bay, Alaska	(303)
Whooper	200			captivity?	(134)
	227	224–230	2	captivity	(339)
Trumpeter	204·5	190–231·5	15	captivity	(339)
	205·5	198·5–212·5	2	captivity, Montana	(14)
	207·5	192–223	4	captivity, Philadelphia	(109)
	215·5		1	captivity, Delta, Manitoba	C. Nelson, pers. com.
	217·5	210–225	2	Copper River, Alaska	(297)

PLATE 47 'The Wild Swans' by Arthur Gaskin (1862–1928) illustrates a common legend of humans changed into swans (page 155). Collection Mrs. J. V. C. Turner. *E. E. Jackson*.

PLATE 48 'Swan Upping' by Stanley Spencer (1891–1959). *The Tate Gallery, London.*

References

1 ACLAND, C. M. 1923. Notes on Bewick's Swan in Glamorganshire. *Brit. Birds 17: 63–64.*

2 AINSWORTH, G. C. and REWELL, R. E. 1949. The incidence of aspergillosis in captive wild birds. *J. Comp. Path. Ther. 59: 213–24.*

3 AIREY, A. F. 1955. Whooper Swans in southern Lakeland. *Bird Study 2: 143–50.*

4 ALBIN, E. 1731–38. *A Natural History of Birds.* London.

5 AMMANN, G. A. 1937. Number of contour feathers in *Cygnus* and *Xanthocephalus*. *Auk 54: 201–2.*

6 ARMSTRONG, E. A. 1947. *Bird Display and Behaviour.* Oxford: Lindsay Drummond.

7 ARMSTRONG, E. A. 1970. *The Folklore of Birds.* New York: Dover Pub.

8 ARNOLD, SIR E. 1882. *The Light of Asia.* London: Trutner & Co.

9 ATKINSON-WILLES, G. L. 1969. The mid-winter distribution of wildfowl in Europe, northern Africa and south-west Asia, 1967 and 1968. *Wildfowl 20: 98–111.*

10 AUDUBON, J. J. 1840. *The Birds of America.* Edinburgh.

11 AVERY, R. A. 1966. Helminth parasites of wildfowl from Slimbridge, Gloucestershire. I. Parasites of captive Anatidae. *J. Helminthol. 40: 269–80.*

12 BAGLEY, G. E. and LOCKE, L. N. 1967. The occurrence of lead in tissues of wild birds. *Bull. Environ. Contam. Toxicol. 2: 297–305.*

13 BALTZER, E. 1955. Verhalten eines Schwans gegenüber weissen Jungen. *Orn. Beob. 52: 62.*

14 BANKO, W. E. 1960. The Trumpeter Swan. *North American Fauna No. 63:* U.S.F.W.S., Washington.

15 BANKO, W. E. and MACKAY, R. H. 1964. Our native swans. In: *Waterfowl Tomorrow*, ed. J. P. Linduska. Washington, D.C.: U.S. Dept. of Interior.

16 BANNERMAN, D. A. 1957. *The Birds of the British Isles. Vol. 6.* London: Oliver and Boyd.

17 BARING-GOULD, S. 1872. *Curious myths of the Middle Ages.* London: Rivingtons.

18 BAUER, K. M. and GLUTZ V. BLOTZHEIM, U.N. 1968. *Handbuch der Vögel Mitteleuropas.* Frankfurt: Akademische Verlagsgesellschaft.

19 BAXTER, E. V. and RINTOUL, L. J. 1953. *The Birds of Scotland. Vol. 2.* Edinburgh: Oliver and Boyd.

20 BEER, J. V. 1960. The aetiology and epidemiology of aspergillosis in the Anatidae and the Laridae. Ph.D. Thesis, Bristol University.

21 BEER, J. V. 1968. Post-mortem findings in oiled auks dying during attempted rehabilitation. *Suppl. Field Studies 2: 123–29.*

22 BEER, J. V. 1968. The attempted rehabilitation of oiled sea birds. *Wildfowl 19: 120–24.*

23 BEER, J. V. 1969. Isolation of pathogenic fungi from waterfowl. In: *Isolation methods for microbiologists.* London: Academic Press.

24 BEER, J. V. and STANLEY, P. 1965. Lead poisoning in the Slimbridge wildfowl collection. *Wildfowl Trust Ann. Rep. 16: 30–34.*

25 BELLROSE, F. C. 1964. Spent shot and lead poisoning. In: *Waterfowl Tomorrow,* ed. J. P. Linduska. Washington, D.C.: U.S. Dept. of Interior.

26 BENT, A. C. 1925. Life Histories of North American Wild Fowl. *U.S. National Museum Bulletin 130, Vol. 2.*

27 BERGLUND, B. E., CURRY-LINDAHL, K., LUTHER, H., OLSSON, V., RODHE, W. and SELLERBERG, G. 1963. Ecological studies on the Mute Swan (*Cygnus olor*) in Southeastern Sweden. *Acta Vertebratica 2: 167–288.*

28 BIGGS, P. M. 1967. Marek's disease. *Vet. Rec. 81: 583–92*

29 BLAAUW, F. E. 1904. On the breeding of some of the waterfowl at Gooilust in the year 1903. *Ibis 46: 67–75.*

30 BLANDFORD, T. B., ROBERTS, T. A. and ASHTON, W. L. G. 1969. Losses from botulism in Mallard duck and other water fowl. *Vet. Rec. 85: 541–43.*

31 BLOCH, D. 1970. Knopsvanen (*Cygnus olor*) som kolonifugl i Danmark. *Dansk. orn. For. Tids. 64: 152–62.*

32 BLOMFIELD, C. D. and BLACK, M. J. S. 1963. Black Swans feeding on willow leaves. *Notornis 10: 189.*

33 BOASE, H. 1959. Notes on the display, nesting and moult of the Mute Swan. *Brit. Birds 52: 114–23.*

34 BOASE, H. 1965. Movements of the Mute Swan in East Scotland. *Scot. Birds 3: 301–10.*

35 BOLAM, G. 1912. *Birds of Northumberland and the Eastern Borders.* Alnwick: Hunter Blair.

36 BOUGHTON, E. 1965. *Sarconema eurycerca* in the Mute Swan. *J. Helminthol. 39: 125.*

37 BOUGHTON, E. 1969. Tuberculosis caused by *Mycobacterium avium*. *Vet. Bull. 39: 457–65.*

38 BOUVIER, G. and HÖRNING, B. 1965. La pathologie du cygne tuberculé (*Cygnus olor* Gmelin) en Suisse. *Mem. Soc. Vaud. Sci. Nat. 14: 1–36.*

39 BOYD, H. and ELTRINGHAM, S. K. 1962. The Whooper Swan in Great Britain. *Bird Study 9: 217–41.*

40 BRAITHWAITE, L. W. and FRITH, H. J. 1969. Waterfowl in an inland swamp in New South Wales. III. Breeding. *CSIRO Wildl. Res. 14: 65–109.*

41 BROUWER, G. A. and TINBERGEN, L. 1939. De Verspreiding der Kleine Zwanen *Cygnus b. bewickii* Yarr. in de Zuiderzee, voor en na de verzoeting. *Limosa 12: 1–18.*

42 BYKHOVETS, A. V. 1966. Periodic cooling of eggs during incubation and increase in viability in poultry. *World Poultry Congress 13: 520–25.*

43 CAMPBELL, B. 1960. The Mute Swan census in England and Wales 1955–56. *Bird Study 7: 208–23.*

44 CAWKELL, E. M. and HAMILTON, J. E. 1961. The birds of the Falkland Islands. *Ibis 103a: 1–27.*

45 CHAPMAN, F. M. 1943. *Birds and Man.* New York: American Museum of Natural History, Guide Leaflet Series No. 115.

46 CHERRY, J. 1969. The Dunstable swan jewel. *J. Brit. Arch. Assoc. 32: 38–53.*

47 CHRISTIANSEN, M. 1952. Coccidiosis in wild waterbirds (Anseriformes). *Eimeria somateriae* n.sp. in the Eiderduck (*Somateria mollissima* (L)). *Nord. Vet. Medo. 4: 1173–91* (in Danish).

48 CHRISTOLEIT, E. 1926. Bemerkungen zur Biologie der Schwäne. *J. Orn. 74: 464–90.*

49 CHUPP, N. R. and DALKE, P. D. 1964. Waterfowl mortality in the Cœur D'Alene river valley, Idaho. *J. Wildl. Mgmt. 28: 692–702.*

50 CHUTE, H. L., O'MEARA, D. C. and BARDEN, E. S. 1962. A bibliography of avian mycosis. (Partially annotated). *Orono, Maine Agricultural Experimental Station, Misc. Publ. 655.*

51 CLARK, R. B. and KENNEDY, J. R. 1968. *Rehabilitation of oiled seabirds.* Newcastle upon Tyne: The University.

52 CLAUSEN, L. and HANSEN, P. M. 1967. Knopsvaner i Guldborgsund. *Feltornithologen 9: 7.*

REFERENCES

53 COATNEY, G. R. and ROUDABUSH, R. L. 1936. A catalog and host-index of the genus *Plasmodium*. *J. Parasitol. 22: 338–53.*

54 COBB, A. F. 1933. *Birds of the Falkland Islands.* London: Witherby.

55 COBURN, D. R., METZLER, D. W. and TREICHLER, R. 1951. A study of absorption and retention of lead in wild waterfowl in relation to clinical evidence of lead poisoning. *J. Wildl. Mgmt. 15: 186–92.*

56 COPLEY, R. A. 1963. Notes on Black-necked Swans. *Avic. Mag. 69: 48–50.*

57 CORDEAUX, J. 1898. *British Birds, their Nests and Eggs. Order Anseres. Vol. 4.* London.

58 CORNWELL, G. 1963. Observations on waterfowl mortality in southern Manitoba caused by *Echinuria uncinata* (Nematoda, Acuariidae). *Canad. J. Zool. 42: 699–703.*

59 COWAN, I. M. 1946. Death of a Trumpeter Swan from multiple parasitism. *Auk 53: 248–49.*

60 CRAWSHAY, R. 1907. *The Birds of Tierra del Fuego.* London: Bernard Quaritch.

61 CUNNINGHAM, R. L. 1962. Breeding Black Swans. *Game Breeders Gazette 2: 23.*

62 CUTTEN, F. E. A. 1966. Clutch size and egg dimensions of the Black Swan *Cygnus atratus* at Lake Ellesmere, Canterbury, New Zealand. *Emu 65: 223–25.*

63 DELACOUR, J. 1948. The Swans. *Avic. Mag. 54: 180–85.*

64 DELACOUR, J. 1954. *The Waterfowl of the World, Vol. 1.* London: Country Life.

65 DELACOUR, J. and MAYR, E. 1945. The family Antidae. *Wilson Bull. 57: 3–55.*

66 DEMENTIEV, G. P. and GLADKOV, N. A. 1952. *The Birds of the Soviet Union, Vol. 4.* Moscow (in Russian).

67 DEWER, J. M. 1936. Ménage à trois in the Mute Swan. *Brit. Birds 30: 178.*

68 DEWER, J. M. 1942. The Mute Swan and the 20–10 seconds rule. *Brit. Birds 35: 224–26.*

69 DIAMOND, L. S. and SERMAN, C. M. 1954. Incidence of trypanosomes in the Canada Goose as revealed by bone marrow culture. *J. Parasitol. 40: 195–202.*

70 DILLON, M. 1948. *Early Irish Literature.* Chicago: University of Chicago Press.

71 DIXON, C. 1893. *The Game Birds and Wild Fowl of the British Islands*. London: Chapman and Hall.

72 DIXON, J. 1931. Save the Trumpeter Swan. *American Forests 37: 492*.

73 DORSSEN, V. A. VAN and KUNST, H. 1955. Over de gevoeligheid van eenden en diverse andere watervogels voor eendenpest. *Tijdschr v. Diergeneesk 80: 1286–95*.

74 DOWNIE, W. B. 1961. Whooper Swan Investigation 1960–61. Unpublished report to Dept. of Agric. and Fish for Scotland.

75 DRESSER, H. E. 1871–81. *A History of the Birds of Europe*. London.

76 ELLIS, J. 1936. Ménage à trois in the Mute Swan. *Brit. Birds 30: 232*.

77 ELTRINGHAM, S. K. 1963. The British population of the Mute Swan in 1961. *Bird Study 10: 10–28*.

78 ELTRINGHAM, S. K. 1963. Is the Mute Swan a menace? *Bird Notes 30: 285–89*.

79 ELTRINGHAM, S. K. 1966. The survival of Mute Swan cygnets. *Bird Study 13: 204–7*.

80 FAIN, A. and HERIN, V. 1957. Deux cas de rhinosporidiose nasale chez une Oie et un Canard sauvages a Astrida (Ruanda-Urundi). *Mycopathologia 8: 54–61*.

81 FALLIS, A. M. and WOOD, D. M. 1957. Biting midges (Diptera: Ceratopogonidae) as intermediate hosts for *Haemoproteus* of ducks. *Canad. J. Zool. 35: 425–35*.

82 FINLAYSON, R. 1965. Spontaneous arterial disease in exotic animals. *J. Zool. 147: 239–343*.

83 FLEMING, J. H. 1908. The destruction of Whistling Swans (*Olor columbianus*) at Niagara Falls. *Auk 25: 306–9*.

84 FORREST, H. E. 1922. Bewick's Swans in Cumberland and Shropshire. *Brit. Birds 15: 189*.

85 FRAZER, J. G. 1898. *Pausanias's Description of Greece*. London.

86 FREME, S. W. P. 1931. Ornithological notes from North Uist, Outer Hebrides. *Brit. Birds 24: 369–71*.

87 FRENCH, C. 1904. Tuberculosis in the Arctic Swan, *Olor columbianus*. *Am. Vet. Rev. 28: 41*.

88 FRITH, H. J. 1967. *Waterfowl in Australia*. Sydney: Angus and Robertson.

89 GAVIN, A. 1947. Birds of Perry River district, Northwest Territories. *Wilson Bull. 59: 195–203*.

90 GÉROUDET, P. 1956. Des Cygnes sauvages sur le Léman. *Nos Oiseaux 23: 323–25.*

91 GÉROUDET, P. 1962. L'hivernage des Cygnes de Bewick sur le Léman savoyard. *Nos Oiseaux 26: 317–19.*

92 GÉROUDET, P. 1963. Retour des Cygnes de Bewick sur le Léman. *Nos Oiseaux 27: 181–82.*

93 GIBSON, E. 1880. Ornithological notes from the neighbourhood of Cape San Antonio, Buenos Ayres. *Ibis 4: 1–38, 153–69.*

94 GIBSON, E. 1920. Further ornithological notes from the neighbourhood of Cape San Antonio, Buenos Ayres. *Ibis 11: 1–97.*

95 GILLHAM, M. E. 1956. Feeding habits and seasonal movements of Mute Swans in south Devon estuaries. *Bird Study 3: 205–12.*

96 GLOOR, K. 1966. Bilder zum Aggressivverhalten des Höckerschwans. *Cygnus olor. Orn. Beob. 63: 76–77.*

97 GODIN, A. J. 1967. Test of grit types in alleviating lead poisoning in mallards. *U.S. Dept. Int. Spec. Sci. Rep. Wildl. 107: 1–9.*

98 GOETHE, F. 1965. Weissfische als Trabanten des Höckerschwans. *Natur Mus. 95: 116–17.*

99 GOODALL, J. D., JOHNSON, A. W. and PHILIPPI, R. A. 1951. *Las Aves de Chile, Vol. 2.* Buenos Aires: Platt Establecimientos Gráficos.

100 GOODMAN, D. C. and FISHER, H. I. 1962. *Functional Anatomy of the Feeding Apparatus in Waterfowl.* Carbondale: Southern Illinois University Press.

101 GORDON, A. 1922. Nesting of the Whooper Swan in Scotland. *Brit. Birds 15: 170.*

102 GOULD, J. 1862–73. *The Birds of Great Britain.* London.

103 GOULD, J. 1865. *Handbook to the Birds of Australia.* London.

104 GRANT, C. H. B. 1911. List of birds collected in Argentina, Paraguay, Bolivia and southern Brazil, with field-notes. Part 2. *Ibis 9: 317–49.*

105 GRAVES, R. 1960. *The Greek Myths.* London: Penguin Books.

106 GRAY, A. P. 1958. *Bird Hybrids.* Commonwealth Agric. Bureaux.

107 GREENWOOD, J. J. D. and KEDDIE, J. P. F. 1968. Birds killed by oil in the Tay Estuary, March and April 1968. *Scot. Birds 5: 189–96.*

108 GRIMM, J. and W. 1819–22. *Kinder- und Hausmärchen.* Berlin.

109 GRISWOLD, J. A. 1965. We raise the first Trumpeter Swans. *America's First Zoo 17: 17–20.*

110 GRITMAN, R. B. and JENSEN, W. I. 1965. Avian cholera in a Trumpeter Swan (*Olor buccinator*). *Bull. Wildl. Dis. Ass. 1: 54–55.*

111   GRUBB, W. B. 1964. Avian botulism in Western Australia. *Aust. J. Expt. Biol. Med. Sci. 42: 17–26.*

112   GUILER, E. R. 1966. The breeding of Black Swan (*Cygnus atrata* Latham) in Tasmania with special reference to some management problems. *Pap. proc. R. Soc. Tasm. 100: 31–52.*

113   GUILER, E. R. 1970. The use of breeding sites of Black Swans in Tasmania. *Emu 70: 3–8.*

114   HALLA, B. F. 1966. *The Mute Swan in Rhode Island.* Paper presented at Northeast Wildlife Conf., Boston, Mass.

115   HAMERTON, A. E. 1941. Report on the deaths occurring in the society's gardens during the years 1939–40. *Proc. zool. Soc. Lond. 109(B): 151.*

116   HANCOCK, C. G. 1969. Observations on Whooper Swans *Cygnus cygnus* in North Central Iceland, August 1969. Unpublished note on visit to Iceland 1969.

117   HANKLA, D. J. 1968. Summary of Canada Goose transplant program on nine National Wildlife Refuges in the southeast, 1953–65. In: *Canada Goose Management,* ed. R. L. Hine and C. Schoenfeld. Madison, Wisconsin.

118   HANSON, H. C., LEVINE, N. D. and IVENS, V. 1957. Coccidia (Protozoa: Eimeriidae) of North American wild geese and swans. *Canad. J. Zool. 34: 715–33.*

119   HANSON, H. C., QUENEAU, P. and SCOTT, P. 1956. *The Geography, Birds, and Mammals of the Perry River Region.* Arctic Institute of North America.

120   HANTZSCH, B. 1905. *Beitrag zur Kenntnis der Vogelwelt Islands.* Berlin: Friedlander.

121   HARLE, D. F. 1951. Mute Swans feeding on standing oats. *Brit. Birds 44: 287–88.*

122   HARRISON, J. G. 1958. Tuberculosis in wildfowl. *Wildfowl Trust Ann. Rep. 9: 70–71.*

123   HARRISON, J. G. 1963. Heavy mortality of Mute Swans from electrocution. *Wildfowl Trust Ann. Rep. 14: 164–65.*

124   HARRISON, J. G. and BUCK, W. F. A. 1967. Peril in perspective. *Suppl. Kent Bird Rep. 16: 1–23.*

125   HARRISON, J. G. and OGILVIE, M. A. 1967. Immigrant Mute Swans in south-east England. *Wildfowl Trust Ann. Rep. 18: 85–87.*

126   HARRISON, J. M. 1963. Aspergillosis in an immature Bewick's Swan. *Wildfowl Trust Ann. Rep. 14: 165.*

127 HARTUNG, R. 1967. Energy metabolism in oil-covered birds. *J. Wildl. Mgmt. 31: 798–804.*

128 HARTUNG, R. and HUNT, G. S. 1966. Toxicity of some oils to waterfowl. *J. Wildl. Mgmt. 30: 564–70.*

129 HATTO, A. T. 1961. The Swan Maiden. A folk-tale of north Eurasian origin? *School of Oriental and African Studies Bull. 24: 326–52.*

130 HATTO, A. T. 1965. *Eos.* The Hague: Mouton.

131 HAWKER, P. 1893. *The Diary of Col. Peter Hawker.* London: Longmans.

132 HEINROTH, O. 1911. Beiträge zur Biologie, namentlich Ethologie und Psychologie der Anatiden. *Proc. Int. Ornith. Congr. 5: 598–702.*

133 HEINROTH, O. 1922. Die Beziehungen zwischen Vogelgewicht, Eigewicht, Gelegegewicht und Brutdauer. *J. Orn. 70: 172–285.*

134 HEINROTH, O. and M. 1928. *Die Vögel Mitteleuropas, Vol. 3.* Berlin.

135 HELLEBREKERS, W. P. J. 1950. *Measurements and Weights of eggs of birds on the Dutch List.* Leiden: Brill.

136 HERMAN, C. M. 1954. Haemoproteus infections in waterfowl. *Proc. Helminthol. Soc. Washington 21: 37–42.*

137 HERMAN, C. M. 1969. Blood protozoa of free-living birds. *Symp. zool. Soc. Lond. 24: 177–95.*

138 HERMAN, C. M. and SLADEN, W. J. L. 1958. Aspergillosis in waterfowl. *Trans. N. Am. Wildl. Conf. 23: 187–91.*

139 HESS, G. 1951. *The Bird; its Life and Structure.* London: Herbert Jenkins.

140 HEWSON, R. 1964. Herd composition and dispersion in the Whooper Swan. *Brit. Birds 57: 26–31.*

141 HILPRECHT, A. 1956. *Höckerschwan, Singschwan, Zwergschwan.* Wittenberg: Neue Brehm-Bücherei.

142 HOLDEN, B. L. and SLADEN, W. J. L. 1968. Heart worm, *Sarconema eurycerca,* infection in Whistling Swans, *Cygnus columbianus,* in Chesapeake Bay. *Bull. Wildl. Dis. Ass. 4: 126–28.*

143 HOWARD, W. J. H. 1935. Notes on the nesting of captive Mute Swans. *Wilson Bull. 47: 237–38.*

144 HUFF, C. C. 1932. Studies on Haemoproteus of Mourning Doves. *Am. J. Hyg. 16: 618–23.*

145 HULME, D. C. 1948. Mute Swan eating dead fish. *Brit. Birds 41: 121.*

146 HUME, O. A. and MARSHALL, C. H. T. 1878. *The Game-Birds of India, China and Ceylon.* Calcutta.

147 HUMPHREY, P. S., BRIDGE, D., REYNOLDS, P. W. and PETERSON, R. T. 1970. *Birds of Isla Grande (Tierra del Fuego).* Washington: Smithsonian Institution.

148 HUXLEY, J. S. 1947. Display of the Mute Swan. *Brit. Birds 40: 130–34.*

149 INTERNATIONAL WILDFOWL RESEARCH BUREAU. 1966. *Legislative and Administrative measures for Wildfowl Conservation in Europe and North Africa.* Le Sambuc, France.

150 IRBY, H. D., LOCKE, L. N. and BAGLEY, G. E. 1967. Relative toxicity of lead and selected substitute shot types to game farm Mallards. *J. Wildl. Mgmt. 31: 253–57.*

151 ISAKOV, Y. A. 1968. Results of the mid-winter waterfowl census in the U.S.S.R. in January 1967. *Booklet of the Moscow Association, Biological Section 4: 92–114.* (In Russian with English summary.)

152 JÄGER, G. F. 1816. Über die Entstehung von Schimmel im Innern des thierischen Körpers. *Deutches Archiv für die Physiologie 2: 354–56.*

153 JARL, M. 1964. *The Legends of Moonie Jarl.* Brisbane.

154 JENNINGS, A. R. 1959. Diseases of wild birds, fifth report. *Bird Study 6: 19–22.*

155 JENNINGS, A. R. 1959. Causes of death of birds at Slimbridge, 1955–57. *Wildfowl Trust Ann. Rep. 10: 37–40.*

156 JENNINGS, A. R. 1969. Tumours of free-living wild mammals and birds in Great Britain. *Symp. zool. Soc. Lond. 24: 273–87.*

157 JENNINGS, A. R. and SOULSBY, E. J. L. 1956. Diseases in wild birds, third report. *Bird Study 3: 270–72.*

158 JENNINGS, A. R., SOULSBY, E. J. L. and WAINWRIGHT, C. B. 1961. An outbreak of disease in Mute Swans at an Essex reservoir. *Bird Study 8: 19–24.*

159 JENSEN, F. 1967. Knopsvanen (*Cygnus olor*) som ynglefugl ved Bognaes. *Dansk Orn. For. Tids. 61: 143–50.*

160 JENSEN, W. I. and ALLEN, J. P. 1960. A possible relationship between aquatic invertebrates and avian botulism. *Trans. N. Am. Wildl. Nat Res. Conf. 25: 171–80.*

161 JOGI, A. 1968. The present distribution of the Mute Swan in the

Estonian S.S.R. *Communication of the Baltic Commission for the Study of Bird Migration 5: 74–79.* (In Russian with English summary.)

162   JOHNSGARD, P. A. 1965. *Handbook of Waterfowl Behavior.* Ithaca: Cornell University Press.

163   JOHNSGARD, P. A. and KEAR, J. 1968. A review of parental carrying of young by waterfowl. *Living Bird 7: 89–102.*

164   JOHNSON, A. W. and GOODALL, J. D. 1965. *The Birds of Chile, Vol. 1.* Buenos Aires: Platt Establecimientos Gráficos.

165   JOHNSON, M. E. 1956. *Translation of Swans, Cygnets, and Owl.* Columbia: University of Missouri Studies 29.

166   JOHNSTONE, S. T. 1953. The Severn Wildfowl Trust – notes on the breeding season 1952. *Avic. Mag. 59: 34–35.*

167   JOHNSTONE, S. T. 1957. Breeding of Bewick's Swans. *Avic. Mag. 63: 27–28.*

168   JOHNSTONE, S. T. 1965. 1964 breeding results at the Wildfowl Trust. *Avic. Mag. 71: 20–23.*

169   JONES, C. A. 1918. *British Birds in their Haunts.* London: S.P.C.K.

170   JONES, T. 1947. Nesting swans. *Avic. Mag. 53: 206–9.*

171   JORDAN, J. S. and BELLROSE, F. C. 1951. Lead poisoning in wild waterfowl. *Illinois Nat. Hist. Surv. Biol. Notes 26: 1–27.*

172   JOURDAIN, F. C. R. 1911. Exhibit of Bewick's eggs. *Bull. B.O.C. 27: 58.*

173   JOYCE, P. W. 1879. *Old Celtic Romances.* London: David Nutt (reprinted 1961, Dublin: Talbot Press).

174   KEAR, J. 1963. The history of potato-eating by wildfowl in Britain. *Wildfowl Trust Ann. Rep. 14: 54–65.*

175   KEAR, J. 1964. The changing status of the Greylag Goose and the Whooper Swan on agricultural land in Iceland. Unpublished report to the Ministry of Agriculture, Reykjavik.

176   KEAR, J. 1964. Colour preference in young Anatidae. *Ibis 106: 361–69.*

177   KEAR, J. 1968. The calls of very young Anatidae. *Beihefte der Vogelwelt 1: 93–113.*

178   KEAR, J. 1970. The adaptive radiation of parental care in waterfowl. In: *Social Behaviour in Birds and Mammals,* ed. J. H. Crook. London: Academic Press.

179   KEITH, A. B. 1917. Indian Mythology. In: *The Mythology of all the Races, Vol. 6.* New York.

180   KENNEDY, P. G., RUTTLEDGE, R. F. and SCROOPE, C. F. 1954. *The Birds of Ireland*. Edinburgh: Oliver and Boyd.

181   KERBERT, C. 1912. Eenige mededeelingen over *Cygnus cygnus* L. *Ardea 1: 87–92*.

182   KERSHAW, N. 1921. *Stories and Ballads of the Far Past*. Cambridge: Cambridge University Press.

183   KEYMER, I. F. 1958. A survey and review of the causes of mortality in British birds and the significance of wild birds as disseminators of disease. *Vet. Rec. 70: 713–20, 736–40*.

184   KIKKAWA, J. and YAMASHINA, Y. 1967. Breeding of introduced Black Swans in Japan. *Emu 66: 377–81*.

185   KING, B. 1957. Feeding association between Bewick's Swan and Mallard. *Brit. Birds 50: 439*.

186   KING, B. 1962. Raw meat as a food for Mute Swans. *Wildfowl Trust Ann. Rep. 13: 171*.

187   KING, J. G. 1968. Trumpeter Swan survey – Alaska 1968. *U.S. Dept. Int., Fish and Wildl.*

188   KLUGE, J. 1967. Avian parasitic (*Sarconema eurycerca*) pericarditis. *Bull. Wildl. Dis. Ass. 3: 114–17*.

189   KORTRIGHT, F. H. 1943. *The Ducks, Geese and Swans of North America*. Washington: American Wildlife Institute.

190   KÖSSLER-ILG, B. 1956. *Indianer Märchen aus den Kordilleren*. Düsseldorf: F. von der Leyen.

191   LACK, D. 1966. *Population Studies of Birds*. Oxford: Clarendon Press.

192   LACK, D. 1967. The significance of clutch-size in waterfowl. *Wildfowl Trust Ann. Rep. 18: 125–28*.

193   LACK, D. 1968. The proportion of yolk in the eggs of waterfowl. *Wildfowl 19: 67–69*.

194   LAPAGE, G. 1961. A list of the parasitic Protozoa, Helminths and Arthropoda recorded from species of the family Anatidae (Ducks, Geese and Swans). *Parasitol. 51: 1–109*.

195   *Larousse Encyclopedia of Mythology*. 1959. London: Batchworth Press.

196   LARRSSON, K. and ODHAM, G. 1970. Larodan for cleaning oiled seabirds. *Marine Poll. Bull. 1: 122–24*.

197   LAVERY, H. J. 1964. An investigation of the biology and ecology of waterfowl in North Queensland. Unpublished M.Sc. Thesis, University of Queensland.

REFERENCES

198 LAVERY, H. J. 1967. The Black Swan in Queensland. *Dept. Primary Industries, Div. of Plant Industry, Advisory Leaflet No. 911.*

199 LEIBOVITZ, L. 1969. The comparative pathology of duck plague in wild Anseriformes. *J. Wildl. Mgmt. 33: 294–303.*

200 LENSINK, C. J. 1968. Clarence Rhode National Wildlife Range. Annual Report 1968. *U.S. Dept. Int., Fish and Wildl.*

201 LEVINE, N. D. 1953. A review of the Coccidia from the avian orders Galliformes, Anseriformes and Charadriiformes, with descriptions of three new species. *Am. Midl. Nat. 49: 696–719.*

202 LEWIN, W. 1789–94. *The Birds of Great Britain.* London.

203 LINDSAY, S. and CHAIKOFF, I. L. 1963. Naturally occurring arteriosclerosis in animals: a comparison with experimentally induced lesions. In: *Atherosclerosis and its Origin.* London: Academic Press.

204 LINT, K. C. 1966. Cygnets from the south . . . Black-necked Swans. *Zoonooz 39: 16–19.*

205 LOCKE, L. N., BAGLEY, G. E. and IRBY, H. D. 1966. Acid-fast intranuclear inclusion bodies in the kidneys of Mallards fed lead shot. *Bull. Wildl. Dis. Ass. 2: 127–31.*

206 LOMBARD, L. S. and WITTE, E. J. 1959. Frequency of types of tumors in mammals and birds of the Philadelphia Zoological Garden. *Cancer Res. 19: 127–41.*

207 LOOMIS, R. S. 1927. *Celtic Myth and Arthurian Romance.* New York: Columbia University Press.

208 LOW, G. C. 1935. The extent to which captivity modifies the habits of birds. *Bull. B.O.C. 55: 144–54.* Edited paper by the Marquess of Tavistock.

209 LUM, B. P. 1952. *Fabulous Beasts.* London: Thames and Hudson.

210 LUTHER, H. 1963. Ecological studies on the Mute Swan. IX. Botanical analysis of Mute Swan faeces. *Acta Vertebratica 2: 265–67.*

211 LYNCH, J. J. 1966–70. Productivity and mortality among Geese, Swans and Brant. Annual Research Progress Reports of the Lafayette Station, Patuxent Wildlife Research Center, U.S. Bureau of Sport Fisheries and Wildlife.

212 MCCOY, J. J. 1967. *Swans.* New York: Lothrop, Lee and Shepard.

213 MCDIARMID, A. 1962. Diseases of free-living wild animals. *F.A.O. Agric. Studies 57: 1–119.*

214 MACDONALD, J. W. 1962. Mortality in wild birds with some observations on weights. *Bird Study 9: 147–67.*

215 MCDONALD, M. E. 1969. Annotated bibliography of helminths of waterfowl (Anatidae). *U.S. Dept. Int. Spec. Sci. Rep. Wildl. 125: 1–333.*

216 MCDONALD, M. E. 1969. Catalogue of helminths of waterfowl (Anatidae). *U.S. Dept. Int. Spec. Sci. Rep. Wildl. 126: 1–692.*

217 MCKEOWN, K. C. 1938. *The Land of Byamee.* Sydney: Angus and Robertson.

218 MCKINNEY, D. F. 1965. The comfort movements of Anatidae. *Behaviour 25: 120–220.*

219 MACMILLAN, A. T. 1968. Whooper deaths. *Scot. Birds 5: 111–12.*

220 MACSWINEY, MARQUIS. 1971. *Six Came Flying.* London: Michael Joseph.

221 MACWILLIAM, G. P. 1959. White cygnets of Mute Swans at Dalbeattie. *Scot. Birds 1: 93–94.*

222 MARSHALL, F. H. A. 1936. Sexual periodicity and the causes which determine it. *Phil. Trans. Roy. Soc. 226: 423–56.*

223 MARSHALL, R. V. A. 1950. Large brood of Mute Swans. *Brit. Birds 43: 19.*

224 MARTIN, A. C., ZIM, H. S. and NELSON, A. L. 1951. *American Wildlife and Plants.* New York: McGraw Hill.

225 MARTIN, E. M. 1970. Results of the 1969 Whistling Swan season. *Admin. Rep., Migratory Bird Populations, Laurel, Maryland 183: 1–3.*

226 MAY, D. J. 1947. Notes on the winter territory of a pair of Mute Swans. *Brit. Birds 40: 326–27.*

227 MAYFIELD, H. 1952. Captive Whooper Swans, *Cygnus cygnus*, kill other waterfowl. *Auk 69: 461–62.*

228 MIERS, K. H. and WILLIAMS, M. 1969. Nesting of the Black Swan at Lake Ellesmere, New Zealand. *Wildfowl 20: 23–32.*

229 MILNE-EDWARDS, M. A. 1897. Note sur une incubation complète faite par un mâle de Cygne Noir (*Cygnus atratus* Lath.). *Bull. Mus. d'Hist. Nat. 5: 165–66.*

230 MINTON, C. D. T. 1968. Pairing and breeding of Mute Swans. *Wildfowl 19: 41–60.*

231 MITCHELL, P. C. 1911. On longevity and relative viability in mammals and birds; with a note on the theory of longevity. *Proc. zoo. Soc. Lond.: 425–49.*

232 MONNIE, J. B. 1966. Reintroduction of the Trumpeter Swan to its former prairie breeding range. *J. Wildl. Mgmt. 30: 691–96.*

233 MOURASHKA, I. P. and VALIUS, M. I. 1961. Natural reacclimatisation of the Mute Swan in Lithuania and neighbouring territories. *Proc. Baltic Orn. Cong. 4: 71–80.* (In Russian.)

234 MÜLLER, (Ed.) 1876–78. Two Irish Tales. *Revue Celtique 3: 342–60.*

235 MUNRO, R. E., SMITH, L. T. and KUPA, J. J. 1968. The genetic basis of color differences observed in the Mute Swan (*Cygnus olor*). *Auk 85: 504–5.*

236 MYRBERGET, S. 1962. Rugende sangsvaner på Senja. *Sterna 5: 45–48.*

237 NAGEL, J. 1965. Field feeding of Whistling Swans in northern Utah. *Condor 67: 446–47.*

238 NEWTON, A. 1893–96. *A Dictionary of Birds.* London: A. and C. Black.

239 NIETHAMMER, G. 1938. *Handbuch der·deutschen Vogelkunde, Vol. 2.* Leipzig.

240 NISBET, I. C. T. 1955. Bewick's Swans in the fenlands: the past and present status. *Brit. Birds 48: 533–37.*

241 NISBET, I. C. T. 1959. Bewick's Swans in the British Isles in the winters of 1954–55 and 1955–56. *Brit. Birds 52: 393–416.*

242 OGILVIE, M. A. 1967. Population changes and mortality of the Mute Swan in Britain. *Wildfowl Trust Ann. Rep. 18: 64–73.*

243 OGILVIE, M. A. 1969. Bewick's Swans in Britain and Ireland during 1956–69. *Brit. Birds 62: 505–22.*

244 OGILVIE, M. A. and MATTHEWS, G. V. T. 1969. Brent Geese, mudflats and Man. *Wildfowl 20: 119–25.*

245 OLIVER, W. R. B. 1955. *New Zealand Birds,* 2nd ed. Wellington: Reed.

246 OLNEY, P. J. S. 1960. Lead poisoning in wildfowl. *Bull. B.O.C. 80: 35–40, 53–59.*

247 OLROG, C. C. 1959. *Las Aves Argentinas.* Tucumen, Argentina: Universidad Nacional de Tucuman.

248 OLSSON, V. 1963. Ecological studies on the Mute Swan. VIII. Nutritional biology of the Mute Swan in Valdemarsviken in Småland and Östergötland. *Acta Vertebratica 2: 256–64.*

249 O'RAHILLY, T. F. 1946. *Early Irish History and Mythology.* Dublin: Dublin Institute for Advanced Studies.

250 PALMER, C. C. and BAKER, H. R. 1923. A case of botulism in ducks and swans. *Poult. Sci. 2: 75–77.*

251 PALUDAN, K. and FOG, J. 1956. The Danish breeding population of wild living *Cygnus olor* in 1954. *Danske Vildt. 5: 3–45.*

252 PATRICK, R. W. 1935. Mute Swans attacking bullock. *Brit. Birds 29: 116.*

253 PAULY, A. F. VON and WISSOVA, G. 1893. *Real-Encyclopädie der classischen Altertumswissenschaft.* Stuttgart.

254 PENZER, N. M. 1927. *The ocean of story, Vol. 8.* London: C. J. Sawyer.

255 PERRINS, C. M. 1969. Mute Swan's method of disposing of broken egg. *Brit. Birds 62: 383.*

256 PERRINS, C. M. and REYNOLDS, C. M. 1967. A preliminary study of the Mute Swan, *Cygnus olor. Wildfowl Trust Ann. Rep. 18: 74–84.*

257 PETERS, N. 1931. 10 Jahre Brutstatistik und Entwicklung der Hamburger Alsterschwäne. *Abh. naturw. Ver. Hamburg 23.*

258 PLACE, E. H. 1920. Reported nesting of the Whooper in Perthshire. *Brit. Birds 14: 22.*

259 PLOT, R. 1686. *The Natural History of Staffordshire.* Oxford.

260 PLUMMER, C. 1910. *Vitae Sanctorum Hiberniae.* Oxford: Clarendon Press.

261 POLLARD, D. F. W. 1967. The W.A.G.B.I./Wildfowl Trust Experimental Reserve – the first eleven years. Part III. An appraisal of the planting programme, 1959–66. *Wildfowl Trust Ann. Rep. 18: 55–62.*

262 PORTIELJE, A. F. J. 1936. Ein bemerkenswerter Grenzfall von Polygamie bzw. accessorischer Promiskuität beim Höckerschwan, zugleich ein Beitrag zur Ethologie bzw. Psychologie von *Cygnus olor. J. Orn. 84: 140–58.*

263 PORTMANN, A. 1950. Développement postembryonnaire. In: *Traité de Zoologie, ed. P. P. Grassé.* Paris: Masson.

264 POULSEN, H. 1948. Bidrag til Svanernes Ethologi. *Dansk Orn. For. Tids. 42: 173–201.*

265 QUORTRUP, E. R. and SHILLINGER, J. E. 1941. 3000 wild bird autopsies on Western Lake areas. *J. Am. Vet. Med. Ass. 99: 382–87.*

266 RADFORD, C. D. 1958. The host-parasite relationships of the feather mites. *Rev. Brazil. Ent. 8: 107–70.*

267 RAPER, K. B. and FENNELL, D. I. 1965. *The Genus 'Aspergillus'.* Baltimore: Williams and Wilkins.

268 RATCLIFFE, H. L. 1946. Tuberculosis in wild birds. Decrease of its incidence following a change in diets. *Am. Rev. Tuberc. 54: 389–400.*

269 RATCLIFFE, H. L. 1961. *Report Penrose Res. Lab.* Philadelphia.

270 RATCLIFFE, H. L., HERASIMIDES, T. G. and ELLIOTT, G. A. 1960. Changes in the character and location of arterial lesions in mammals and birds in the Philadelphia Zoological Garden. *Circulation* *21: 730–38.*

271 RAWCLIFFE, C. P. 1958. The Scottish Mute Swan census, 1955–56. *Bird Study 5: 45–55.*

272 REES, A. and B. 1961. *Celtic Heritage.* London: Thames and Hudson.

273 REYNOLDS, C. M. 1965. The survival of Mute Swan cygnets. *Bird Study 12: 128–29.*

274 RIZHIKOV, K. M. and KASLAUSKAS, J. 1968. Occurrence of *Syngamus palustris* Rizhikov 1949 in swans. *Acta Parsit. Lith. 7: 91–95.* (In Russian.)

275 ROBERTS, B. B. 1934. Notes on the birds of Central and South-east Iceland with special reference to food-habits. *Ibis 76: 239–64.*

276 ROSEN, M. N. and BANKOWSKI, R. A. 1960. A diagnostic technic and treatment for lead poisoning in swans. *Calif. Fish and Game 46: 81–90.*

277 ROSEN, M. N. and MORSE, E. E. 1959. An interspecies chain in a fowl cholera epizootic. *Calif. Fish and Game 45: 51–56.*

278 ROSENIUS, P. 1937. *Sveriges Fàglar och Fögelbon, Vol. 4.* Lund.

279 ROSS, A. 1967. *Pagan Celtic Britain.* London: Routledge.

280 ROSSI, J. A. H. 1953. Contribución al conocimiento de la biología del cisne de cuello negro. *El Hornero 10: 1–17.*

281 RUTTLEDGE, R. F. 1963. Whooper Swans feeding on refuse dump. *Brit. Birds 56: 340.*

282 RUTTLEDGE, R. F. 1966. *Ireland's Birds.* London: Witherby.

283 SALOMONSEN, F. 1968. The moult migration. *Wildfowl 19: 5–24.*

284 SANDEN, W. VON. 1935. Beobachtungen an dem Schwanenbestand des Nordenburger Sees in Ostpreussen seit seiner Besiedlung mit *Cygnus olor. Orn. Mber. 43: 82–85.*

285 SCHIØLER, E. L. 1926. *Danmarks Fugle, Vol. 11.* Copenhagen.

286 SCHÖNWETTER, M. 1960–61. *Handbuch der Oologie,* ed. W. Meise. Berlin: Akademie-Verlag.

287 SCLATER, P. L. 1880. List of the certainly known species of Anatidae with notes on such as have been introduced into the Zoological gardens of Europe. *Proc. zoo. Soc. Lond.: 496–536.*

288 SCLATER, P. L. and HUDSON, W. H. 1889. *Argentine Ornithology.* London.

289 SCOTT, D. 1967. The Bewick's Swans at Slimbridge 1966–67. *Wildfowl Trust Ann. Rep. 18: 24–27.*

290 SCOTT, D. 1969. Wild swans at Slimbridge, 1968–69. *Wildfowl 20: 157–60.*

291 SCOTT, P. 1954. South America – 1953. *Wildfowl Trust Ann. Rep. 6: 55–69.*

292 SCOTT, P. 1966. The Bewick's Swans at Slimbridge. *Wildfowl Trust Ann. Rep. 17: 20–26.*

293 SCOTT, P., FISHER, J. and GUDMUNDSSON, F. 1953. The Severn Wildfowl Trust expedition to Central Iceland, 1951. *Wildfowl Trust Ann. Rep. 5: 79–115.*

294 SENEVIRATNA, P. 1969. *Diseases of Poultry (including Cage Birds).* Bristol: Wright.

295 SERMET, E. 1963. Des Cygnes de Bewick à Yverdon. *Nos Oiseaux 27: 181.*

296 SHARLAND, M. S. R. 1924. *The Vertebrate Animals of Tasmania.* Hobart: Lord and Scott.

297 SHEPHERD, P. E. K. 1962. An ecological reconnaissance of the Trumpeter Swan in south central Alaska. Unpublished M.Sc. Thesis, Washington State University.

298 SHERWOOD, G. A. 1960. The Whistling Swan in the west with particular reference to the Great Salt Lake Valley, Utah. *Condor 62: 370–77.*

299 SIBLEY, C. L. 1938. Hybrids of and with North American Anatidae. *Proc. Int. Orn. Cong. 9: 327–35.*

300 SIEGFRIED, W. R. 1970. Wildfowl distribution, conservation and research in southern Africa. *Wildfowl 21: 89–98.*

301 SIMON, J. R. 1952. First flight of Trumpeter Swans, *Cygnus buccinator. Auk 69: 462.*

302 SLADEN, W. J. L. and COCHRAN, W. W. 1969. Studies of the Whistling Swan, 1967–68. *Trans. N.A. Wildl. Nat. Res. Conf. 34: 42–50.*

303 SMART, G. 1965. Body weights of newly hatched Anatidae. *Auk 82: 645–48.*

304 SOKOLOVSKI, J. 1960. The Mute Swan in Poland. *State Council for Nature Conservation, Warsaw 1: 1–28.*

305 SOPER, M. F. 1960. Long incubation period of Black Swan. *Notornis 9: 61.*

306 SOULSBY, E. J. L. 1955. Deaths in swans associated with trematode infections. *Brit. Vet. J. 111: 498–99.*

307 SPÄRCK, R. 1958. An investigation of the food of swans and ducks in Denmark. *Trans. Cong. Int. Union Game Biol., 3: 45–47.*

308 STABLES, E. R. and NEW, N. D. 1968. Birds and aircraft: the problems. In: *The Problems of Birds as Pests.* London: Academic Press.

309 STAMM, D. D. 1966. Relationships of birds and arboviruses. *Auk 83: 84–97.*

310 STEJNEGER, L. 1882. Outlines of a monograph of the Cygninae. *Proc. U.S. Nat. Mus. 5: 174–221.*

311 STEVENSON, H. 1866. *Birds of Norfolk.* London: Van Voorst.

312 STEWART, H. L. 1966. Pulmonary cancer and adenomatosis in captive wild mammals and birds from the Philadelphia Zoo. *J. Natn. Cancer Inst. 36: 117–38.*

313 STEWART, R. E. and MANNING, J. H. 1958. Distribution and ecology of Whistling Swans in the Chesapeake Bay region. *Auk 75: 203–12.*

314 STUART, D. M. 1957. *A Book of Birds and Beasts.* London: Methuen.

315 SWAINSON, C. 1886. *Folklore of British Birds.* London: Folklore Society.

316 SWINHOE, R. 1870. Zoological notes of a journey from Canton to Peking and Kalgan. *Proc. zoo. Soc. Lond.: 427–51.*

317 SWIRE, O. F. 1964. *The Inner Hebrides and their Legends.* London: Collins.

318 TATE, J. and D. J. 1966. Additional records of Whistling Swans feeding in dry fields. *Condor 68: 398–99.*

319 TAYLOR, J. 1969. Salmonella in wild animals. *Symp. zool. Soc. Lond. 24: 51–73.*

320 TEMPLE, SIR R. 1884–86. *The Legends of the Panjab.* Bombay.

321 THOMPSON, S. 1929. *Tales of North American Indians.* Cambridge, Mass.: Harvard University Press.

322 THYSELIUS, B. 1968. Falsk albinism hos knölsvan (*Cygnus olor*) vid Kvismaren. *Vår Fågelvärld 27: 265.*

323 TICEHURST, N. F. 1957. *The Mute Swan in England.* London: Cleaver-Hume Press.

324 TRAINER, P. O. and HUNT, R. A. 1965. Lead poisoning of Whistling Swans in Wisconsin. *Avian Dis. 9: 252–63.*

325 TROYER, W. The Trumpeter Swan on the Kenai peninsula. In prep.

326　TURGARINOV, A. J. 1941. *Fauna of U.S.S.R. Aves, Vol. 4.* Moscow. (In Russian.)

327　TYLER, C. 1964. A study of the egg shells of the Anatidae. *Proc. zoo. Soc. Lond. 142: 547–83.*

328　URBAIN, A. 1938. Sur une epidémie de paratyphose constatée sur des cygnes blancs (*Cygnus olor* Gmelin), des Pelicans (*Pelecanus rufescens* Gmelin) et des canards sauvages (*Anas platyrhynchos* L.). *Bull. Soc. Path. Exot. 31: 268–70.*

329　URBAIN, A. and GUILLOT, G. 1938. Les aspergilloses aviaries. *Oiseau 8: 558–91.*

330　VALIUS, M. I. 1959. Data on the biology of the Mute Swan in Lithuania. *Ornitologiya 2: 221–27.* (In Russian.)

331　VAURIE, C. 1965. *The Birds of the Palaearctic Fauna: Non-Passeriformes.* London: Witherby.

332　VENABLES, L. S. V. and U. M. 1950. The Whooper Swans of Loch Spiggie, Shetland. *Scot. Nat. 62: 142–52.*

333　VENN, J. A. J. 1955. Pathological investigations. *Wildfowl Trust Ann. Rep. 7: 55–56.*

334　VIKSNE, J. 1968. Counts of the Mute Swan and White-tailed Eagle in Latvia. *Communication of the Baltic Commission for the Study of Bird Migration 5: 80–107.* (In Russian with English summary.)

335　VOS, A. DE. 1964. Observations on the behaviour of captive Trumpeter Swans during the breeding season. *Ardea 52: 166–89.*

336　WAGNER, SIR A. R. 1959. The swan badge and the swan knight. *Archaeologia 97: 127–38.*

337　WATSON, J. B. 1931. Mute Swan eating fish. *Brit. Birds 24: 367–68.*

338　WELLER, M. W. 1968. Notes on some Argentine anatids. *Wilson Bull. 80: 189–212.*

339　WILDFOWL TRUST. Unpublished data.

340　WILLEY, C. H. 1968. The ecology, distribution and abundance of the Mute Swan (*Cygnus olor*) in Rhode Island. Unpublished M.Sc. Thesis, University of Rhode Island.

341　WILLIAMS, G. R. 1964. Extinction and the Anatidae of New Zealand. *Wildfowl Trust Ann. Rep. 15: 140–46.*

342　WILLIS, R. A. 1968. *The Pathology of Tumours*, 4th Ed. London: Butterworth Press.

343　WILSON, J. E. and MACDONALD, J. W. 1967. Salmonella infection in wild birds. *Brit. Vet. J. 123: 212–19.*

344 WISELY, B. and MIERS, K. H. 1956. Lead poisoning in New Zealand waterfowl. *N.Z. Dept. Int. Affairs Wildl. Pub. 41: 1–11.*

345 WITHERBY, H. F., JOURDAIN, F. C. R., TICEHURST, N. F. and TUCKER, B. W. 1940. *The Handbook of British Birds, Vol. 3.* London: Witherby.

346 WYNNE-EDWARDS, V. C. 1962. *Animal Dispersion in Relation to Social Behaviour.* Edinburgh: Oliver and Boyd.

347 YARRELL, W. 1841. On a new species of swan (*Cygnus immutabilis*). *Proc. zoo. Soc. Lond. 9: 70.*

348 YARRELL, W. 1871–85. *A History of British Birds.* London: Van Voorst.

349 YEATES, G. K. and JEANS, T. W. B. 1949. Field notes of the birds of the Hrútafjördhur district, North Iceland. *Scot. Nat. 61: 1–9.*

350 YOUNG, J. 1964. *Translation of The Prose Edda.* Berkeley: University of California Press.

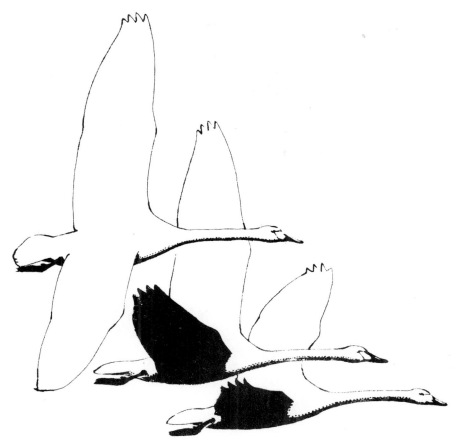

Index

Abbotsbury, 4, 35, 85, 92
Acanthocephala, 140
Accident, 128, 129, 183
Acuaria, 77, 139–40
Aesop, 151–2
Aggression towards other species, 63, 102–3, 177
Agriculture, interactions with, 36, 60–1, 64, 67–8, 73, 75, 176, 188
Alexander the Myndian, 151
Analysis of droppings, 69, 70, 74;
    of stomach contents, 63, 65
Andersen, Hans, 156
Angus, The Dream of, 152–3, 159
Apollo, 146, 148, 151
Apsarases, 161
Aristotle, 150
Aspergillosis, 136–7
Atherosclerosis, 142
Aviculture (*see also* Captivity), 191, 192

Bacterial disease, 134–6
Bands and Banding, *see* Rings and Ringing
Bewick, Thomas, 10
Bill, 19, 27, 58–9, 172;
    use of, in feeding, 58–60, 61;
    variable patterning of, 4, 11, 27, 123
Botulism, *see* Bacterial disease
Brahma, 146, 161
Brigid, 155
Buddha, 161
Byahmul, 162

Captivity (*see also* Aviculture), 13, 76–7, 132, 191
Capture for ringing, 13, 54–5
Census, *see* Counts
Cestodes, 138–9
Chastity test, 155
Children of Lir, 153–5, 156, 160
Cholera, *see* Bacterial disease
Cleves, Anne of, 158
Closeburn Castle, 150
Clutch size, 96–9, 126, 210–11
Coccidiosis, *see* Protozoal disease
Collisions with aircraft, 133, 178
Colony, 4, 5, 34, 35–6, 39, 48, 90–2, 93, 190
Colour preference, 61
Counts, 38, 40, 42, 53–4, 184
Courtship, 81–4, 123
Cycnus, 148, 149, 151
Cygnet, calls of, 110–13;
    carrying, 109–10;
    colour phase, 105–9;
    death rate, 127, 129;
    description, 22–3;
    weight, 113–15, 213
Cygnus, the constellation, 148
Cygnus davidi, 108;
    immutabilis, *see* Polish Mute Swan;
    sumnerensis, 25, 96, 169

Daylength, effects of, 87–8, 117–18, 121
Display, nest relief, 99–100, 101;
    sexual, 81–4;
    territorial, 89–90, 124;
    threat, 82, 89–90, 102–3, 122

Distribution of Bewick's Swan, 42–6;
  Black Swan, 32–4;
  Black-necked Swan, 31–2;
  Coscoroba Swan, 30–1;
  Mute Swan, 34–41;
  Trumpeter Swan, 46–7;
  Whistling Swan, 41–2;
  Whooper Swan, 47–9
Divorce, 13, 84–5
Domestication, 4, 34, 108, 170
Dunstable Swan Jewel, 164
Dyers' Company, 5, 173, 174

Education, 194
Egg, 95–6, 127, 206–9;
  laying, 86–8, 94–5;
  loss, 127, 129;
  retrieval, 103–4;
  tooth, 104, 111
Eggs, collection of, by man, 34, 174–6
Euripedes, 146
Extinction, 169, 183, 191, 193

Family, break up of, 124
Feeding associations with other species, 63;
  behaviour, 59–63;
  development in young, 61–2;
  in captivity, 76–7;
  of wild swans, by man, 4, 11, 14, 15, 66, 70–1, 74, 186, 188;
  of young, 113
Filarial worms, see Nematodes
Fisheries, interaction with, 36, 65, 67, 177
Fledging, 117–18

Flight speed, 50, 129
Flukes, see Trematodes
Food, amount required, 62;
  of Bewick's Swan, 69–71, 202–4;
  of Black Swan, 74–5, 202–4;
  of Black-necked Swan, 75–6, 202–4;
  of Coscoroba Swan, 75–6, 202–4;
  of Mute Swan, 64–7, 202–4;
  of Trumpeter Swan, 73–4, 202–4;
  of Whistling Swan, 71–3, 202–4;
  of Whooper Swan, 67–8, 202–4

Gape worms, see Nematodes
Gibbons, Orlando, 150
Gilmore, Mary, 166
Gizzard worms, see Nematodes
Grimm, J. and W., 156
Grit, 76, 131, 132
Growth of young, 115, 117–18

Hatching, 104;
  success, 129
Height of migratory flight, 50–1
Helios, 148, 157
Homer, 151
Homosexual pairings, 85–6
Hunting, 4, 46–7, 168–9, 174, 183, 184–6, 194
Hybridisation, 20, 86
Hyperboreans, The, 146, 148

Imprinting, 104–5
Incubation, 99–101, 212
International Union for the Conservation of Nature, 8, 187
International Wildfowl Research Bureau, 187
Introductions, 5, 32–4, 40–1

Jankowski's Swan, 25, 43
Juvenal, 161

Key to field identification, 20–1

Latin names, meaning of, 4, 5, 6, 7,
    8, 9, 10
Lead poisoning, *see* Poisoning
Leda, 146, 147, 148, 155, 164
Leeches, 140–1
Legends, Australian, 162–3;
    Celtic, 152–5;
    Classical, 148–151;
    Norse, 144;
    South American, 163
Leto, *see* Leda
Lice, 141
Life expectancy (*see also* Longevity),
    126, 128, 201
Longevity, 3, 124

Malaria, *see* Protozoal disease
Martinez, E. G., 165
Maturity, age of, 80–1
Measurements, 22, 199–200
Migration, 49–52, 121–2
Mites, 141
Moore, Thomas, 153
Moult, 55, 118–21, 168, 183;
    migration, 37, 50

Neck, 22, 59
Nematodes, 139–40
Nemesis, 146
Nest building, 92–4, 100;
    defence, 101–3
New Zealand Swan, *see* Cygnus
    sumnerensis

Norns, The, 144
Numbers of Bewick's Swan, 42–6;
    of Black Swan, 33–4;
    of Black-necked Swan, 32;
    of Coscoroba Swan, 31;
    of Mute Swan, 36–41;
    of Trumpeter Swan, 46–7;
    of Whistling Swan, 42;
    of Whooper Swan, 47–9

Oiling, *see* Pollution
Ownership, 5, 172, 173

Pair formation (*see also* Courtship),
    123
Pausanias, 151
Pesticides, 132–3, 187
Phaethon, 148, 151
Plato, 151
Plumage, 21, 23, 117
Poisoning, 131–3
Polish Mute Swan, 105–8, 127, 174
Pollution, 130–1, 138, 187, 193
Polygamy, 86
Predation and predators, 34, 50, 91,
    129, 130
Preening, 116–17
Project MAR, 187
Protection of Animals Act, 1911,
    176
Protection of Birds Act, 1954, 176
Protozoal disease, 137–8

Race, *see* Subspecies
Radio tracking, 52
Ransom, Elmer, 182
Recipe, 174
Reproductive rate, 126

Rings and ringing, 13, 14, 36, 37, 52, 53–5
Round worms, *see* Nematodes
Royal status, 5, 172, 173

St. Hugh of Lincoln, 171–2
Salmonella, *see* Bacterial disease
Salt excretion, 59
Scythians, 5
Shakespeare, 151
Shooting, *see* Hunting
Sibelius, 164
Silver Swan, The, 164
Slimbridge, *see* Wildfowl Trust
Socrates, 151
Starvation, 114, 127, 129, 133
Sthenelides olor, 150
Subspecies, 18–20, 25, 43
Sun worship, 144–6
Swan as food, 173–4;
   Children, 156–7;
   farming, 173–4, 191;
   Knight, 157–8, 164;
   Maiden, 159–60;
   marks, 158, 172–3;
   pit, 174;
   Service, 165;
   song, 150–1;
   upping, 5, 172–3

Tapeworms, *see* Cestodes
Taxonomy, 18, 24

Tchaikovsky, 162
Territory, 88–91, 124
Trachea, 26–7, 112
Trade, 169–70
Transplantation of swan populations, 47, 192–3
Trematodes, 138
Tuberculosis, *see* Bacterial disease
Tumours, 142

Urd, Spring of, 144–5

Valkyries, 160
Vintners' Company, 5, 158, 173, 174
Virgil, 151
Viruses, 134
Voice, 26–7, 122–3

Wagner, 164
Weight, 21–2, 115, 198, 213;
   of eggs, 95–6, 208–9
Wildfowl Trust, 3, 6, 7, 9, 10–14, 27, 50, 87, 94, 96, 97, 99, 100, 114, 117, 129, 134, 138, 188, 189, 191
Wing noise, 27
Wires, accidents due to overhead, 70, 129, 130, 177, 186
World Wildlife Fund, 187

Zeus, 146, 148

P.S.